D0335263

STIE

Please renew or return items by the date shown on your receipt

www.hertsdirect.org/libraries

Renewals and enquiries: 0300 123 4049

Textphone for hearing or speech impaired 0300 123 4041

Hertfordshire

521 444 60 6

VICTOR BOYS

PREVIOUS BOOKS BY TONY BLACKMAN

Flight Testing to Win (Autobiography paperback)
ISBN 978-0-9553856-4-3, 0-9553856-4-4
Published Blackman Associates September 2005

Vulcan Test Pilot
ISBN 978-1-906502-30-0
Published Grub Street June 2007

Tony Blackman Test Pilot
(Autobiography revised and enlarged, hard cover)
ISBN 978-1-906502-28-7
Published Grub Street June 2009

Nimrod Rise and Fall
ISBN 978-1-90811779-3
Published Grub Street October 2011

FICTION
A Flight Too Far
ISBN 978-0-9553856-3-6, 0-9553856-3-6
Published Blackman Associates

The Final Flight
ISBN 978-0-9553856-0-5, 0-9553856-0-1
Published Blackman Associates

The Right Choice
ISBN 978-0-9553856-2-9, 0-9553856-2-8
Published Blackman Associates

Flight to St Antony
ISBN 978-0-9553856-6-7 0-9553856-6-0
Published Blackman Associates

Now You See It
ISBN 978-0-9553856-7-4, 0-9553856-7-9
Published Blackman Associates

VICTOR BOYS

True Stories from Forty Memorable Years
of the Last V Bomber

TONY BLACKMAN

with

GARRY O'KEEFE

Grub Street • London

Published by
Grub Street
4 Rainham Close
London SW11 6SS

Copyright © Grub Street 2012
Copyright text ©Tony Blackman 2012

British Library Cataloguing in Publication Data

Blackman, Tony.
  Victor boys : true stories from 40 memorable years of the
  last V bomber.
  1. Victor (Jet bomber)--History.
  I. Title
  358.4'283-dc23

ISBN-13: 9781908117458

Jacket and book design by Sarah Driver

Printed and bound by MPG Ltd, Bodmin, Cornwall

Grub Street only uses FSC (Forest Stewardship Council) paper for its books

CONTENTS

FOREWORD

I was delighted when I was asked to write a foreword to *Victor Boys*. It is now sixty years since 'Hazel' Hazleden did the first flight of the aircraft and it is great to have a book written by operators telling the stories of all the splendid things that the aircraft did. In some ways the Victor has had less publicity than the Vulcan because of the latter's unusual shape but, in fact, in the end the Victor outlasted the Vulcan in military service by over ten years, doing sterling service in the Middle East until it was eventually retired in 1993.

The success of the aircraft relied enormously on the design concept by Godfrey Lee and the realisation of what was needed to keep the aerodynamic drag down as the aircraft approached the speed of sound. In addition, the shape of the fuselage enabled a very large bomb bay and so, later in life, room for two huge fuel tanks, an absolute must for an effective tanker.

I was a little surprised when Tony Blackman told me he was masterminding the book and putting it all together since we had spent many a year in rivalry as he helped to develop the Vulcan while I was developing the Victor. However, when Handley Page stopped operating it was Avros who took over the task of making the Mk2 into a tanker and it was Tony who started the development work. Everybody knows now what a magnificent tanker the Victor became, enabling not only the Black Buck bombing raids during the Falklands campaign and the Nimrod long-range reconnaissance flights along the coast of Argentina, but also doing an invaluable job supporting our fighters in the Middle East. It has given me great pleasure to see recorded how my aeroplane distinguished itself so splendidly during these long and troubled times.

In the event, Tony has done a splendid job in recounting the story of the Victor from its beginning as a bomber to its second coming as a really effective tanker. I am delighted that he has finally recognised all the virtues of the Victor and its great effectiveness during the years, even perhaps conceding its overall superiority over the Vulcan.

I am confident that this book will help to make the general public aware of what a superb aircraft the Victor was and realise that it was almost certainly the most useful and best of the three V bombers.

Johnny Allam
June 2012

ACKNOWLEDGEMENTS

When I was asked to write this book I realised I could not possibly manage without getting assistance from someone who knew the Victor history in detail and who would be able to give me contacts and get photographs. This was particularly true since, while I was helping to develop the Vulcan, Handley Page was Avros', greatest competitor though my attitude changed when I found that my first job as chief test pilot was to bring the Victor Mk2s from Radlett to Woodford and turn the aircraft into tankers. I have been extremely fortunate therefore, to get unstinted help from Garry O'Keefe who has been writing the immaculate *Victor Association Newsletter* for many years. Indeed I wouldn't have undertaken this book without the encouragement of the Victor Association.

This book could not have been written without the enormous help of Victor operators – in fact much of it has been written by them. I was also fortunate to have great help from Johnny Allam who took over from Hedley Hazelden and did all the development flying until the Mk2 was turned into a tanker. Charles Masefield then completes the development story by relating the K2 flight testing which I started and he took over.

Another phase of development to the aircraft was when the Victor was fitted with the Blue Steel air-launched stand-off missile. This testing was done in Australia and John Saxon helped splendidly in relating the trials.

On squadron service, David Bywater and his navigator, Norman Bonnor, have supplied stories on both the B1 and B2 aircraft. Norman has also explained how the Victors, and the Vulcans for that matter, were navigated but unfortunately there has not been room to put this definitive article in the book. However, he has kindly allowed me to make it available on my website.

For the Falklands campaign and the key role that the Victors played I have been very fortunate to have had several inputs including Alan Brooks, Barry Neal and Bob Tuxford. In addition Dick Russell, who was with Martin Withers in Vulcan 607 Black Buck 1 as the refuelling specialist, has been a really great help and has given me invaluable support, not only in nearly every chapter of the book, such is his vast experience and knowledge of the aircraft, but also by checking the proof for mistakes. Gary Weightman has also told a story or two and provided the highly illustrative cartoon commenting on Black Buck 1 .

In the years following the Falklands up to and including the wars in the Middle East and the retirement of the aircraft, there are splendid accounts by David Williams, Steve Carty, Syd Buxton and Bill Scragg who was on the very last flight. In addition Syd Buxton has been extremely supportive providing inputs, contacts and information.

There have been valuable contributions from George Worrall, John Jeffrey on the K1 tankers and from many many others.

With regard to photos, I am indebted to all our contributors and apologise for not acknowledging them all and for any omissions. Barry Neal and Dick Russell provided so many pictures that I hope they won't mind if I have not acknowledged every one. Special mention should go to Stuart Osborne for his superb Middle East collection taken from a Tornado[1].

I would especially like to thank my publisher for all his support, with his suggestions, superb editing and the speed in which he has turned the draft into a book to be proud of.

Finally I would also like to thank Margaret Blackman for her indefatigable editing and for giving me so many ideas and so much encouragement. Inevitably there will be errors and omissions for which I apologise and take full responsibility.

DEDICATION

To the many Victor aircrews, some sadly no longer with us, who flew the aircraft for over 40 years helping to guard the United Kingdom through many troubled times.

www.thevictorassociation.org.uk

---

[1]   Stuart says: "I'm glad the photos are being put to good use. The camera was a Minolta Dynax 7000i SLR and the film either Ektachrome slide or plain old Kodacolor 100. I wish we'd had digital back in those days – I'd have taken a lot more shots."

PREFACE

This book is about the third of the three V bombers which were built to guard the United Kingdom during the Cold War. The first of the three aircraft, the Valiant, was commissioned as a stop gap using conservative aerodynamics and systems. In the event, the aircraft had only a short service life as it was found to have a limited fatigue capability and had to be grounded prematurely, accelerating the Victor into its role as a tanker.

The Vulcan and the Victor were developed almost in parallel, with the Vulcan always a few months ahead so that the first Vulcan flew on 30th August 1952, four months before the Victor. Avros decided to respond to the RAF requirement with a completely novel delta design while Handley Page also chose a very advanced concept, the crescent wing, described in the first chapter of this book. There was very keen competition between the two development teams which went on for many years. The first Vulcan went into RAF service in September 1956, immediately flew to New Zealand and back but crashed at London airport on 1st October 1956. The first Victor went into the RAF in 1959.

Both the first Mk2 aircraft with bigger engines flew in 1958. I remember the event well as it was the first time I had flown at the SBAC show at Farnborough; I was demonstrating the power of the new engine in the Vulcan Mk2 by doing rolls off the top. I thought we had stolen a march on the Victor only to find that Johnny Allam in his Victor had also done a roll off the top, though I felt the situation was ameliorated by the fact that he only did one while I had done two in quick succession from a standing start.

The Vulcan was fitted with two Douglas air-launched ballistic missile Skybolts, one under each wing, and therefore had to have its wing strengthened to carry the 11,000lb weapon. Consequently, after the Skybolt programme was cancelled and the nuclear deterrent had to be flown at low level, the Vulcan was able to do this and still have a reasonable fatigue life, unlike the Victor. However the Victor then came into its own as it was realised that the Mk2 version with powerful engines and with both underwing and bomb bay tanks would be invaluable as a tanker. Unfortunately for Handley Page, because of its reluctance to work with either of the two major aerospace companies at the time, this work was given to Avros. The tanker modification proved to be a great success with the aircraft giving invaluable service during the Falklands campaign making the Vulcan Black Buck raids on Port Stanley possible as well as refuelling the Nimrod for its very long reconnaissance flights up the Argentinian coast. Having done a great job flying thousands of miles up and down the Atlantic, it carried on for another ten years supporting fighters all round the world culminating in the first Iraq war.

The question is frequently asked, which was the better aircraft? Clearly both aircraft did superb jobs in fulfilling the primary role for which they were designed, proving to be invaluable contributors to the Defence of the Realm through many turbulent years. However, though the initial role of the Victor was, like the Vulcan, to pose an attack threat to the enemy during the Cold War, its role was expanded to become a vital link in the defence of the UK for many years by refuelling our fighters long after the Vulcans had been scrapped. Of course, having been a Vulcan man initially, my knee-jerk reaction was always to defend my aircraft but, while writing this book, I have come to realise what an amazing aircraft the Victor was. In the Mk2 version with the large Conway engines, the aircraft could out climb the Vulcan reaching 63,000ft compared to 60,000ft for the Vulcan at the extreme altitude. When the underwing tanks were not fitted it could break the sound barrier, unlike the Vulcan, and could carry a lot more fuel than the Vulcan when they were. The crew layout was vastly superior to that of the Vulcan in that the rear crew, if they turned round, could see the pilots and look through the windscreens whilst the Vulcan rear crew were below the pilots in a 'dungeon' with just two tiny skylights.

As a pilot, for sheer flying qualities I preferred the Vulcan because the controls were lighter, had better roll control and, on landing, the braking parachute was not necessary. In addition the flying qualities of the Vulcan had fewer vices than the Victor, particularly at the lower speeds. Attempting to sum up, the Vulcan performed better in the Cold War but the Victor stayed in service as a tanker for ten years after the Vulcan was retired, supporting our aircraft around the world.

However, notwithstanding the Victors' outstanding service the general public worldwide, perhaps unfairly, know and recognise the Vulcan with its distinctive shape while the Victor and its sterling work during the Falklands campaign and the Iraq war is largely unknown. I hope that this book will help in some way to redress the balance.

Tony Blackman, June 2012

NB: For other relevant contributions and photos which could not be fitted into the book please visit my website
www.blackmanbook.co.uk

PROLOGUE

Handley Page's chief test pilot Hedley 'Hazel' Hazelden's statement after making the first flight of the Victor on 24th December 1952

I locked my radio on to transmit so that all that was said could be heard on the ground. In a matter of seconds now we would know if the Victor would fly. I opened the engines to fairly low power and released the brakes. The aircraft rolled up the runway, rapidly gaining speed. I pulled the control column back and the nosewheel left the ground. So far, so good. I held the Victor like that for a few seconds; the rumbling of the wheels ceased and I knew we were off. I kept close to the runway, still gaining speed, for a few more vital seconds, and then I knew it was all right. An imperceptible movement of the control column, and the ground started to fall away as we climbed.

Smoothly, effortlessly, the Victor had slid into its natural element. By so doing it had become an aeroplane instead of just the expression in metal of so many drawings and hieroglyphics on paper. Whatever happened now, we all knew it could fly.

After a few minutes in the air, my thoughts turned to landing. I had got the Victor up there; now, could I get it back again? I tried reducing speed to see how it would behave at a suitable speed for the approach. Once more it was all right and, coming in on a long, straight approach, I headed for the runway. Lower and lower we came, until the beginning of the runway was only a few feet below the wheels. I throttled right back, and in a few seconds the wheels started rumbling again and we were down. The Victor had come back to earth as smoothly as it had left. We had had a comfortable flight, with no anxieties.

Chapter One

A New Shape in the Sky

The first flight of the Victor was a landmark in the development of British-designed aircraft after the war. Its wing was unique and it made the aircraft possibly the best of the three V bombers. It is difficult not to make comparisons but the facts speak for themselves; compared with the Vulcan the aircraft could carry more bombs, more fuel, fly further, fly faster and could fly higher; furthermore it was in service much longer.

First prototype Victor WB771.

There have been many descriptions of the Victor and what seemed, at the time, to be its futuristic wing design; Charles Masefield, who took over from me as chief test pilot at Avros and had a large part in developing the Victor K2, has written not only an account of his Victor development test flying but also gives here an excellent description of this key feature that made the Victor so successful.

After the war, Handley Page turned its hand to the production of the Hastings military transport, already somewhat obsolete with its tail-wheel undercarriage at a time when the much more capable nose-wheel-configured Douglas DC4 had been giving wartime service with the USAF for some years. By the time the Hastings had evolved into the Hermes civil airliner for BOAC it was, yet again, behind the times as Douglas was by then producing the larger and more capable DC6. HP's last civil airliner was the 40-passenger Herald which could not match the Avro 748 or the Fokker F27 which, between them, went on to capture the whole of the 1,000 aircraft DC3 replacement market throughout the world.

It was against this somewhat modest background that Handley Page produced, out of the blue, what was undoubtedly one of the most aerodynamically advanced and highest performing four-engine jet aircraft in the world at that time – the Victor bomber. The inspiration behind the Victor design came from the brilliant mind of chief aerodynamicist, Godfrey Lee. He had been a member of the Air Ministry-inspired scientific and technical fact-finding team which had visited the German aeronautical research establishments at Gottingen and Volkenrode immediately after the end of the war. It became clear from this visit that these German research establishments were considerably more advanced than those in any of the allied countries in the study of the use of swept wings to delay the onset of compressibility-induced drag at high subsonic speed.

Fired by what he had seen and learnt in Germany, Godfrey Lee returned to the UK and immediately began to formulate ideas for a very high performance four-engine jet aircraft. Although there was no Air Staff requirement for such an aircraft at that time, he nevertheless put forward his ideas in the form of a comprehensive brochure sent to the director of operational requirements at the Air Ministry. That this initiative made a major impact within the Operational Requirements Branch is in no doubt. Indeed it was as a result of this proposal that OR 230 was issued to the aircraft industry to which at this time six companies were able to respond. The resultant specification B35/46 ambitiously called for an aircraft able to cruise at 50,000ft close to the speed of sound and, amidst much lobbying at the highest levels of government and solely to protect the manufacturing industry and its jobs, the Air Ministry came to the bizarre – indeed to us in this day and age incredible – decision to order all three. Thus were born the three V bombers, the Valiant, the Vulcan and the Victor.

Recognising that the high mach number drag rise of any aircraft coincided with its velocity at which the first shock wave would begin to form at some point on the airframe, Godfrey Lee took the decision to attempt to design an aircraft in which the local airflow over every portion of its airframe reached its shock wave forming supersonic velocity simultaneously. With a chain only as strong as its weakest link he sought to eliminate every location of potential premature shock wave formation. With this aim he decided to bury the engines in the wing roots to avoid shock wave formation around external engine nacelles. Furthermore, if a constant critical mach number was to be achieved across the entire wing span it would have to feature an extremely steep sweep of 47.5 degrees at the six-foot-deep wing root. As the wing thickness reduced further outboard, so did its sweep to 40.5 degrees at mid span and to 32 degrees sweep for the very thin outboard section of the wing. So was born the unique crescent wing.

A similar 'constant critical mach number' approach was applied to the design of the fuselage, resulting in the characteristic very smooth, pointed Victor nose with the windscreen glass and Perspex panels merely forming part of an unbroken aerodynamic skin shape. In this aircraft there was to be no compromise of a raised cockpit windscreen to improve pilot view as any such discontinuity or blemish of the sleek lines would inevitably trigger the formation of local and draggy shock waves. The success of Godfrey Lee's 'no compromise' design was vividly demonstrated when, on June 1st 1957, Johnny Allam exceeded the speed of sound in a Victor for the first time. In doing so the Victor became the largest aircraft in the world at that time to have flown at supersonic speed and, indeed, the first four-engine aircraft to do so. To add to this record Johnny's navigator, Paul Langston, became the first man to fly supersonically backwards! It subsequently became a common occurrence for residents throughout eastern England to experience the characteristic double

Godfrey Lee standing in front of one of the last Victors. (*Darren Simons*)

bang as Victors regularly exceeded the speed of sound on routine production test flights. What a remarkable aircraft it was.

The HP80's first flight on Christmas Eve 1952 and the announcement to the world's press was a great event but few people realised how much planning and design of the highest order was required to achieve this historic event. Though the aircraft had been tendered for by an experienced and talented company, Handley Page was of a very modest size to be taking on such an advanced and large-scale project, certainly in comparison with its American counterparts. That the resulting HP proposal would eventually come to fruition was both a remarkable and a colossal achievement, despite causing later bewilderment to one visiting American general who, while praising the later Victor production line at "Fred's Shed" asked why they had to be "built in a barn".

The pilot who was to advise, contribute towards and finally test-fly the first prototype was Hedley 'Hazel' Hazelden. He began working for HP in the spring of 1947 at the very time the revised tender B.35/46 had been agreed and was issued as OR 230. In fact, this was only a few months after the company's visit to Germany and aerodynamicist Godfrey Lee's initial doodles on the back of an envelope had begun, with further development being transferred onto the drawing boards at Cricklewood.

It is clear that Handley Page had been fortunate in having Hazleden whose technical ability was of the highest order while his general experience was second to none, most of which had been honed by the exigencies of war. At Handley Page he soon got involved with the new aircraft and their adaptations that the company busily strove to introduce in the aftermath of war; Sir Frederick and the Board were ever-mindful of the loss of orders that had befallen the company together with the rest of the then infant British aircraft industry after the previous carnage of WW1.

Developing the HP80 prototype in preparation for flight required not only a lot of wind tunnel testing but also airborne engine testing of the proposed Sapphire engine and, as far as was possible, flying the proposed crescent wing. Production of the original Metrovick F.9 turbojet engine planned for the HP80 had been taken over by Armstrong Siddeley Motors at Coventry who re-named the engine the Sapphire after scaling it up by 25% to give more thrust. When ready, two of these excellent jet turbines were attached to the second Hastings prototype TE583 in the outboard position and first flown in this configuration in November 1950 after which Hazelden later recalled that the aircraft could happily cruise at 175 knots on one engine only, thanks to the tremendous increase in power afforded by this revolutionary watershed in powered flight. Such test flying, coupled with high-speed development work with a Sapphire-engined Canberra, prepared the engine and made it ideal for the projected bomber.

When faced with the programme's exacting specification the company had set up a special team to make an exhaustive aerodynamic study of the problems involved. In

Sapphire-engined Hastings. (*A.Dowsett*)

tandem with this team, other members of a project group were charged with more general design features, with special reference to complementary structural and installation problems. The official preliminary design won approval in principle at a conference in December 1947 with no major issues raised apart from questioning what escape provisions should be provided for the rear crew. HP considered this idea of a jettisonable crew cabin, years ahead of its time, but in the end the concept together with its 'bug-eye' canopy blisters had to be abandoned and the uniquely shaped nose section was fitted with further refined large, flush-fitting Triplex windscreens developed to taper and sweep down towards a sharp proboscis. Sixty years later it seems amazing that adequate escape provision was not given to the rear crew but at that moment the country was only just recovering from a terrible war and was faced with the urgent need to prepare for the Cold War, so time could not be spared to develop ejection seats or the equivalent for the rear crew members.

The project moved forward with senior staff at HP wading in to make notable contributions, innovations and improvements with the help of the German research scientist Gustav Lachmann, chief designer Reginald Stafford and assistant chief designer Charles Joy, all working closely with aerodynamicists C.Vernon and Godfrey Lee. The latter had worked as a research engineer during the war before being promoted to chief aerodynamicist in 1949. Ray Sandifer and Frank Tyson as chief and assistant stressmen respectively began to carry out pioneering work on wing structures while Sir Frederick Handley Page added many of his own forthright opinions and suggestions.

It was realised that it was vital to get some aerodynamic testing on the proposed wing design. One plan was to develop the wing on a glider but this concept was abandoned and later replaced with the HP88, a Supermarine Attacker fuselage with a scaled-down crescent wing and tail, the testing of which would hopefully be able to give some positive comparisons between theoretical calculations and the 'crescent wing'. After its eventual construction and initial testing by sub-contractor Blackburn in the summer of 1951, the job of test flying the HP88, XV330, was given to Dougie Broomfield DFM because, unfortunately, Hazelden's 225lb weight and height of six feet one inches meant that he was too large to be comfortably accommodated in the airframe and was forced to watch and advise from afar.

HP88 research aircraft XV330.

In the meantime a decision had been taken in early 1948 to delete the original wing-tip fins and replace them with a central fin and rudder while, later in June, Victor engineer Lachmann also decided to raise the tailplane to the top of the fin. As the months passed into years, the concept drawings and wind-tunnel models continued to resemble those of a very futuristic aircraft to Hazelden's eyes, while the planners of this sophisticated design fully expected their theories to result in Britain gaining an aircraft which would offer at least two-and-a-half times the performance of the most successful wartime Bomber Command 'heavies'.

Hazelden, while not being able to fly the HP88, made his own contribution to the HP80 design thanks to a cockpit mock up which had been constructed at Cricklewood. He spent much time acquainting himself with it and making various recommendations that would be incorporated into the prototype. Crucially, he ensured that the real cockpit had a simple layout with an absence of complication or elaborate 'gadgets' that might cause future pilots problems, particularly on long and tiring missions. He also paid close attention to the control forces in flight which, when close to the speed of sound, would be impossible for humans to control without mechanical aids. All aileron, rudder and elevator control surfaces would have to be fully power-assisted, with the motors obeying the control decisions demanded by the pilot; the consequence of this was that artificial feel had to be provided to protect the aircraft structure and to make it possible for the pilots to fly precisely and safely without overcontrolling and damaging the airframe. He therefore advised the design office on what he considered would be the optimum forces for the control wheel and rudder, commensurate with the size and type of aircraft that was being flown. As a result, he frowned on controls being too light for a large aircraft, though ironically the RAF would later ask that the HP80s were 'heavied up' further. The artificial forces built into the Victor's flying controls would make it feel like a slower aeroplane in terms of response and this was also complemented by his insistence on traditional 'spectacle' control columns, which clearly reminded pilots of the type of aircraft they were flying. This was in marked contrast to the Vulcan with its fighter-type control stick which, despite its huge wing area, could be manoeuvred around to out-turn many fighters of the day at altitude.

Unfortunately, the project suffered a setback when the HP88 crashed in August 1951 killing Dougie Broomfield. Though naturally saddened by this tragic loss, the HP team were relieved to hear from the Accident Investigation Branch findings that the HP88's loss was not in any way due to any fault in the design or construction plan of the wing, rather it was a structural failure due to a tailplane servo control system failure.

The Victor and Vulcan contracts were approved at the same time and in June 1952 production orders were received by Avro and HP for twenty-five examples of their V solutions – the former before the prototype had flown, while the latter was now an HP80 no more – the 'Victor' being soon announced as the official name for the last of Britain's V bomber designs, now completing a triumvirate of world class medium bombers for the RAF – the 'V Force'. For HP the many years of thought, theorizing and experiment were concluded and were now narrowing down to their ultimate test of its 'new shape' which was about to make its mark in the flowering of British aviation's post war 'Jet-Age'. While Hazelden was undoubtedly saddened by Broomfield's death, he was also concerned at the loss of any potential information which might have assisted him as to how the aircraft would behave when first taken aloft in its natural element, and he pondered over this while preparations were made for the first flight.

Handley Page intended to fly the first aircraft from Radlett but suddenly it was decided that the runway there was too short to fly it safely for the first time and the change of venue would be worth the extra delay to remove unnecessary risk. People blamed the ministry for the decision but it could be that Hazel was behind the change since the runway was being extended but the work wasn't finished. The aircraft had to be taken apart again and transported in trucks down to the Armament Experimental Establishment, A&AEE, at Boscombe Down, Wiltshire; the situation was compounded by the desire of the Ministry of Defence to keep the aircraft secret. All the parts, wings, fuselage and the rest were covered up and labelled as fuel tanks and a lot of it went via Southampton Docks. Wrapped in canvas to disguise its still-secret shape from the world and labelled 'Gelepandy, Southampton', the Victor fuselage of WB771 finally left the factory at Cricklewood on June 7th 1952, on its way to Boscombe with its very long runway. Other component sections arrived in the following weeks and Hazelden regularly flew across from Radlett in a light aircraft to watch the re-assembly. Sir Frederick was understandably anxious to have the aircraft cleared for a first appearance at the September Farnborough air show to match the Vulcan's first outing; this proved impossible however due to the great time expended in testing and retesting each component before the aircraft could be given the final go ahead to fly.

It was at this time in 1952 that Johnny Allam, who was eventually to take over from Hazelden and was an RAF test pilot at Boscombe, had his first encounter with the Victor, since the aircraft was being re-assembled in B Squadron hangar and all their aircraft had to be moved onto the ramp outside. There was an enormous cloak of secrecy which made normal B Squadron operations very difficult.

Then tragedy struck once more some days after the missed Farnborough event, when leaking hydraulic fluid led to a fire in a small compartment at the rear of the aircraft. Within seconds a fierce fire had developed and three workers caught in the flames suffered severe burns before the blaze was quelled. One of them, Eddie Eyles, died in hospital of his injuries. Though the damage to the aircraft was not serious, further delays ensued and it was not until December 1952 that Hazelden found himself strapping in to the aircraft to commence taxiing trials. At last the aircraft was ready but alas, not the weather; finally on Christmas Eve Hazel took the aircraft into the air for the first flight with great success and no untoward happenings. Much was made of the crescent wing design in the press and in early 1953 R.S. Stafford, Handley Page's chief designer, said of it: "This wing is the complete and only answer to the demands of a most exacting specification. It calls not only for operation at high subsonic speed and very great heights over long ranges, but also for good control over the whole speed range, particularly at approach and landing speeds near the ground."

Apparently some time later the secretary of the US Air Force, Harold E. Talbott, visited Radlett. After flying in the first prototype both in the rear seats and at the controls he likened the Handley Page Victor to a baby, meaning that he was impressed with the viceless flying qualities of the machine and with its consummate ease of handling. The high, all-moving tail

First prototype WB771 in flight.

provided exceptionally good elevator control from the stall up to sonic speed while the powerful air brakes on the rear-fuselage sides gave accurate control in the dive and on the approach glide, with no adverse effect on trim.

Even more noteworthy than the all-round ease of handling was the claimed capacity of the Victor to "land itself", once placed in a correct approach configuration. Sir Frederick managed to have this quality demonstrated to many American delegates attending an RAeS conference following the 1953 SBAC show. The weather was fine but exceptionally gusty and Hazelden brought the Victor back from Farnborough to Radlett where he put on a flying demonstration which was brief but noticeably not subject to the normal restrictions of the previous week in that it was able to fly lower than 200ft and turn towards the spectators.

Dai Davies, chief test pilot of the Air Registration Board, who had been wisely invited to act as an impartial observer by Sir Frederick so that the demonstration could not be termed 'bull', then got into the Victor and settled himself into the right-hand seat.

They were absent for some time while Hazelden carried out handling tests and steep turns and briefed his passenger on the intricacies of the Victor's cockpit. Hazelden then – according to Davies – turned on to final at 1,100ft and held the aircraft in a steady approach. At 800ft there was slight re-trimming and the power levers for the four Sapphires were then locked. At 600ft and some 130 knots, Hazelden ceased all elevator movement and merely applied slight aileron and rudder deflections to counteract the violent wind which was blowing directly across the runway. From then on the Victor was left to its own devices. Untouched by human hand the 300ft per minute reduced to zero as the ground was approached and the aircraft settled on to its bogies after which Hazelden was able to bring it rapidly to rest with the help of the braking parachute.

To all the onlookers the landing appeared quite normal, and it could not derisively have been called an 'arrival'. There was some transfer of weight from one bogie to the other, with consequent load on the electro-hydraulics anti-pitch dampers, but the brakes were on after some 500 yds and the Victor pulled up with about one third of the runway remaining. Later, Hazelden went across to the spectators and said how pleased he was with the aircraft.

The "self-landing" characteristic, he said, resulted from the aircraft having a strong tendency to trim nose-up as ground effect became noticeable. The characteristic was valuable in that, in rain or bad visibility, he could bring the Victor in gently with power on and all the flaps and air brakes open. All that was required then was to correct for local air disturbances affecting lateral trim until eventually the bogies could be heard rumbling on the concrete. The nosewheels would then be brought down on to the runway, the parachute streamed and the wheel brakes applied.

For his part Davies said that the Air Registration Board, as it was called then, were particularly interested in powered controls and those of the Victor appeared excellent, with progressive feel simulation. His impression of the Victor had been most favourable and, obviously speaking 'off the cuff', he said he did not expect that Sir Frederick would have much difficulty if and when the HP97 airliner came to his department for certification!

Though Hazel did the first flight of the Victor and undertook the initial development, it was Johnny Allam who made it possible for A&AEE to give the aircraft a 'certificate of airworthiness' and clear it for squadron use. He was on the 9th Empire Test Pilots Course in 1950, four years before mine. Like me he went to B Squadron, Boscombe Down and had Roy Max as his squadron commander. I had a chat with him before writing this chapter and he told me how he got involved with the Victor.

In conversation, Johnny told me that he had been promised a flight in the Victor but it kept on being delayed so he went home one weekend and sure enough the flight took place and a guy called Joe Tischo flew instead. Hazel did about eleven flights from Boscombe, one of the most memorable being when he had to do an overshoot on coming in to land. It was very important on the Victor to have stopped the wheels after take-off before retracting the landing gear. To ensure this was done the parking brake lever was positioned over the undercarriage up-selection button so that until the parking brake was on it was impossible to select the gear up, which seemed a good idea at the time. Hazel carried out his overshoot, put the parking brake on and then realised it wasn't necessary to raise the gear as he had so much power. He went round the circuit with the undercarriage down and then proceeded to land with the parking brake still on. From then on he was known as Dunlop's friend as he wrote off sixteen tyres and wheels.

Hazel by then knew Johnny very well but in spite of that he recruited another pilot from B Squadron called Kenneth Dalton-Golding who couldn't wait to leave the air force and join industry. He started to do a lot of Victor flying and actually did more than Hazel. However Handley Page, like a lot of UK aviation firms, were also manufacturing Canberras, seventy-five in total, and Dalton-Golding at the end of a production test flight on one of the Canberras started a barrel roll which he failed to complete and hit the railway embankment on the east side of the airfield.

Hazel then went to Farnborough and recruited a test pilot from Aeroflight called Taffy Ecclestone and he too was killed, this time in the first Victor doing position error measurements when the tail came off at the top speed. By chance Hazel should have been doing that flight but he didn't as he so often had something else to do at the last minute; he had elected to go to Woodley that day and briefed Taffy who had only done about four or five Victor flights by then, though of course he was very happy to do the flight. In fact Taffy apparently did one more test point at a faster speed than he was briefed to do. When they examined the wreckage they found that one of the bolts already had a great crack in it so in fact there were only two bolts holding the tailplane on. On this occasion Hazel blamed Taffy for not keeping to the briefing though at other times he was absolutely first class at defending his pilots.

At this stage the second Victor hadn't flown. Johnny was getting to the end of his tour at Boscombe in 1953 but realising that he rather liked test flying he spoke to Bill Pegg at Bristols. Then out of the blue Hazel called him and said he was looking for someone to start in July 1954. Johnny then started negotiating with Hazel as he was posted from Boscombe to become a jet instructor at Little Rissington and then on to Oakington. During this time the first prototype Victor crashed so that the flight of the second aircraft was considerably delayed while the crash was investigated and an extra bolt added to hold the tailplane on to the fin. In the end Johnny left the RAF on Saturday 28th August 1954 after being required to attend a station commander's parade and joined Handley Page at Radlett on the Monday morning.

Hazel finally took up the second prototype on the last Sunday of Farnborough week in September 1954; he flew it for an hour and then got permission to display it at the show itself. It was then grounded for a couple of weeks before Johnny started flying it. He flew twice with Hazel in the left-hand seat and then twice with Hazel in the right-hand seat. Apparently he then asked Johnny how much longer he wanted him to go on sitting there and that really was the end of Hazel's involvement as Johnny took the aircraft over.

One of Johnny's first inspired changes was to get the firm to fit a yaw damper because it suffered excessive oscillations in roll and yaw, Dutch Roll. He pointed out that there was no hope of the aircraft entering service without one so the firm fitted one which worked perfectly from its first flight. Johnny was explaining this to Hazel who asked to test it so after a few days grounding he flew the aircraft and apparently the yaw damper made matters much worse. He switched it off and returned to find that some mistake had been made with the wiring. However Hazel never tried it again and Johnny then became the Victor project pilot.

As Charles Masefield remarked earlier, the Victor, unlike the Vulcan, could easily go supersonic in quite a shallow dive. The first time this happened Johnny was doing a trim point at .985IMN for some reason which he didn't understand since it was way above the maximum speed that would be cleared for the RAF. He set up the condition but clearly he was distracted since a moment later he saw over 1.0 on his machmeter. He wasn't sure at that stage whether the aircraft had gone supersonic so he turned it round and pointed it at Radlett. It was a Saturday morning and when they landed and spoke to the tower there had been no reports of supersonic bangs. To quote Johnny's exact words.

It wasn't until Monday morning when they had analysed the aeroplane recorder results that they said we had been supersonic. Well I said I had wondered but no-one had heard the bang. It turned out, once they started talking about it around the design office, that the chief designer, Charles Joy, said "I was shopping in Watford during the morning and we heard a great supersonic bang there". When we compared times it was exactly right, it was widespread but that wasn't surprising considering how shallow was the dive we were in.

Apparently nobody complained and Johnny felt that this was because shallow dives tended to disperse the noise. The other test pilots then started to go supersonic quite deliberately and, possibly, one or two squadron pilots though it was not permitted in service. Johnny said that apart from anything else the ailerons would lock up, presumably because they didn't have sufficient power but that luckily the elevators were still very effective.

The flying controls operated in the same way as the Vulcan with each surface being driven by an electrically powered hydraulic pump. However one day Johnny had a complete failure of both hydraulic systems which worked the landing gear, flaps, air brakes and nose flaps. Johnny describes the situation clearly.

Yes I did lose both systems once. I was at 52,000ft on a production flight test when suddenly my AEO said that the hydraulic pumps were not cutting in as they should every 50 to 55 seconds to do a top up because you get internal leakage from the pressure units. We were fairly heavy on fuel of course so I just tried the air brakes for instance and they didn't move, main flaps – didn't move, nothing moved. I realised we hadn't got any hydraulic pressure at all. It was a Victor that still had nose flaps on it and we could put those down because they had stored energy – you couldn't pull the nose flaps in until the energy was stored to put them down again, those aeroplanes would have deep stalled quite easily without nose flaps. So I had that but no other hydraulics, no undercarriage, no nothing.

The first thing I did was to get on to Radlett to see if they could get anybody from the hydraulics design team on to the VHF. We had a complete breakdown, brakes, undercarriage, flaps, and nose flaps which we couldn't have retracted again once they were down. I think everybody on the ground at Radlett realised it was most likely an electrical failure but all our electrics indicated correctly and were obviously operating because the flying controls were all working. One of the electrical designers was on the end of the RT for me and told me I had to get into the fuse box immediately on the right-hand side of the AEO on the wall and it meant him getting out of his seat which was all right, but he couldn't open the thing. The wretched design man came back and said, "well get the axe out and chop it open". I said no way was anybody going in there with an axe and chopping the electrics about. A ridiculous suggestion, he was just getting desperate really. Anyhow in the end we realised we were stuck with this situation so we alerted the RAF since we couldn't put it back on the ground at Radlett; we didn't have foam or anything like that and we needed a place with foam on the runway. Waddington was selected so I then wanted to get rid of a lot of fuel, since it was clearly desirable to have as little fuel as possible when doing a wheels-up landing.

There was no way of dumping fuel, so we had to burn it off so what I did for that was simply to come back to about 1,500ft, give it full power and make it climb to about 10 or 12,000ft; if you do this several times it gets rid of a lot of fuel very quickly. I got it down to what I thought was enough for an approach, an overshoot and another approach so that if I got it wrong the first time I would have one more chance. For my co-pilot I had a bomber command liaison officer who was twitching furiously about all this; he may have been absolutely scared. Well I told everybody what they must do and that one of his jobs when we landed was to stop the engines and close them down; that's really all he had to do and then he could get out. The navigators didn't really have much to do but the AEO had a bit of closing down to do.

When we got to the first approach at Waddington we were in hazy weather, I could see the ground perfectly well but couldn't see far enough forward. We had a GCA talking us down but the GCA man desperately wanted me on a 3 degree glide slope which I didn't want at all, I wanted to be underneath that by a long way, with a very flat approach since I had no flaps, landing gear or air brakes. On my first approach this wretched controller was nattering away and yelling at me because I was below the glide slope you see, but I knew what I wanted to do and knew where I wanted to be. I could have adjusted it all within the last mile, I could see about a mile probably and sort it out if it wasn't quite right. But he made such a thing of all this that I just couldn't land, it was a pickle. I said "Right, we are going to overshoot, that's what we planned for". This bomber command liaison officer nearly pulled the jump seat – I thought he was going to go. Anyhow he did manage to stay there so we went round and I talked to the air traffic controller when we were down wind and said "now look all I want from you is directional guidance, I don't want anything else at all. I can see

Dramatic if poor quality photograph of Johnny just touching down.

the ground and I know what I'm doing." He did that and I got it superbly lined up with the runway when it appeared and was not far off the height I wanted to be, so it was pretty good.

The runway had been covered with foam and we landed just at the beginning of the foaming edge exactly, I gradually put the nose down and said "okay chop everything". We were going pretty fast at this stage. The aircraft was horrendously light and so I was probably doing 125kts or something like that but I couldn't go much slower. So we put it on the runway and it kept beautifully straight. I really didn't have to do anything with it, it slid straight down this line of foam. When we touched the ground and I knew that we weren't going to fly any more I told them to cut everything. We landed, we had the door open of course before landing and I looked round for this man in the co-pilot's seat and he wasn't there. He'd gone. He was the first out of the aeroplane and he should have been after the three back end chaps. I thought crikey, I was the only one in the aircraft so I thought get out, everything is closed down. I got out of the aeroplane and thought that's funny I can hear a noise, the engines were all still running, every one of them. I thought I must get back in but before I could do anything, there was a flash in front of me and this bomber command man got back in and did the final bit he was supposed to have done. He must have been deadly scared he was going to get into awful trouble. Anyhow, I closed them down and we looked at the aeroplane when we got out of it – there had been a bit of a fire; right at the back end, there is a fuel vent underneath, aft of the bomb bay and there was obviously some vapour there which kept flashing bits of flame.

It's quite interesting really, the radome suffered a bit and the fuselage just behind it plus we wore off the nosewheel doors and the nosewheel settled onto the runway.

It stayed on this nosewheel all the way and nothing else touched the ground until just behind the bomb bay where this wretched fuel vent was. Neither wingtip was touched; it was only fuselage damage, no bomb bay damage, it was just fore and aft bits, it was absolutely amazing. Radlett sent a team up by road, they had set off before we landed, because I was quite a while getting rid of fuel. They knew where we were going to land and they had some air bags which lifted it up and then they put jacks underneath. They got it up on the air bags, got the jacks in position and then took the air bags away. As bad luck would have it the furthest outboard jack on the starboard wing slipped and went right up through the wing. And do you know that was the worst bit of damage that was done.

It was an electrical fault of course; the Victor had two relays, outside the pressurised part of the aeroplane in the nosewheel bay. They are the ones that are signalled to cut out on a pressure switch. They'd somehow arced across the points and joined themselves up and of course blown the fuses. It was a fuse problem in the end but we wondered why it happened, because we had been flying the thing for ages without this trouble ever before. Back at Radlett we found that the manufacturers of these faulty relays had changed the relay design slightly and the points were a trace closer together than they had been previously. Of course we relied on air insulation and now it wasn't good enough, so they started to arc across. Immediately it was found out we stopped that batch of relays on the production line; this was a production aeroplane, not one of our flight test aeroplanes so we went back to the old relays for a while. The strange thing was that normally when a new component came in or a modified one, it would go into Radlett's test department where it would be checked. But these hadn't and somehow they had got straight onto the production line and I suspect the inspection department was at fault because they should have diverted them to the test department and they would probably have picked it up. However that was sorted out and we flew the aeroplane out of Waddington six weeks later, it would have been much sooner if they hadn't put the jack through the wing. So we got it back to Radlett, put it somewhere in the production line and it came out again like a new aeroplane and the last time I saw it, it was standing at Marham as the gate guardian, 673 it was called.

In talking to Johnny I asked him about auto-landing which was programmed for both the Victor and Vulcan Mk2s. I had done a lot on the Vulcan quite a few months before the Victor tests.[2] In fact we had had to sort it out since the auto-throttle, which the world's experts at the time had designed, didn't have a rate-of-pitch sensor. We also sorted out the pilot's interface with the auto-throttle to make it safe to use. What we could not change was the Vulcan's ILS aerial, situated for some inexplicable reason in the wingtip and, much more serious, the leader cable system which eventually proved to be unnecessary and was so expensive to install that it caused the auto-landing programme for both aircraft to be cancelled. Johnny described the Victor auto-landing flight tests.

[2]   See *Vulcan Test Pilot* p106.

We had two problems to start with – we found it all on the first flight. The first thing was when we went down the leader cables to wherever it was, about 300ft I think, they used to change over to the leader cables for the last bit of guidance and the aeroplane suddenly jinked right and left and upset the whole approach at 300ft. I thought about it in flight and realised that our localiser aerial was right out on the wing and why someone hadn't thought about it I don't know, in service the Mk1s were just like this.

The other problem we had on the first flight was that when we landed it was the smoothest and softest landing, so soft the aeroplane was not sure it was on the ground and it would skip off a bit and you didn't know where it was going to land next. So we cured that by simply setting the radio altimeter datum to a foot below ground level and that worked immediately so, after the first flight, we just got down to running a whole series of them and cleared it to go to Boscombe Down, phoned up the ministry to say it was ready to go there and they told me they'd just added something to the requirement. We had to do 200 landings straight without a single failure before Boscombe would accept doing it themselves. So I told them we'll do that but they had to give us a contract to do it because it was a lot of work doing 200 of these in about ten flights and we did it in about five installations, mostly at Bedford but also at various other places where there were leader cables. While doing this somewhere where the leader cables were unserviceable, I said right let's just go there and see what happens without them, we did this and it did it just as well – leader cables were not necessary.

The second prototype WB775 flew soon after the loss of the first and appeared at the Farnborough air display of 1955. Prior to this, development had progressed apace and during a demonstration flight in April that year with the Hon. George Ward, then under-secretary of state for air on board, the Victor flew close to the speed of sound and climbed to more than 50,000ft.

Production line at Radlett.

Handley Page handed over their first Victor to Boscombe Down for acceptance by the RAF in 1956. From then on Radlett concentrated on developing and improving the aircraft, resulting in the Victor K1 tanker and the Victor Mk2 with Blue Steel and the Victor SR2 reconnaissance aircraft. Shortly before the RAF proudly showed its new bombers to the press in the autumn of 1958, Air Vice-Marshal K.B.B. Cross, Air Officer Commanding 3 Group, RAF Bomber Command, wired his opinion of his new aircraft to Sir Frederick Handley Page: 'Victor intensive flying trials ended as planned yesterday STOP This success is a great tribute to those who designed and built the Victor and I send you congratulations from Aircrew and Airmen who fly and service them STOP'.

An Air Ministry statement prepared for this press visit to Rutland gave some indication of the aircraft's still secret performance. "At its operational height this bomber can outfly and out-manoeuvre any fighter in service today." Later, during routine flights in RAF service, Victors would cut the flying times between countries and continents. One flew from England to Malta in exactly two hours at 655 mph, a speed only slightly subsonic, while another crossed the Atlantic in 188 minutes at 644 mph. Radlett as a design and development centre for the Victor finally closed in 1970 when Handley Page stopped operating and Avro took over the development of the Victor K2 at the Woodford facility. In this connection Charles Masefield sums up the end of this great company.

It is always sad when one of the longest established aircraft manufacturing companies comes to an end but, in this case, it has to be said that the directors of Handley Page, including the great man himself, largely brought this fate upon themselves. The rationalisation of the highly fragmented British aircraft industry into two large groups, Hawker Siddeley and the British Aircraft Corporation, was as inevitable as it was overdue. Clearly Britain could no longer support the multiplicity of factories, design teams, workforces and projects which owed their existence to the wartime imperative of mass production of military aircraft supported by unlimited funds. Economies of scale were now essential if the industry was to survive in a peacetime environment of ever fiercer international competition.

Handley Page alone refused to join either of the new industrial groupings, naively believing that they could remain competitive as an autonomous and stand-alone business. They based this strategy entirely upon their knowledge that new flight refuelling tankers of greatly increased capacity had become the top military procurement priority – and that the tanker conversion of the Victor B2 bomber had already been selected as the ideal solution. Furthermore, the directors held the flawed conviction that the embedded knowledge and expertise of the Handley Page team which had designed, built, developed and supported the Victor programme throughout its life made Handley Page at Radlett the only viable location capable of executing this large and complex programme. This conviction was further strengthened by the fact that the selected twenty-four Victor B2 and SR2 aircraft had already been flown into Radlett in preparation for their conversion and the company held grimly onto the old adage that possession was nine-tenths of the law. Sadly for the company and its dedicated workforce, their directors had badly underestimated the government's determination to complete the aircraft industry rationalisation plans in totality – with absolutely no exceptions. In pursuit of this the government adopted the simple expedient of withholding the award of the tanker contract until either Handley Page relented and joined one of the groups – or ran out of money waiting for the contract award. It is now history that the HP stubbornness persisted to the bitter end when, on February 11th 1970, the company went into liquidation. The government then moved with lightning speed and within three weeks the contract was ours.

That great Victor expert Harry Fraser-Mitchell recounts his memory at the time. He explained why Sir Frederick never agreed to a merger.

Johnny Allam flying the Victor Mk2 at Farnborough 1960. (*George Trussell*)

In his talks with HSA in 1960, HP asked 16/- per share from HSA when the market price was 13/-; HSA offered 10/- which HP turned down. At this point the government cancelled twenty-eight Victor BMk2s so HSA reduced their offer to about 8/- when the shares were trading at 10/-. The RAF selected the Herald rather than HSA's Avro 748 but the government would not pay HP their full Victor contract cancellation claim and the merger talks collapsed. Next HSA offered 5/- which was rejected and the government cancelled the Herald order.

Sir Frederick Handley Page died in 1962, aged 77. A few years later the company ran into financial problems while developing their civil Jetstream small airliner and eventually had to stop operating. A US company, the Cravens Corporation, took over but not long after the owner died and the business collapsed. Charles Masefield concludes.

During the First World War the company had become known for the production of large biplane bombers which arrived upon the scene rather too late to make any significant impact upon the outcome of the conflict. Between the wars their best known aircraft was the huge four-engine HP 42 biplane which ponderously plied the Imperial Airways routes from London to Karachi like sedate galleons of the sky cruising at just 90 mph. At that time, the UK industry as a whole – and HP in particular – were clearly well behind the times. The modern all-metal DC2 and DC3 monoplane airliners, with a fully retractable undercarriage and variable pitch airscrews, were already rolling off the Douglas production lines in California in their hundreds, soon to be in their thousands, with the onset of World War 2. By the outbreak of that conflict RAF Bomber Command was equipped with another outdated HP design, the Hampden with its extremely cramped crew conditions. These were eventually succeeded by the four-engine Handley Page Halifax, an aircraft of honest endeavour, but outclassed in every respect by the mighty Avro Lancaster. Therefore one of the great ironies of the Handley Page history is that their demise came during the vibrant ongoing development life of what was undoubtedly their greatest ever aircraft in a not always stellar sixty-year history.

Chapter Two

Victor B1/B1A

There were fifty Victor Mk1s built and thirty-four
Victor Mk2s. The first Victor B1, XA931 was delivered
to the Royal Air Force at 232 OCU Gaydon on 28th
November 1959. The first Squadrons were Nos 10
and XV. Operationally the aircraft was a high altitude
bomber, painted anti-flash white and capable of
carrying nuclear weapons or thirty-five 1,000lb bombs
in its large bomb bay. The size of the bomb bay proved
very important when the aircraft was later converted to
a tanker because two very large fuel tanks were able to
be fitted. Like the Vulcan, ECM equipment was fitted
in the tail after the initial deliveries and twenty-four
B1s were converted to B1As.

In 1964 six aircraft were converted as tankers with
two underwing pods but no centreline hose drum
unit. These were called B1A(K2p), K for tanker 2p for
two point; this nomenclature was adopted because
in theory the aircraft could be converted back to the
bombing role. Next, eleven aircraft had a central hose
drum unit added and were initially called BK1 but were

Handley Page not only built
good aircraft but they had a
very good publicity department
eulogising their undoubted
capabilities and achievements.

renamed K1 when the bombing capability was removed. Fourteen more aircraft were
then converted to tankers named BK1A and then renamed K1A, again after the bombing
capability was removed. The K1s were missing some minor modifications on the K1A
and were only used by 214 Squadron. All the tankers could both take and receive fuel.

David Bywater started his career as a young co-pilot on XV Squadron eventually
becoming a captain on the B1A and he describes the aircraft in a very interesting and
penetrating way, not surprisingly since after qualifying as a test pilot he spent his later
RAF years at A&AEE Boscombe Down first as superintendent of flying and then as
commandant.

I graduated from the Royal Air Force College Cranwell in April 1958 and was posted
to 232 OCU at Royal Air Force Gaydon on No 5 Victor Mk 1 course. I joined the

crew of Wg Cdr D A Green, the newly appointed OC of XV Squadron, prior to my posting to Cottesmore in October 1958. As a very junior pilot, and having flown nothing larger or more sophisticated than a Vampire, my first impressions were of a very large and complex aircraft which was technically very advanced for its time. The need to operate as part of a five-man crew also brought its challenges. The forty hours of OCU flying at RAF Gaydon passed relatively uneventfully, but did little to change these impressions; it also gave a hint that such a new and advanced aircraft might produce some maintenance and handling problems.

As the CO and first crew on XV Sqn, the 'Boss' decided that he and his crew would collect as many as possible of the new aircraft from the HP factory at Radlett and in the event we delivered five or six of the original eight Mk1s to Cottesmore. I recall the intriguing sight and smell of a brand new aircraft with perhaps as little as one hour's previous flight time, and my surprise that such an advanced aircraft could be produced at such a small factory and flown from such a short runway on such a small airfield.

Despite reliability issues with the airframe and the NBS (navigation and bombing system), I managed 200hrs in the first year of operations on the squadron, 140hrs in the second year and 177hrs in ten months of the third year. During the first year this flying consisted of high level navigation with simulated bomb runs over RBSUs (radar bomb scoring units) either as a single aircraft or as part of Group or Bomber Command exercises involving large numbers of aircraft from 1 and 3 Group airfields plus air displays of the new aircraft, scramble demonstrations for visiting VIPs and the early use of our dispersal airfield, St Mawgan. One notable event was the first overseas flight to Vancouver via Goose Bay by two aircraft, for flying displays as part of the celebrations to mark the Golden (50th) anniversary of flight in Canada. We also took part in the Bomber Command Bombing Competition for the first time, gaining valuable experience, but no high scores due mainly to poor NBS performance. A 10,000lb Blue Danube practice atom bomb was carried for the first time on a high level profile in November 1959 with no problems evident at the time.

In August 1960 I returned to Gaydon for a 22hr intermediate co-pilot's course, which then qualified me to fly in the left-hand seat of the aircraft under the watchful eye of my captain in the co-pilot's seat. A number of detachments were made to Akrotiri at this time to familiarise ourselves with the Middle Eastern theatre and use the practice bombing range at Episkopi, during which we dropped 100lb practice bombs visually from 40,000ft, as opposed to using the NBS. During 1961 trial flights of the extensive ECM fit were carried out for the first time, with encouraging results judging by some of the complaints received by various military and civil agencies.

In general, during this time as a co-pilot, apart from the issues described later, I found the aircraft pleasant to fly and the cockpit layout and comfort to be satisfactory, although the lookout was rather restricted by the heavy canopy framework. However, perhaps to be expected in those early days with a new and very sophisticated aircraft, some of the problems which led to a fairly high rate of unserviceability are worth exploring in more detail.

Two independent, 4,000 psi hydraulic systems were provided, each powered by an electro/hydraulic pump, with a high pressure nitrogen emergency system for undercarriage extension in the case of hydraulic failure. Unfortunately, there were a number of hydraulic failures in the early days culminating in several wheels-up landings on other units. Part of the problem was the constant cycling of the pumps, which were left off-load when not required to power their relevant system; eventually constant running pumps provided a more reliable system.

The undercarriage also produced a number of problems. Fortunately, these were normally a failure to retract rather than lower. However, as the aircraft had no means of jettisoning fuel with take-off weights in the region of 170,000lb and a max landing weight of 135,000lb, a failure to retract meant an hour or two at low level with the undercarriage and flaps down and airbrakes out, carrying out circuits to burn off the excess fuel. This may have pleased the pilots, but seldom endeared them to the rear crew. Having two engines side by side using a common intake often led to losing both engines on one side following an engine failure. If this occurred on the take-off run or shortly afterwards, the inability to reduce the all-up weight by jettisoning fuel meant that the aircraft required very careful handling, particularly when carrying out a heavyweight circuit prior to an overweight landing.

The retraction system was an ingenious procedure, whereby each main bogie, consisting of four axles and eight wheels, trailed to a near vertical position once the aircraft was clear of the ground. A number of 'tip lock hooks' then engaged with the bogie to hold it in the vertical whilst the leg retracted, with the result that the main bogie was upside down as the leg retracted along the fore and aft axis into the wing, thus saving the space that would otherwise be occupied by a sideways retracting leg. Each tip lock hook was fitted with a micro switch to indicate to the system that it had engaged the bogie correctly. Unfortunately, if any one of these eight micro switches failed the undercarriage would not retract and the early micro switches proved susceptible to the ingress of water and damp.

The Victor was not a difficult aircraft to land but, with threshold speeds varying from about 130kts to 160kts depending on the weight, it did require some care and good crew co-ordination to achieve an accurate touchdown point and avoid lengthy landing distances. The brake parachute

10 Squadron Victor B1As at Cottesmore.

provided excellent retardation requiring only moderate braking to achieve predicted landing distances. However, there were many brake chute failures in the early days due to malfunctions of the parachute compartment doors and, it was thought, to the poor airflow around the tail area. In addition, in strong crosswinds the strong weather cocking effect of the parachute sometimes made it necessary to jettison the chute early, particularly if the runway was wet and the nosewheel was not held firmly on the ground whilst elevator control was still available. Heavy braking would be needed if the brake parachute failed to stream. Initially, the aircraft was fitted with organic brakes, which faded badly and overheated under heavy braking, leading in some instances to brake fires. Later, inorganic brakes were introduced, the door opening system was changed from electric to hydraulic and handling techniques were improved, producing a much more reliable system.

Being the last of the V bombers into service brought additional attention from politicians, senior service officers and other UK and international VIPs, with the result that the squadron was required to carry out a very large number of scramble take-offs to demonstrate that four aircraft could get airborne in under four minutes and, in the early days, some theatrical licence was introduced. Following the firing of a Very light, the aircrew were required to sprint from one side of the runway to the aircraft and waiting groundcrew on the other. Apart from the possibility of cardiac arrest for some of the senior ex-WW2 captains, this imposed considerable problems for a multi-crew aircraft when the clock was already ticking, and five people with flying kit and navigation bags were trying to settle into a space which at the best of times was fairly confined. A ground power unit consisting of a bank of 24V batteries provided the electrical power for engine start, the engines being started individually from a control panel above the pilots' heads. Each engine had to be selected in turn and the next engine could not be selected until the start cycle for the previous one was almost complete. It was therefore quite an achievement to get four aircraft airborne within the set time limit.

There was also considerable competition between 10 and XV Squadrons to achieve the fastest time for the first aircraft to move on a scramble, which added to the excitement on the day. As the co-pilot (and possibly, as the youngest and the fittest crew member!), I was required to be first up the ladder and into the cockpit, closely followed by the air electronics officer who needed to switch on electrics to enable me to start the first engine whilst the remainder of the crew were still arriving at their crew positions. During practices, I discovered that if I selected the first engine and pressed the start button and external power was immediately cut off, the aircraft was

in a primed condition so that, if the crew chief selected the external power on as we raced across the runway, the first engine would be starting as we climbed the ladder, albeit there was nobody in the cockpit. This was, of course, highly illegal and a closely guarded secret which enabled XV Sqn to consistently beat the scramble times achieved by 10 Sqn.

Perhaps the most significant drawback of the Mk1 Victor was the low thrust of the Sapphire,

XV Squadron scramble take-off. Notice nose flaps, deleted on later aircraft.

which was, however, a fairly reliable engine. There have been various estimates published of the installed thrust ranging from 7,900lbs to 8,500lbs at sea level; I always assumed the former was more realistic. At normal max take-off weight (170,000lb) the thrust to weight ratio was therefore about 0.2 but at high airfield elevations and temperatures this was dramatically reduced, and I vividly recall a take-off at Nairobi when, at brake release, having run the engines up to maximum power against the brakes, I was amazed to observe what appeared to be a measurable pause before the aircraft moved. It had been necessary to extrapolate take-off figures from the operating data manual as the published data did not cater for such extreme circumstances. Suffice it to say that we became airborne just before the end of the 11,000ft runway and there was a very large and long gap between the V Stop and V Go speeds; this gap meant that had we had a single engine failure after the V Stop speed and before the V Go speed we would not have been able to take-off nor stop before the end of the runway. Even in the UK this gap often existed on hot summer days, but an airfield altitude of 5,000ft and a temperature of well over 30° C made the occurrence all the more dramatic.

However, I experienced only one engine failure during my five years on the aircraft, when an engine ran down to windmilling speed at high level, the high pressure fuel pump drive having sheared. Others experienced failures, including fire warnings but, so far as I can recall, until deployments started to the Far East these were relatively rare events. Far East operations necessitated flight through very cold air masses and, I believe, a number of serious engine failures occurred when the shroud surrounding the inlet guide vanes shrank to the point where all clearance was lost and the engine imploded. I understand the relatively simple but effective solution was to coat the inside of the shroud with 'Rockard' a substance used on the nose cone of rockets to enable them to withstand the heat stress of atmospheric re-entry. The theory was that the Rockard would ground down the tips of the low pressure compressor which might lead to some loss of performance, but would allow the engine to continue to run; so far as I am aware this proved to be a crude but effective solution to the problem.

One failure that did have an interesting conclusion occurred in June 1962 after I had returned to XV Sqn having completed my captain's course at the OCU at Gaydon. During the take-off run for a planned night high level training sortie, the oil pressure on the no 3 engine dropped to zero at about 120kts. I returned to dispersal and handed the aircraft over to the engineers. After two further abortive attempts, when the same fault occurred at the same point, we abandoned the sortie, as neither I nor the crew were looking forward to landing in the early hours of the following morning after a 20hr working day. Two days later, after rectification, the same aircraft and one other were offered to the CO, Wg Cdr John Matthews, and myself for a high level Group Exercise. A coin was tossed to see who had first choice of aircraft, and, having won the toss, I elected to take the alternative aircraft, leaving the one that had misbehaved previously to the CO. We followed John on the descent into Cottesmore at the end of the exercise and, shortly after he levelled out at 1,500ft, were more than a little surprised to hear him call "Mayday, Mayday – four-engine failure – abandoning the aircraft" – or words to that effect. Moments later we overflew the burning wreckage some five miles short of the runway, attempting to count the parachutes on the ground as we did so, before diverting to Wittering as all Cottesmore's fire cover had rushed to the scene of the crash. All three rear crew members had escaped via the crew entry door and the two pilots had ejected. I felt a particular sympathy with the 'Boss' as he and the navigators were part of my old crew and, but for the toss of a coin, it might have been my new and relatively inexperienced crew in the aircraft.[3]

During rectification of the oil pressure gauge problem, the fuel tray had been removed to allow access to the rear of the instrument panel. This involved disassembling a multi-pin plug and socket through which electrical control of all the fuel booster pumps passed from the fuel tray. The locking ring securing the plug and socket had apparently not been properly tightened, allowing it to rotate with the vibration during the flight and the two elements to begin to separate. A combination of the end of sortie low fuel state and the high demand for fuel as the throttles were advanced on levelling out, together with the change of aircraft attitude and intermittent electrical signals to the booster pumps, had caused fuel starvation and all four fuel low pressure warning lights to illuminate followed by all four engines flaming out.

One other exciting incident occurred in June 1963 during the climb en route to Goose Bay for a Western Ranger to Offutt airbase in the USA. For this flight I had positioned my co-pilot, who had completed an intermediate co-pilot's course, in the left-hand seat whilst I occupied the normal co-pilot's seat. At about 30,000ft there was a very, very large bang and the first pilot's hatch departed the aircraft. Even though we were not at very high level, the depressurisation, coupled with the suck effect of the airflow over the very large opening, was sufficient for every loose article in the cockpit to disappear through the hole in the roof. This included clothing, navigation bags, maps and charts; it was even more exciting for the co-pilot as the departure of the hatch was the first part of the ejection sequence for his seat. We were also carrying a sixth crew member, a crew chief, who, from his elevated and forward-looking seat between the pilots, had a ringside view of events. Having carried out an emergency descent to about 5,000ft and slowed down, it became possible to talk on the intercom and I asked the navigator plotter for our position to which he replied, rather rudely, that he had no idea. He had been plotting our position on a Gee chart when the hatch blew off and had stabbed his pencil point into the chart with the shock of the event; he was left with only one square inch of chart firmly attached to an otherwise clean chart table. On the way back to base we flew through, or close to, several low level cumulus clouds which brought some complaints from the rear crew. Having slowed down to a relatively low speed, rain was entering the cockpit well above the heads of the pilots, but soaking them thoroughly; the crew chief stoically said very little! I believe the cause of the incident was put down to the incorrect rigging of the hatch latching system.

I left the Squadron in December 1963 and joined No 23 fixed wing course at the Empire Test Pilots School which lasted for the whole of 1964 but was soon back on Victors.[4]

---

[3] See page 181 Victor B1A XH613 14th June 1962.
[4] See next chapter.

Norman Bonnor was a navigator and did a tour on both B1s and B2s. Here he gives a very comprehensive account of life on XV Squadron with David Bywater as his captain.

In 1960 I disappeared into the winter gloom of South Yorkshire at RAF Lindholme to complete the ten month V Force radar bombing course, flying in the Hastings T Mk 5 equipped with the same H_2S Mk9 and navigation and bombing system (NBS) that were being fitted to the Valiant, Vulcan and Victor. In June 1961, I arrived at 232 OCU at RAF Gaydon for No 36 Victor course. There were fifteen guys on the Victor course and twenty on the related Valiant course; the age-old traditions of Bomber Command still applied; on the first night, we all gathered in the officers' mess bar, where the staff expected us to sort out our five-man crews. Across the room, I recognised a blond-haired chap who had marched me around the drill square at Cranwell; this was Flight Lieutenant David Bywater, who was coming through as the first co-pilot on Victors to make it to captaincy. He looked like a good bet, so I bought him a beer, and we spent the rest of the evening picking out a co-pilot, a nav plotter and an AEO.

The ground school that summer of 1961 was a breeze, visiting a different Warwickshire pub each night and usually ending up having Chinese nosh in Leamington Spa or Stratford-upon-Avon at midnight. The flying phase was a bit more serious but still great fun and, after seventeen trips and fifty-five hours, our crew was posted to XV Squadron at RAF Cottesmore in October. The next phase was to qualify as a combat ready crew; this involved: completing a nuclear weapons training course, target study of both NATO and national targets, proving we could undertake first-line servicing of the aircraft if deployed or diverted and flying 16 sorties/60 hours undertaking various profiles and exercises and, finally, proving to the Boss that we were ready!

January 1962 saw the Squadron deployed to the Far East for a month but, as the junior crew, we were not allowed to fly a Victor all that way and had to suffer the rubber chicken meals of Transport Command on a Britannia for four legs through El Adem, Khormaksar (Aden), and Gan to Butterworth on Malaya. Somehow, the word got out that our crew had the youngest average age of all crews in the V Force, and the press descended on us for interviews and pictures; although it was good to see ourselves in the tabloids and broadsheets, my proudest moment was getting our picture in the *Eagle*! Finally we got to fly a couple of sorties and were surprised how much the Victor liked the much colder conditions at altitude and climbed easily to 45,000ft and above. With the very hot and humid ground level conditions of Malaya, we realised that the best technique to stay cool when returning to the circuit after five hours was to reduce the cockpit temperature before commencing descent and then turn off the air conditioning to retain the cool air. Unfortunately, we made a bad mistake on one of these trips; somehow, a rat – or perhaps it was a large mouse – got into the cockpit probably with our in-flight rations and appeared on the cockpit coaming. The two pilots reacted very quickly and depressurised the cockpit to kill the rodent before it could bite through some vital cables; mistake! A few hours after landing, the groundcrew were driven out of the aircraft by the smell of rotting rodent, and it took two days to find the offending corpse! When the detachment ended in early February, we flew back home in a Britannia.

Back at Cottesmore, training flights continued including fighter affiliation exercises with Gloster Javelins, for which we had to descend to lower than 40,000ft so they could catch up. The UK's first nuclear weapon was a 10,000lb lump called Blue Danube; by late 1961, it was rapidly being replaced by the first version of Yellow Sun making the original concrete replicas used for max all-up-weight take-offs redundant, so it was decided to use them for bombing practice at Jurby range off the NE coast of the Isle of Man. We were instructed to apply an offset of 200 yards from their raft target to reduce the risk of a direct hit putting the range out of use for a day or two. I took great care setting up the attack ensuring that the correct ballistic film was loaded on the NBS Calc 3 and keeping the radar markers accurately on the raft with the offset applied right up to release. Ted Edwards, our nav plotter, lay in the visual bomb-aimer's position and saw the 10,000lb lump fall away but, unfortunately, nobody at the range had seen it, so it must have made a perfect water entry with virtually no splash! That said, we regularly dropped 100lb practice bombs at various UK weapons ranges from a nuclear weapon simulator fitted in the bomb bay which gave us very realistic indications in the cockpit. A detachment to Wildenrath in Germany was interesting because we parked in the wrong place and, rather than restart the engines, the five of us plus the crew chief and a couple of local lads, managed to push the 70-ton aircraft several hundred feet. At the end of the six-month training period, in June 1962, we met the individual and crew classification requirements to move up to Combat Star and we were no longer the junior crew on the squadron.

After achieving Combat Star, we were rewarded with a 4-day Ranger sortie to Karachi via Akroitiri. After the Suez Crisis of 1956, this involved flying back westward from Cyprus then over Libya (I wonder if we would do that today) and Sudan to go round 'Nasser's Corner' at 22N/25E to avoid Egyptian airspace. On landing at Karachi, we were directed to a refuelling point and quickly completed the first-line servicing only to be told that we couldn't stay parked in that spot. With no suitable tow-bar available, we recalled our experience at Wildenrath and asked for some help to push the aircraft. A gang of locals appeared led by an overseer with highly polished boots and with much '2-6 Hupping', they pushed the aircraft some 150 feet to our parking spot. We arrived at the Speedbird Hotel rather hot and sweaty in our blue flying overalls, where the receptionist greeted our captain with great reverence and told him which suite was reserved for him; the rest of us were two to a room! After inspecting the accommodation, we persuaded our man that Bomber Command would never accept the bill for a suite and, much to the surprise of the receptionist, he asked to be downgraded to a room like ours. Unfortunately, the aircon didn't work too well in his new room, and he was none too happy when we smirked about this at breakfast. The hotel had its own outdoor swimming pool, but you had to share it with some rather large black ants that appeared to enjoy swimming. When you looked over the perimeter wall, it brought home the amazing difference in living standards between the jet-setting airline passengers of the 1960s and the local folk living in hovels nearby.

On 12th October 1962, we returned from a Western Ranger to Offutt, Nebraska, just as the Cuban missile crisis was beginning. We flew a training mission on 16th October but didn't fly again until 7th November. I was still single and living in the mess at Cottesmore and remember watching the situation unfold on TV with

U2 recce pictures of IRBM sites being prepared and missiles unloaded. I have the recollection that there was a quiet recall of personnel over the weekend of 20/21st October. Apparently, the Prime Minister, Harold Macmillan, had asked the C-in-C, Sir 'Bing' Cross, to bring the V Force squadrons to maximum readiness with the least publicity as he didn't want to alarm the general public. The engineers began to generate all available aircraft, including those in deep servicing, and load them with live nuclear weapons. As aircraft became available over the next few days, aircrews scramble-checked them and went on alert at RS15, Readiness State 15 minutes. From the normal one crew on QRA, quick reaction alert, on the Monday morning, we had built up to seven by the end of the week; there was only one XV Squadron aircraft that was not recovered from the hangar before the crisis ended. 10 Squadron was in a similar state by Friday, 26th October as were all the V Force squadrons in 1 and 3 Groups. 59 of the 60 available Thor missiles were in a similar or higher state of readiness. The political situation came to a head on Saturday, 27th during which we were called to cockpit readiness RS05 for an hour or so. Krushchev backed down that afternoon; we, and the rest of the world who were in the know, breathed a sigh of relief that WWIII had been averted. In the aftermath of the crisis, High Wycombe introduced monthly no-notice exercises such as 'Mick' and 'Mickey Finn'. These usually lasted up to a week and culminated in four-aircraft scrambles at Cottesmore and at least one of our dispersal bases such as St Mawgan or Bedford.

In the early 60s, the tactic for penetrating Soviet early warning and surveillance systems was still based on a large wave of aircraft at high altitudes covering its approach with high-power, broadcast jamming on radar and communications frequencies. The Valiant and some early Mk1 Victors and Vulcans had not been fully equipped with this ECM kit so regular exercises such as Spellbound were flown to test the capability of the force to fly in a large wave, up to 100 aircraft, with the jammers above and around the non-jammers to protect them. Obviously, this had to be tested away from main areas of population so a facility was set up at Stornoway against which we could prove how well the jamming covered these big waves of aircraft. Clearly, we didn't have a station-keeping capability, so the positioning of individual aircraft in the wave relied entirely on the navigation accuracy of the NBS on-board each aircraft. These exercises were often flown at night so the first time we did one in daylight it came as a bit of a shock to the pilots who could suddenly see many aircraft and contrails rather close by. When the run against Stornoway was complete, the jammers would be switched off and the wave would split up and complete other planned training as individual aircraft or return to base. On one such exercise, the AEO of one of our aircraft could not switch off one of the Red Shrimp jammers and flew down the UK from Glasgow wiping out all the TV relay systems, but fortunately the press didn't find out who caused the black-out of Coronation Street that night. The jamming finally turned off when the weight-on-wheels switch operated on landing.

The other tactical change that had taken place was in bombing; up to now, straight in attacks were made using radar (Type 2) from an identification point some 50 or 60 miles away; however, the Soviet deployment of SA1 missiles around Moscow and SA2 around some other major cities meant that high-flying aircraft could be vulnerable to these missile systems even at 50,000ft and above. To defeat the prediction capability of these systems, we changed our bombing tactic to a weaving approach (Type 2A) never remaining on heading for more than a minute or so; this made accurate bombing far more difficult as sensible corrections could only be made in the brief periods when straight and level.

Our crew achieved the select crew classification at the end of 1962 and, by this date, we were one of the most experienced crews on the squadron as many of the longer-serving crews had already moved on to the Mk2 squadrons at Wittering. That winter, it was 10 Squadron's turn to go to the Far East and, of course, the station commander – Group Captain Bob Weighill – wanted to visit them, so one of our crews was selected to take him out to Butterworth in early February. The winter of 1962/63 was particularly cold and icy, and clearing the runway and taxiways at Cottesmore was a 24/7 task and not always completely successful. When the aircraft took off for the Far East, it had a problem – the Maxaret anti-lock braking unit had failed on one side – but on the icy runway it wasn't obvious; it became very obvious when they landed at Akrotiri, when all eight tyres on the starboard side burst and caught fire. In their enthusiasm, the local fire crews managed to spray foam over everything including down the engine intake, so the aircraft was out of action. The frustrated group captain called for a replacement aircraft, and we were tasked to take one out to Akrotiri and wait for the damaged aircraft to be repaired to fly it back. The first part was easy, but the second became a nightmare as a bureaucratic row began between Bomber Command and the Near East Air Force HQ about who was responsible for assessing and repairing visiting aircraft in Cyprus. We enjoyed a day or so swimming and water-skiing but then decided to start working on the aircraft ourselves which caused yet more trouble with the local engineers. Under the supervision of the crew chief who travelled with us, we repacked the brake parachute, changed the wheels and tyres using a knuckle jack under the bogie and started working on the two engines that needed replacing. However, we reached our competence limit after a couple of days and returned home on 11th February as priority aircrew in transit on a Comet from Nicosia, much to the relief of my fiancé as we were due to be married in Melton Mowbray on the 23rd.

Training on high level profiles continued until late April 1963, when the decision was made to change the plans for penetration and attack of the Soviet Union by Mk1 Victors and Vulcans to low level (500 feet and below); the reason was the dramatic increase in deployment of the SA3 missile system around Soviet borders and cities.[5] This change involved a very different approach to training and, in particular, our navigation techniques. The nav plotter still used 4H pencils and Lambert's plotting charts for the high level phase but, for low level, he used chinagraph pencils and ½ million maps laminated with clear plastic. The normal mode of operation was for him to provide a running commentary of what the guys in the front should see and for them to confirm. My role as nav radar was still to update the NBS with regular radar fixes, but this now involved a new set of radar prediction techniques as the picture at low level was severely affected by hill shading, so that the height of an object or feature was far more important than what it was made of. Thus railway

---

[5]   After Gary Powers had been shot down in U2 in 1960.

embankments and even hedgerows became important when interpreting the picture. Our primary armament remained the 1.1-megaton, Yellow Sun Mk2 which, unlike the later WE177, was not a lay-down, delayed-fuse weapon. So we had to learn new bombing tactics involving popping up to 26,000ft just in time to release the weapon; later we were cleared to release it at 12,000ft in a full-power climb and effectively throw the bomb before escaping back to low level.

At the end of June 1963, we were scheduled for another Western Ranger to Offutt via Goose Bay, but the trip didn't go as expected. Planning for the trip was routine except that our co-pilot – Pete Armstrong – was now cleared to fly in the left-hand seat, so David Bywater said he should take the first leg to Goose Bay. (See David's earlier account.) In those days, the crew chief in the 6th seat faced forward; clearly, this was not a very comfortable position as he was directly in the airflow from the missing hatch and he didn't have a bonedome; the two pilots had lowered their seats as much as possible and were below the worst of the problem; fortunately they always carried some goggles so these were passed to the Chiefie causing much hilarity in the tower as through binoculars it looked as though he was sat up in an open cockpit flying the aircraft like something from the 1st World War! As a bomber, the Victor couldn't dump fuel so we spent an hour and a half in the circuit burning off the surplus to get down to max landing weight. Unfortunately, it was raining so we were very wet by the time we finally climbed out in the squadron dispersal. The hatch was found by a farmer near the Wash some years later. We were re-scheduled on the Ranger in August, but this time with SASO 3 Group – AVM Johnnie Johnson – who wanted to go salmon fishing at Goose Bay.

A foggy evening at Cottesmore in October resulted in us being diverted to RNAS Lossiemouth from the end of Bomber Command Exercise Anchor. With the long transit to Scotland, we descended to land with our fuel state almost at minimum and declared a PAN. As a result of our problem, air traffic gave us priority over a returning FAA Hunter which put him on minimums too. Fortunately, we both landed safely and later we met up with a relieved lieutenant commander in the wardroom bar. After congratulating one another for a good outcome, he asked what our fuel state was on landing; when David said it was 8,000lbs, he exclaimed "That's more than I took off with!", and we had to spend the next hour explaining why 8,000lbs spread around 21 tanks was our absolute minimum with a risk of flameouts if we had to overshoot. He wasn't happy, but I think he finally got the point.

By the end of 1963, the Bywater crew had achieved Select Star rating, the highest and most difficult classification, which only some ten percent of V Force crews ever managed. We had been together for more than two years and the co-pilot, Pete Armstrong, had completed his intermediate captain's course and David had been selected for the Empire Test Pilots School so we were ready to move on. At this time, President Sukarno of Indonesia was threatening the newly formed Malaysian republic as a means of diverting attention from his own internal problems as a failing dictator, so Sir Alec Douglas-Home's government decided to confront this threat by sending a few 'aerial gunboats', eight Victors in the conventional role, four from XV and four from 55 Squadron. The crews from XV included the Boss, now Wing Commander Marshall, and the A Flight commander, Squadron Leader Dave Mullarkey; however,

35 x 1,000lb bombs being dropped from a Victor.

the nav radar on this crew was due to get married around Christmas time so, as a spare nav radar, I was drafted in to take part in the Far East Operation Chamfrom.

The Victor bomb bays were quickly converted to the non-nuclear role and we started training for visual and radar attacks with 100lb practice bombs at the China Rock range in the South China Sea and at Song Song north of Penang Island. Soon after we arrived, FEAF HQ agreed that we should make our presence known to the population of Singapore so, on Christmas Eve, all eight aircraft flew at 1,000ft, one minute line astern, on a route that criss-crossed the island several times. For the same purpose, a number of practice attacks were made with 35 and 21 x 1,000lb sticks from high level; one of the drops of 35 was photographed by a PR7 Canberra of 81 Squadron also based at Tengah, and the resulting picture (above) was published in the *Straits Times* and other local newspapers.

That picture became an iconic symbol of the V Force, displayed in almost all Bomber Command operations blocks including at those stations operating the Vulcan, which could only carry a load of 21 x 1,000lb. The picture was carefully staged over Song Song range with the main aim of ensuring that all the bombs fell in the five-mile danger area; to achieve this, they were released at 15-millisecond intervals using the 90-way bombing system, but this would never have been done operationally as the aim of stick bombing was to have at least some overlap between the 30 to 50ft craters or 400ft fragmentation area depending on the target, so more realistic release intervals would have been between 100 and 500 milliseconds. Unfortunately on the day, the Canberra pilot banked too steeply as the release was called and, while the Victor was perfectly centred in the many frames of the F95 oblique camera film, the first few bombs were off the bottom before the last had left the bomb bay. Fortunately, the sergeant in the photographic reconnaissance laboratory said, "Leave them with me overnight sir", and the next day a picture showing all 35 bombs was available with no sign of the join between two frames; this long before digital airbrushing was available.

Early in January 1964, it was finally agreed that eight Victors parked in a neat row at RAF Tengah were a very tempting target for the Indonesian air force, so the four aircraft of XV Squadron moved to RAAF Butterworth on the mainland near Penang Island. Training flights continued with low level profiles culminating in further drops of 21 x 1,000lb bombs at high level. By the end of January, the chap I had replaced was married and, with the honeymoon over, he was flown out to rejoin his crew and I moved to FEAF Headquarters at Fairy Point on the east side of Singapore Island to provide expertise on the Victor's performance and capabilities and a rewrite of the operation orders and target plans for Operation Chamfrom and other operational plans involving V bombers in the Far East. The task took about four weeks, after which I was posted home to attend the Victor 2 ground school at RAF Gaydon followed by the flying phase on the Victor Training Flight at RAF Wittering before joining 100 Squadron with its Mk 2 Victors (see chapter on Victor B2).

Manual bomb sight.

Chris Le Comu, a nav plotter, describes dropping a full load of live bombs as a show of strength to the Indonesians.

Whilst on detachment with 57 Squadron in Tengah, Singapore during the confrontation with Indonesia in 1965, our crew was detailed to take part in a firepower demonstration (codenamed Exercise Showpiece) off the east coast of Malaysia. The plan was for all the participating aircraft (Hunter, Buccaneer, Victor and others) to fly, one by one of course, between two columns of warships in line astern formation, about four miles apart, and each headed by two aircraft carriers. The RN and Royal Australian Navy could muster quite a few ships in those days and if my memory serves me right, there were something like six ships in each line ranging from the carriers down to frigates. The VIPs for whom the demonstration was staged were on the carriers so the focal point for the demonstration was between the two line-astern flotillas and abeam of the carriers.

As the primary role of the Victor, in those days, was strategic bombing, we had little expertise in the conventional role and we were presented with a number of problems, such as the minimum safe release height for such a load of HE bombs, fusing options and stick spacing. We had to release from as low as possible because that gave us the best chance of getting the firepower where it was wanted. Dropping from 40,000ft would not have provided adequate accuracy.

Fortunately, the tasking agency, HQ 224 Group based at Seletar, had a weapons expert on the staff who did a few sums and decided that 5,000ft was the minimum altitude for the drop to achieve best effect and safe separation (between aircraft and bomb burst). We were also advised that air burst fusing (controlled by pressure-measuring equipment within each bomb) was preferable to impact fusing and that we should use minimum stick spacing – something like a quarter of a second between each release.

Equally fortunately, it was decided that a rehearsal should be carried out the day before the big event, and that the bomb load for the rehearsal would be 35 x 1,000lb, but only the first and last two of the stick would be live, the rest would be inert.

Everything went very well on the rehearsal, but the explosions and shockwave from the HE bombs were very pronounced and caused us to consider making the drop the next day from a slightly higher altitude. We chose 7,000ft.

So on the morning of 27th March 1965, we went through the normal crew briefing, emergency procedures and what ifs. Luckily the exercise area was not too far off the coast and the transit time from Tengah a matter of minutes rather than hours. Just as well, because with a large bombload, we could only carry a limited amount of fuel and therefore had little loiter time.

We soon located the 'fleet' and at the appointed time, aligned ourselves to make a run between the two flotillas. Usual pre-bombing checks were performed, bomb doors opened and when we judged the position to be right, pressed the bomb release button. A few seconds of silence and then a series of almighty big explosions, a short pause and then more explosions. I really thought we were going to fall out of the sky so violent were the effects, both noise and buffet. We closed the bomb doors, climbed away and headed for base knowing that something was wrong. Why the pause of explosions in the middle of the stick? Examination of the bomb control panel showed we still had 14 bombs on board; there had been a hang-up and the interlock system had prevented them from releasing. We did not want to land with all these HE bombs on board so made immediate plans to try and jettison on a coastal range nearby called Song Song (or was it China Rock? – one or the other). Approaching the range and this time nearer 15,000ft, we opened the bomb doors ready for a normal safe jettison, and a single bomb fell away from the aircraft. It must have fallen off its rack after the bomb doors were closed following the big drop. Whether it landed inside the range area or not we never knew, but the remainder were all jettisoned inert at the range, and we made a normal recovery, albeit a little low on fuel, into Tengah.

We spent many hours subsequently debating what might have been the outcome if all the bombs had released as planned. What seems fairly certain is that because the stick spacing was so small and the fusing set to 'air burst', sympathetic detonation was occurring so that each subsequent bomb was exploding a couple of hundred feet higher than its predecessor.

If all thirty-five had gone, it was quite feasible that the last few bombs of the stick might have inflicted serious damage to the aircraft, or even have created a fire-power demo beyond all expectations! Just for once we were grateful that things had not exactly gone to plan.

The crew were:

Captain	Sqn Ldr Tony Fraser
Co-pilot	Flt Lt Sandy Mason
AEO	Flt Lt Ted Gregory
Nav rad	Flt Lt Geoff Armitage
Nav plotter	Flt Lt Chris Le Comu

And the aircraft; XH591

Only a few month before this, the *Daily Telegraph* had published on the front page, a photograph of a Victor I dropping 35 x 1,000lb bombs (probably inert). This was before the aircraft had been painted in camouflage, they were still white. It was very obvious from the picture that the bombs had been released in groups of seven.

Dick Russell, who later was the refuelling expert on board Black Buck 1 discussed in a later chapter, was a qualified flying instructor and air-to-air refuelling instructor on K1s and K2s. However, he started on the Victor B1, joining 55 Squadron in 1962, and when they were converted to K1s he won an Air Force Cross for 'services to refuelling'. He relates some early memories.

In 1961 I was a QFI on Provosts when I was posted to 82 Valiant course as a co-pilot. However, just before going on leave prior to Gaydon another posting came in changing it to Victors, 41 course as a captain and Sqn QFI. It was like going from the third division to the premier league. When I phoned a friend at Honington he laughed when I said that I would finish the course in July. He said that they were going to paint them blue to match the ground equipment since at the time they had a reputation of being electrically unreliable. In fact, my course went without a hitch but on my first sortie solo I landed with a total fuel gauge reading of 12,000lb to be met by my CFI who said that I must be short of fuel since I had done five hours fifteen minutes on internal fuel. The Victor had a total fuel gauge in the back of the aircraft and climbing in we looked at the total gauge to see it reading only 4,000lb.

My crew backed me up well as they had read out the gauge reading. I flew with him on the next sortie in the same aircraft. We landed with a total of about 11,000lb but after shut down the total read 3,000lb. I gathered that the fuel capacitor belts were the problem.

The unreliability of the Victor Mk1 at this stage was re-emphasised by the fact that whilst I was on the course, we lost three aircraft.[6]

One at Akrotiri, a flap problem; the second at Honington an alternator drive shaft failure; and the third at Gaydon, mismanagement of the fuel (they ran out after an engine fire).

Furthermore, as mentioned, the electrical system had an unenviable reputation mainly because the power was derived from four engine-driven AC alternators driving through TRUs two 112V DC busbars with only batteries as a back-up; the crews were very suspicious of the system from a reliability point of view because there had been some failures and without electrical power there would be no flying controls. Nos 1 and 2 alternators were connected to the port busbar and 3 and 4 to the starboard busbar. For safety, the two busbars were normally kept separate but could be parallelled in an emergency. The alternators were not constant frequency so, after take-off, 3 alternator was set to 93% to give the AEO the correct frequency to drive his ECM equipment. All subsidiary services were driven from two 28V busbars. The system left a lot to be desired and the constant frequency AC system on the Mk2 with ram air turbines and an emergency auxiliary power unit was an enormous improvement.

Another problem was that each engine on the aircraft had a fuel pump driven by a quill drive which was prone to failure and this always resulted in a three-engine landing. This happened to me several times and the last one could have been awkward. I was with my friend Denys Mobberley on a heavyweight circuit on two engines on the approach at about 400ft when a quill drive went and the engine failed. Fortuitously it happened on the throttled back engine so I still had the two to overshoot with. Had it been on one of those I was expecting to give me take-off power it could have been more than awkward. The system was modified to improve the situation.

The early aircraft had brakes that were to say the least terrible. If the parachute, which was operated electrically did not come out, which happened about once in every ten landings, then there was a pretty good chance of a brake fire. The brakes were later upgraded to a ceramic material on the Mk1a together with the use of hydraulic power to operate the brake parachute.

For take-off we calculated a Go and Stop speed using the operating data manual; the Stop speed was the maximum speed at which the aircraft could stop on the runway for the weight, runway length, and ambient conditions; because the brake parachute was so unreliable it was discounted in the calculation of the Stop speed and so it worked out that our Stop speed was around 90kts. The Go speed calculated from the manual gave the speed which, when reached, enabled the aircraft to continue the take-off and climb away in the event of an engine failure. On the Mk1 this speed was about 120kts leaving a very nasty gap between the two speeds; clearly a very undesirable situation particularly when operating overseas at high ambient temperatures. Of course, these days such a situation would be unacceptable and, in fact, it was corrected when the aircraft was fitted with the Conway engines on the Mk2.

At Marham a line had been drawn across the runway at about 800yds and if the aircraft was better than 90kts on reaching the line then it was considered that everything would be all right. I remember thinking that this made no mention of weight and in a relatively short time after one aircraft made the line but on three engines it was scrapped since patently it was useless.

Which leads on to practice scrambles. Every now and then a visiting dignitary would be shown the ability of the V Force to get airborne within a certain time, I think that it was four minutes.

My first practice was at Honington and the signal to go was a flare. All four aircraft were parked, combat readied, on the hard standing at the beginning of the runway. My co-pilot was my CO, Wg Cdr Wilson who, for his sins, was with the dignitaries on the other side of the runway and I, fresh out of training, had been on the squadron exactly twenty-seven days. The flare went off, my boss ran across the runway as I began the actions to start. We were to be third off. He clambered in to the co-pilot's seat out of breath just as the engines (but only three of them) were running up. All aircraft were cleared to take-off on three engines for these demonstrations and we, or I, taxied on to the runway with my CO strapping in and as we straightened up moving at about 40kts I put the PFCUs on. We got airborne comfortably with the light fuel load and rather than try to restart landed back on three. All for show!! Not sure what I would have said in later years as a QFI watching the performance.

One early sortie on arrival on 55 Squadron in 1962 was with a max bombload take-off with the objective to drop all thirty-five in one go on the Jurby range by the Isle of Man. The Mk1A had a max take-off weight of 180,000lb; the airframe weighed about 96,000lb with the ECM pack and with our 35,000lb bombload we had 49,000lb available for fuel. Since we had to be back on the ground with 12,000lb we only had 37,000lb to use. Start and taxi took 3,000lb, climb to height another 10,000lb, leaving 24,000lb for the sortie which was to have a run in of about 100 miles to Jurby range prior to the drop. The planned sortie was to just north of Newcastle down to The Isle of Man (Jurby) and back to Honington, to land with the minimum fuel so the exercise was fairly demanding. Of course, the main task of the Victor was as a nuclear bomber weighing 10,000lb so with only that payload we could carry full fuel.

Interestingly, as the bombs were released the c of g went from maximum forward to maximum aft but the change of trim was barely noticeable.

Life on 55 Squadron was dominated by QRA and we had four aircraft, two from each squadron available day and night, 24/7 in modern terms. Each aircraft was in what was called a combat ready state and was started by a bank of batteries controlled by the crew chief outside. Initially, the fuel cocks were left open so that as the crew rushed to the aircraft after call out the captain would shout "start" to the chief, the engines would begin to turn as the captain climbed in and as he got into his seat he would punch the circuit breakers starting the fuel pumps.

On one unforgettable occasion the captain shouted start but the nav radar broke the key in the door lock. Result, engines running, nuclear bomb on board, no one in the cockpit. The recuperators kept the engines running backed up by some fuel until the groundcrew got an engine door down and shut them off.

In the winter of 1963 the whole station froze. The runway was unusable because of ice. Wg Cdr Flying got about forty aircrew (not groundcrew) out on the runway with shovels. Someone had the bright idea to get two Victors out as well and the thought was that the four engines would melt the snow and blow it off. In fact, all the two aircraft did was to melt the snow and move it about six feet whereupon it froze again. The whole idea was a fiasco and we were out of action for the better part of a week or more.

During the Cuba crisis we were alerted not by the siren as normally practised but by a knock on the door. All the serviceable aircraft were bombed up and crews congregated in the mess. Initially, the bar was open (we needed it) but reason prevailed and we dispersed to the target study rooms. Most of the crews had plans for their families; mine was for my wife to drive back to her parents with the children.

1964 came and the four Victor squadrons took it in turn to go to Singapore on Exercise Chamfrom; 55 Squadron's turn came and it was a nice little jolly although the Victor B1 was not really suited to operating out of tropical 30°C as it was grossly underpowered.

Whilst in Singapore we had a little trouble. Confrontation with Indonesia came and crews were briefed that if the balloon went up each crew had a target. Mine was Jakarta International airport with either fourteen or twenty-one thousand pounders, I cannot remember the number. The brief we had early on was that Indonesia had no radar since Decca had pulled out of the installation about eighteen months before.

We had four aircraft and were briefed that we were not allowed to use our Red

Dick Russell's crew at Butterworth with XH594 and a white XV Squadron Victor in the background. From left, Dick, Flt Lt Bendall nav rad, Fg Off Payne AEO, Fg Off Morris co-pilot, Fg Off Elwig sqn eng, Flt Lt Walters nav plotter.

Shrimp jammers because we were told it would give away the frequencies since there were so few aircraft attacking. At the same time we had a later update and intelligence showed us that the Russians had put in 200-mile search radar and there were Russian-built Migs on the holding point at the airport.

Two aircraft were detached to Butterworth and I was detachment commander. On arrival we discovered that with our fuel and bombload the runway, a new north/south replacement of 7,500yd for the 2,000yd east/west was too short to get off with our fuel and bombload. My phone call to our 55 Squadron commanding officer I leave to the imagination.

Incidentally, when we dispersed from Tengah in 1964 and arrived at Butterworth I said to my crew chief "uprate the engines" which he could do quite easily. They were nominally rated to give their take-off output at 100% rpm, however prior to confrontation in 1964 they were uprated to 101.5% if needed and for operational necessity; the total time allowed was 30 minutes for the life of the engine. However the engineering officer at Butterworth would not allow it because he said he did not have the authority. There were some very heated words said by me to him and I finally complained to my boss down at Tengah, Alan Housten, but despite the short length of the runway and the high temperatures the engines were not uprated.

Terry Filing, the captain of one of the crews from 57 Squadron who had come out to Tengah to relieve us had an incident. Climbing out from Tengah one night he had a fire in number three engine. The drill in those days was to shut down the adjacent engine as well. He shut down three and four and turned for home. On the way down number two caught fire. Problem, he obviously could not shut down the adjacent engine but after the fire drill he was left with only one going. In order to start the good one, that is number four engine, he had to parallel the low voltage busbars which in those days was a no no except in exceptional circumstances. Anyway he did parallel, restarted number four engine and got back OK; remember, the bomber aircraft had no fuel jettison facility.

It took this incident to bring to the fore a well known problem with the Sapphire engine. The Javelin with the Sapphire engine had had this problem before. It was called centre-line closure. The Javelin with its greater rate of climb had experienced this several times before back in the UK. It was caused by the outer casing of the engine contracting and touching the compressor blades due mainly to the rapid change of outside temperature. The Victor in the UK did not climb quickly enough to be affected but in Singapore the temperature change with height was more rapid, at least it was in this case.

Months later back in the UK I was teaching engines as part of my job on the OCU as well as the autopilot and the fuel system. I discovered that the remedy for the blades touching the casing was to coat the inner part of the outer casing with carborundum so that if and when the compressor blades touched they would wear away.

The Sapphire if I remember correctly had an overhaul life when I was involved of 1,200hrs; it had been raised over the preceding years from somewhere around 800hrs and around 1967 it was extended again to 1,400hrs for 'selected engines'. Now I used to talk to the techies quite a lot about the things I was teaching and so I went to the engine bay and asked what a selected engine was. I might have guessed the answer; the chief in the engine bay said all those that reach 1,400!!

However, the Sapphire was a great and reliable engine. On one co-pilot left-hand seat sortie we collected eleven seagulls down one of the port engines at unstick. Since I could not jettison we went up to 5,000ft and burnt off fuel. The engine had to be changed but it did continue to run for the hour or more spent circling over the coast.

Life on a B1 squadron was for the most part at a fairly gentle pace. We flew about five times a fortnight, each flight taking more than about ten hours. Every flight had to be at least six hours which would consist of a navigation stage or stages culminating with a practice bomb drop scored by a radar unit at the range. It would be normal to have three targets and they all had to be booked. So if all the ranges were booked until 1800 then we could not get airborne until an hour or so before then.

A crew would get in three hours prior to take-off apart from the two navs; they would, depending on the complexity of the sortie, have to sort out the navigation stage(s) so that the target was attacked on the correct heading and they might be in thirty minutes ahead of the others.

Because the flight times were over a 24hr period there was an aircrew buffet and we could have a meal prior to and after flight. There were no fat aircrew!!

Over and above the flying we were required to target study, in essence we studied the targets that we had been allocated and we were required to answer a series of questions every now and then posed by the targets officer.

On fifteen-minute standby each crew was allocated a Standard Ensign estate car which at night was connected to a battery charger and a bray water heater, and they had to stay together throughout the day and night. A practice call out was held every 24hrs and if a crew and aeroplane did not make the threshold of the runway within

57 Squadron Victor B1A XH588 near Butterworth.

the fifteen minutes the captain had to account for it to the station commander.

They were long days, and not particularly rewarding and I hated them. Two opportunities came up. The first was an Air Ministry order asking for volunteers for the test pilot's course; the requirement was that they should have four-engine experience. The second was a volunteer for the Mk 2 simulator at Wittering.

I put in an application for both but they did not get off the station. My station commander, Freddie Ball, caught me outside our operations block one day and put it to me that it would be unlikely that Group would release me as I had only been on the squadron six months and there was a shortage of crews so I cancelled them both. We flew together many times and he came with me to Singapore the following year, going home with another crew.

At Honington there were two Victor squadrons and a Valiant tanker squadron, 214. We were like chalk and cheese and presumably because of our totally different roles seemed to keep to ourselves.

Finally, in 1964 fatigue caught up with the Valiant and they finally stopped flying with four or five on the airfield jacked up. After one rather stormy night one fell off the jacks and it sat there resting on one wing. In the meantime 55 and 57 Squadrons moved to Marham and the Valiants there, in the same state, were cut up on the airfield. Occasionally, when taxiing out in my Victor there would still be a piece of Valiant on the taxiway.

The Victor Mk1 bomber did a good job as a deterrent in its time carrying Yellow Sun and it was replaced by the new build Victor Mk2 aircraft carrying Blue Steel. The only Mk1 airframes left were the K1 tankers but because of the relatively low-powered Sapphire engines they had to be very careful in deciding how much fuel could be carried always taking into account the length of the runway and the ambient temperature. The larger engines in the Mk2 Victor revolutionised the aircraft.

Chapter Three

Victor K1

In the mid-60s there was a shortage of refuelling tankers due to the Valiant having to be retired prematurely with metal fatigue, so six B1As were converted to tankers with two Mk20 hose and drogue units, one under each wing, while leaving the bomb bay available for weapons; 55 Squadron then became operational in April 1965. However, these aircraft with a low refuelling rate were only suitable for refuelling fighters so that later fourteen further B1As and eleven B1s were converted to dedicated tankers by fitting two permanent fuel tanks in the bomb bay and a Mk 17 centreline hose dispenser unit so that fuel could be delivered at a much higher rate; these aircraft were designated K1 and K1As, K1's modification state being slightly less than the K1A.

The Victor K1 tankers carried 85,000lb of fuel but the aircraft only had the Sapphire engines and so max weight take-offs at 180,000lb were very demanding. The problem was that in the event of certain engine failures, like compressor blades becoming detached, the adjacent engine would also be affected.

Victor K1 with centre hose drum unit and wing flight refuelling pods.

David Bywater[7] by this time was a test pilot at Boscombe and relates some of the very necessary test work.

In January 1965 I joined B Squadron of the Aeroplane and Armament Experimental Establishment at Boscombe Down, initially as a project officer and later as the senior pilot. During this time I was involved in trials flying on a wide variety of aircraft types including the Victor B1/B1A, and 2, the Vulcan B1/B1A and 2, and all marks of Canberra. Early flight trials on the Victor Mk1/1A were concerned with various improvements to the communications, intercom fits and work on the development of the centre station HDU and hose in conjunction with Flight Refuelling Ltd, often using Victor 1 XA 918, a long term development aircraft used by both Handley Page and A&AEE for a wide range of the early flight trials of the Mk 1/1A.

Following the decision to replace the Valiant in the air-to-air refuelling role with the Victor, trials were carried out in 1965 and 1966 to provide a CA release of the tanker fitted with a Mk 20 flight refuelling pod under each wing and the centre station Mk17 hose drum units removed from the Valiants. Early trials enabled a CA release to be given for refuelling from the wing pods whilst work continued at Boscombe to assess the centre station. Meanwhile the Marham squadrons (55 and 57) were anxious to commence their AAR training and had aircraft fitted with centre stations which could not be used. One squadron commander, Wg Cdr Des Hall, decided that, despite having no receiver training, there was no reason why he should not go ahead and make contact on the centre station of one of his tankers. Apparently his approach to the drogue was probably rather too fast, which resulted in a hose ripple which broke the tip of his probe off. This left the tanker pumping fuel through the drogue valve which was held open by the broken probe tip. As the receiver overtake speed took it closer to the tanker, the hose oscillation resulted in the drogue striking the top of the receiver and breaking through into the pressure cabin, meanwhile continuing to dispense fuel at a rate of 4,000lb/min, which soaked the rear crew and cabin in Avtur and could have had disastrous results. Des Hall was nevertheless adamant that the hose oscillation was abnormal and dangerous and should not have occurred. The other Victor project officer, Alan Fisher, and I were thereafter involved in an interminable trials programme, flying either the tanker, receiver or a chase aircraft taking high speed cine film, in an effort to excite and record any centre station hose oscillation. Finally, after many flights, I chased Alan Fisher whilst he ran through the flight test schedule, which finally on this occasion, using a variety of pitch-control inputs, produced a runaway oscillation. This quickly increased to the point where the hose and drogue were rising at one extreme to point forward over the top of the tailplane, and at the other striking the bomb bay doors on the underside of the aircraft. After much analysis of the system, it was concluded that the dynamics of the airflow behind the Victor with the ex-Valiant 90ft cotton-sheathed rubber hose resulted in a system which was inherently unstable and capable of becoming self exciting. The fix was to use a shortened 75ft rubber hose, but air-to-air refuelling was treated far

---

[7]   See last chapter.

more seriously after this, and every receiver and drogue combination required a very thorough evaluation thereafter.

Barry Neal, who was later a squadron leader/flight commander on 57 Squadron at the time of the Falklands campaign, describes his earlier experiences on the Victor K1 and K1A.

AAR CAPABILITY

1,200 LB/MIN
4,000 LB/MIN
1,200 LB/MIN

Victor K1 refuelling rates.

In early spring 1969 several fresh-faced young pilot officers and flying officers, including me, were contemplating their futures as co-pilots on various multi-engined aircraft across the RAF. The previous six months or so had been spent learning and honing our skills on the venerable Varsity TMk1. After 100 hours I realised that the multi-engined world was where my flying skills would be best spent. The choice of aircraft type was pretty much the same for all graduates of multi-engine flying training courses at RAF Oakington, Cambridge – transport, maritime or bombers. But this time there were some openings on Victor tankers. After some enquiries and a visit to RAF Marham in Norfolk, a couple of us opted for what we hoped would be varied and exciting flying rather than plodding along carrying live (and dead!) freight halfway around the world. And so it was to be, but not until early 1970 when I started training at 232 Operational Conversion Unit (OCU) at RAF Marham.

Having been de-compressed, thrown in the sea for fun, and putting my head in the books yet again, I started flying in earnest on the Victor 1A in the right-hand seat. There were no tanker variants of the aircraft on the OCU in those days; the air-to-air refuelling (AAR) conversion was done on the squadrons. I soon started enjoying the aircraft and, once you got used to the rather cramped conditions – confined to an ejection seat – and the restricted visibility, the aircraft was good to fly. Under-powered, yes, as was soon to be proved, but good nonetheless. We graduated from the OCU as a complete crew – myself and the navigator radar as the 'new' boys – and went off to 55 Squadron. 57 and 214 Squadrons were also in residence with a total station establishment of twenty-four aircraft plus some in-use reserves, with each squadron having a two-point version of the aircraft (the K2p – no centre hose) for squadron pilot training. My first AAR sortie for real was a K1A maximum weight take-off and circuit with me sat on the 6th seat. Welcome to the real world of the Victor tanker!! It was probably one of the most frightening things I had ever seen in my (then) short flying career. If a single engine failed on the K1 then its adjacent engine was (nearly) always shut down for safety to avoid the complications of an uncontained failure damaging that adjacent engine – so we trained in that way. The heavyweight circuit was a simulated single-engine failure with both engines on one side throttled back to idle. The lack of engine power was aptly demonstrated, not only did we struggle to leave the runway even in early June, but in the event of a real engine failure then fuel had to be jettisoned to struggle round the circuit; a lesson that would not be forgotten by any pilot new to the aircraft and one that ensured you treated it with respect.

Most of our time in those days was spent training and deploying on exercises with the UK's fast jets. Hours were spent over the North Sea on routine AAR 'towlines' (racetrack patterns established around a fixed point enabling aircraft to find the tanker and get fuel), with lots of time spent in either Malta, Cyprus, Masirah off Oman, Gan in the Indian Ocean or Singapore, having deployed with or assisted in the deployment of fast jets on exercise. Careful planning was needed as, at all times, all aircraft in a formation had to have sufficient fuel to divert to a nominated airfield should the need arise. If the geographical nominated diversion point was reached and fuel had not been taken on then a mandatory diversion was made; a simple procedure to calculate and extremely accurate and effective. Tanker refuelling equipment was extremely reliable and it was rare that a diversion was necessary due to that equipment failure, usually other circumstances conspired to force a diversion. We had a continual standby commitment to support the UK's quick reaction alert (QRA) force (Lightnings and Phantoms depending who was on 'Q') with one tanker at three hours notice and another at six hours. Support for QRA was often needed at the extremities of UK airspace and detachments to Leuchars, near Edinburgh, in support of QRA were frequent. Short notice, ten-day detachments were not unusual.

I quickly progressed through an intermediate co-pilots' course (ICC) at the OCU to a captaincy. Back to the OCU for the third time in early 1973 and back to 55 Squadron with a new crew and, yes, that heavyweight take-off and circuit again. One day that September our deployment of fighter aircraft from the Far East was delayed, with us in a very hot and dusty Dubai. The take-off was put back and back and back until we had to take off at probably the hottest part of the day. At the 11,500ft point of a 12,000ft runway I pulled back the control column to take off although we were still a few knots below the 'calculated' rotate speed for the conditions. In no-man's land between the 'decision point' and rotate speed, I had no alternative but to go. In fact, I had already learned from plenty of similar instances that a heavy K1's acceleration after the decision point was not always as advertised!!

As a captain, decision-making skills were quickly advanced and, more importantly, new flying skills emerged. All tanker captains had to be trained and qualified to receive fuel from another tanker by day and night. A new dawn arrived when the time came for that training and by the end of the year I was qualified; a remarkable skill that gave enormous satisfaction as a pilot when a successful receiver sortie was accomplished – especially in poor weather conditions. More was to come as in the middle of 1974 I became an AAR instructor (AARI) instructing other Victor captains in that particular skill. It gave immense personal satisfaction when captains which I had trained were checked-out and qualified.

And then, along came the K2 – a quantum leap in aircraft performance, capability and fuel capacity. For performance and capability, yes, and that was the understatement for the latter! "We would not now need aircraft captains to be receiver trained," said our Masters. "OK," we thought, "let's see." I had been planned to convert to the K2 pretty quickly, but some bright spark decided that I would be better off in a 'career improving' desk job. So I was short-toured and given seven days notice of a posting to the tanker pilot staff desk at the then HQ 1 Group. I mention that because while I was there the first Harriers were deployed to Belize and, guess what, plans for the deployment included tanker/tanker receiver sorties to get the Harriers there expeditiously. So we said to our Masters in MOD "Excuse me, but?" All K2 captains were soon qualified in the receiver role – but only by day as "we would not need a night capability"!

I moved, on promotion, to an exchange tour with the USAF, flying KC135 tankers and, from California, the family came back to Marham in a miserable October in 1980. I had been appointed a flight commander on 57 Squadron and went off to the OCU (again) to convert to the K2. The OCU had fully AAR role-capable K2s, and crews qualified in the tanker role during the conversion. Day receiver training for captains was subsequently done on the squadrons – 57 and 55. The role, procedures, day-to-day flying, standby commitment and deployments and exercises were pretty much the same as before. The K2's engines were a dramatic improvement – 'contained' so it wasn't necessary to shut down an adjacent engine in the event of a single-engine failure. The increased power meant that the aircraft could be handled more "aggressively" (if I can use that word) and confidently. At medium fuel loads, a K2 could out-climb a fully loaded Phantom and, in some circumstances, out-accelerate in level flight, but more of that later.

Canadian F5 and RAF Phantoms.

George Worrall who was a navigator plotter also spent a lot of time on K1s and he relates his experiences.

I had four years of ground tours and a navigation refresher course at Stradishall before being posted to 57 Victor tanker squadron at Marham. I had been at Marham before but only very briefly, after Air Navigation School in Winnipeg (52/53); the backlog was such that we soon got out of practice and a short term remedy to keep us air minded was to send us on familiarisation flights as observers, which is how a Marham Washington (B29) came to feature in my logbook. Marham was not the best place to enjoy an adventurous social life. It was known as 'El Adem with grass'. The important thing here is that this clouded any enthusiasm I might otherwise have had for joining a Tanker Squadron. Nevertheless, it was for me a new and interesting role which had a tangible meaning not found when performing the no less important role of nuclear deterrent. Passing fuel to aircraft in flight seemed perhaps more purposeful than dropping practice bombs.

There is another downside to recapturing the events of those years of the Cold War. Much of the training material and documentation we used was classified. By habit we were very security conscious indeed and had of course all signed the Official Secrets Act. I well recall how after having retired from the RAF I found quite a lot of classified material which had been part of my professional equipment – lesson notes, check lists and so forth. I burnt the lot forthwith. One's memory, however faulty, has to be relied on.

As a navigator/plotter I attended the Tanker Training Flight (TTF), also at Marham, in October/November 1968; the flying phase comprised fourteen training flights. Apart from exercising our usual roles as either navigator radar or navigator plotter, both navigators received training in operating the refuelling system controls, though they were located at the navigator radar's station and were his responsibility. This was because the downward-facing periscope for monitoring what was going on at the receiving end of the refuelling hoses was at his station. It was a fascinating learning process not least because of the several fail-safe features of the system to prevent mishaps. Fuel could only be passed when a green light indicated a positive connection between tanker and customer. If the link was broken the fuel flow would cut off immediately. Any excess acceleration or deceleration forwards, backwards or sideways at the point of contact would have a similar consequence. It was a comfortable and comforting system to operate.

During this phase we went down to RAF Mountbatten at Plymouth for some sea survival training. We leapt from a launch each clutching our one-man dinghy packs which we inflated and scrambled aboard as quickly as we could. We were required to stabilise our craft by deploying a small sea anchor; however our pilot neglected to do so until the fresh breeze had carried him way downwind. The crafty devil had realised that the 'rescue' helicopter would fly into wind to pick each of us up in turn. As he was now the closest to the incoming helicopter he was the first to enjoy the sanctuary of its cabin.

Victor K1A and Lightnings on Tansor.

It was also a requirement for tanker pilots to receive training in taking on board fuel from fellow tanker aircraft. This not only gave them the feel of being at the receiving end of transfers but was a necessary procedure for extending the range at which tankers could themselves operate, which was so dramatically illustrated in the Black Buck bombing raids on the Falkland Islands when they were occupied by Argentinian forces in 1982.

The Victor tanker fleet was first fitted out with only two refuelling points mounted on the underside of the outer wings, but by the time I joined the Squadron all aircraft had a heavy-duty refuelling point in what had been the bomb bay. These were called hose drum units (HDUs).

The fuel hoses which terminated in a nozzle surrounded by an aerodynamic stabilising drogue were retractable by being rewound on to the drum from which they were deployed during flight as required. Fighter aircraft could use any drogue whilst larger aircraft would employ the larger centre drogue only. Refuelling three 'small' aircraft at once was perfectly feasible. The tankers were choc-a bloc with fuel of course which could be moved around the several tanks as required for transferring and for keeping the tanker aircraft's centre of gravity within prescribed limits. Synchronising and maintaining airspeeds during fuel transfers was occasionally difficult for aircraft with a marked difference in speed range from the tanker aircraft and a gentle descent known as 'tobogganing' was sometimes used.

Because we could expect to be deployed anywhere, navigational exercises were as routinely carried out as when I had been on bombers, with the usual requirements of practice in astro navigation and using limited navigation aids. Throughout Strike Command, all aircrew had strict training commitments to meet and, furthermore, were monitored at intervals by on-board specialist teams known as tactical evaluation teams or 'trappers'.

Sorties dedicated to refuelling practice would take place in well defined zones known as tow-lines monitored by ATC services. The tanker would fly a trombone pattern rather like an elongated racecourse whilst customers would practice making contact with the trailed drogues. We would fly up and down these trombones for hours at a time. The navigator operating the refuelling equipment was busy all the time, otherwise the procedure could get monotonous. But practice for all concerned was, of course, absolutely necessary. The tow-lines were identified by the fighter station with which they were associated such as Binbrook tow-line and Wattisham, Leuchars, Boscombe, and RAF Germany tow-lines.

From time to time the non-stop overseas deployment of our fighters would require en route refuelling and tankers would be pre-positioned along the intended route. The stretches of route calculated for optimum fuel transfers would be charted and defined within brackets. The receiving aircraft would aim to start taking on fuel as soon after reaching the opening bracket as possible but if the requisite transfer had not been achieved by the closing bracket the customer would have to divert to a designated en route airfield. This was a critical fuel management and safety procedure if fuel starvation was to be avoided; this would also apply to any tankers who took on fuel during flight.

Fuel management was always critical, especially during such 'operational' transfers.

On one occasion we flew to Masirah to top up Phantoms travelling non-stop to the Far East. The requirement was such that we had to take off at maximum all-up weight with a full fuel load. Unpopular pre-dawn departures were the safest option due to the local ground temperatures. On one occasion during pre-flight planning I discovered that HQ Staff had seriously miscalculated the fuel log which fortunately was corrected in good time. I also recall a refuelling exercise in the Penang area when we couldn't wind in the central hose and had to head for a maritime danger area to jettison both it and excess fuel at low level in a fearsome tropical storm. My log book also records just four occasions when we had to RTB (return to base), twice for bird strikes and twice for engine problems.

In many ways the refuelling role was perhaps the most mission-oriented role I had experienced, with the sole exception perhaps of two Canberra raids on Egyptian targets during the Suez crisis of 1956. One could get anxious about the fate of aircraft whose refuelling needs were critical to their mission even if they were only in peaceful transit. One hoped to get one's own part right, to be in the right place at the right time, that was the navigator plotter's job.

On occasions we were deployed overseas for a period so that the aircraft which we had refuelled en route to the same destination could exercise in the local environment using local air-to-ground firing ranges where possible and air refuelling between mock attacks. Tanker crews were a bit like transport crews, meeting each other half way at places such as Cyprus or Gan, some outbound some inbound. Such exercises were identified by arbitrary codenames such as Piscator, Chicanery, Magic Palm, Blue Nylon, Forthright, High Noon, Ultimacy, Arctic Express, Panther Trail, Bersata Padu, Co-op, to name but a few. On occasions we enjoyed task-free deployments known as Rangers. A Western Ranger would have Offutt AFB Nebraska as its final destination. Other codeword items in my logbook are Tankex, Phantex and Litex. I was in the crew which made the first visit to Hong Kong by a Victor tanker (10th April 1970). We were greeted by a small reception party and a pretty girl bearing a tray of glasses of beer.

One episode which perhaps merits special attention was the *Daily Mail* Air Race[8] of early May 1969, in which Victor tankers were used to refuel the Harrier of 1 Squadron and RN Phantom of 892 Squadron in their dash across the Atlantic. It may have been the first time in which the tankers were used at such extended range across open water, employing the same techniques for greatly extending their range via tanker to tanker transfers as was later to be used even more dramatically in the Black Buck raids. Our crew gave the Harrier its first top up just before it reached the Atlantic.

I do recall a phase when we were put to maritime reconnaissance, in which the nav/radar would use his NBS screen to plot the traces of surface vessels, trying to determine their course and speed. Our nav/radar was pretty good at it. Whatever were our airborne tasks we had to surrender our logs and charts for checking and very little was handed back.

Unlike the Vulcan, in which I had clocked up quite a lot of flying time, the Victor enjoyed the benefit of having the entire crew at the same level. One could swivel

---

[8]   Discussed in more detail later.

round and see forward through the cockpit; not that there was ever much to see or much of an aperture to see it through. In other respects, apart from the refuelling instrumentation fitted at the navigator/radar's position, the rearward-facing crew stations were not dissimilar to those of the Vulcan.

The pilot of the first crew to which I was assigned had considerable experience of flying the Victor so it was not entirely a surprise when on his last flight before leaving the service he performed an unathorised barrel roll, which happily, apart from creating a bit of a dust-storm in our crew compartment, was accomplished without incident of consequence.

George was being kind about the barrel role since clearly the pilot did not pull the nose high enough before starting the roll to keep on positive g as he should have done. Godfrey Moffatt was a pilot on 214 Squadron on K1s as the K2s were being delivered.

Time in staff work led to a posting back to Marham as flight commander, on 214 Sqn. We were still busy, but now the big boys – Victor K2s flown by 55 & 57 Squadrons – were on the job. There were some new faces but also a lot from the past and there was plenty of work to go around. There was a lot of rivalry but it was always centred on getting the job done efficiently, flexibly and with style. A missed first contact to take fuel as part of the job, especially in a formation in which more than one tanker squadron was present, would be noted and subsequently used in evidence at an appropriate moment!!

All this increasing activity went hand in hand with constant operational training and evaluation of the front line's capability. The base and its squadrons were subjected to an ever-increasing number of evaluations by national and occasionally NATO staff. To cope with the operational implications and to learn the necessary lessons, the stations created their own mini evaluations – minivals – which lasted only a day or so. Tactical evaluations by Command grew more frequent and were bigger, better and much longer. We even took part in one that covered almost two weeks and kept a peacetime station on a 2 x 12-hour shift system for the whole period, including operating in a very warm spell in full NBC equipment (nuclear, biological, chemical). It was a difficult time for all, but the groundcrew, faced with the reality of 'war in rubber suits', found it really trying, but still met all the requirements.

We still worked at our deployments to the Mediterranean and beyond, but fast jet training and Red Flag scenarios in the USA meant more tanking across the Atlantic and beyond; different lessons to learn, different tactics to devise. In reality we were preparing the ground for that demonstration of the ability of air-to-air refuelling to extend a force capability – the bombing of Port Stanley in the Falklands.

The tanker force came of age then, and those of us who had been in at the beginning or very close to it were extremely proud of the way it was handled – professionally, flexibly and ultimately, when the plans went somewhat awry, with considerable bravery, to ensure the task was successfully completed.

This demonstration of the worth of AAR took place after our Squadron had been disbanded yet again but we all played our part in developing the tactics that were used and many of the main players, at all ranks, in that operation, were proud to include 214

Squadron in their log book.

Like most I had a total belief in my own and my crew's abilities to cope with all eventualities – overconfidence which led inevitably to a nasty shock to my ego.

I was on my first trip as detachment commander to Leuchars – four aircraft from the squadron on a quick reaction alert in support of the Phantom squadrons during a period of high Russian activity – Bears and Badgers operating in the Atlantic, close to the British Air Defence Identification Zone (ADIZ), testing our ability to react.

It was a busy time and we were flying at least one, and occasionally two, sorties a day. Interesting, high intensity work as the threats changed and our 'chicks' profiles and airborne requirements changed accordingly.

On Day 3 we were scrambled in the late afternoon to support the Phantoms well out to the west looking for Bears who had been picked up further north heading south into the ADIZ. All went fairly well and we joined up with our receivers who were not having much joy making contact with the 'enemy' – fuel was a problem; we were a long way from base. They could take large amounts of fuel from us – so the plan was to keep them well topped up to allow them maximum operational capability but also keeping us well aware of our fuel state.

No contact with Russian aircraft had been made after some long time 'on task' and we were beginning to think about getting the chicks and ourselves back to base – both our base and our alternative diversion weather forecasts were good. As we announced the final plan, the fighter leader called contact, simultaneously requesting another fuel top-up. A very hurried appraisal of our fuel state and checks on base and diversion weather allowed us to cope with most of their fuel requirements. The new plan, however, also required us to land at Lossiemouth, our diversion, with normal landing fuel. Lossiemouth was en route to Leuchars, and there would be sufficient to go to Leuchars and land on minimums should Lossiemouth become non-available. Good plan!

The trip back to the mainland was normal. As we approached Lossiemouth I checked the weather at both bases, both were clear and with good forecasts. At that stage the devil in the head said "Don't be silly just confirm the forecasts with 'actuals' and then you can get back to Leuchars albeit with minimum fuel and get on with being detachment commander" – what a good idea I thought. The actual weather at Lossiemouth was gin clear with no trend; Leuchars was clear with a forecast of 3/8 cover at 800 feet later. So the decision to continue to the forward operating base was made: after all it was only another forty minutes or so, and we could monitor the trends.

Some ten minutes later the AEO announced that Lossiemouth had called saying that they were now below minimums and were closed! I think I calmly suggested that perhaps we should check the Leuchars weather now some twenty-thirty minutes away – just to be sure!

"AEO to captain – Leuchars report the Haar is moving in with the cloud base 600ft with drizzle – continued deterioration expected."

A brief acceptance of a 'fickle finger of fate' intervention in the plan – realisation that the issue was to beat the weather as we were not going to go anywhere else, a brief pause for thought and then the plan – for even briefer consideration by the crew:-

1.Get Air Traffic clearance for a clean 300kt descent on a curve of pursuit to join Leuchars RW 27 at 1,000ft and three miles, at approach speed and configuration. Land on first approach.

2.Radar nav to plan approach in minimum time and best speed – safety height considerations.

3.AEO to monitor weather with base only letting me know of significant deterioration.

4.Co-pilot to monitor the fuel and his captain.

No real discussion just a series of navigator inputs to position us and then, in what seemed like an eternity as we descended from 30,000ft at 300 knots, a constant flow of weather inputs – all deterioration. Fuel was as planned – we would have enough for a climb out, position the aircraft safely and abandon it. As we passed 1,200 feet we reduced speed and configured for landing hitting the three-mile point at 900 feet on-speed and on the ILS glide path and centreline together with an announcement from the tower that the cloud base and visibility were now minimums. We saw the lights at just under the mile, touched down, ran out and turned off the runway accompanied by the tower telling us that the base was now closed for weather!!

It really was a close-run affair with many lessons learnt; the most important being that decision-making still relies on the favour of the gods; that a professional, integrated well-trained crew not only shares the load in trouble but also shares the outcome of bad decision-making or plain bad luck.

The quick reaction of the navigator radar, his and the rest of the crew's professionalism in that hectic half hour, ensured a safe return to the haven of the mess bar and to the plans for the next day's programme for a tired and certainly wiser young man. And this time I was very happy for it to be my round – all evening!

Not only the fighters saw the Badgers and Bears. This is a Bear D. (*Simon Watson*)

Godfrey's account of his landing at Leuchars will ring a bell with many pilots; it certainly did with me making me remember all my close shaves.

As mentioned, Dick Russell, after his tour on B1s became a qualified flying instructor and air-to-air refuelling instructor on K1s and K2s and was chosen as the refuelling expert to fly with Martin Withers on board Black Buck 1, discussed in the Falklands chapter. Here he relates some early K1 memories.

When the Valiants succumbed to fatigue, the Victors moved to Marham and took over the refuelling role in 1965/66. 55 and 57 Squadrons moved from Honington in the summer of 1965. The Victor OCU initially remained at Gaydon but then transferred, the ground school to Finningley and the flying to Marham to join 55 and 57 Squadrons and later 214.

The OCU name changed now to Tanker Training Flight, TTF, a misnomer since we on the training flight did not have tankers. The training flight continued the conversion to the aircraft and the tanking conversion was done on the squadrons. Initially the first tankers were two point, with a hose under each wing and no centre hose: they were named BK1(2p) as they still had the ability to fly in the bombing role providing the bomb bay tanks were removed. The first flew on 28th April 1965 and joined 55 Squadron in May. Work continued and the first three hose tankers flew on 2nd November that year. 55 Squadron received only K1As while 57 Squadron flew a mixture of K1 and K1As and 214 flew K1s.

Tanker trails in the early 70s were plagued with shortages of fuel in planning, but only in the hotter climates. Each aircraft was given a fuel load and planned to complete the trail and offloads to reach its destination with a fuel reserve. Very seldom did this happen and the reason really never became apparent until after the K2 was operating.

All the Mk1s had tank capacity calibrated in pounds so that in the UK with fuel at a specific gravity of 8lb per gallon the wing tanks of the aircraft when full held approximately 32,000lb. In the Middle and Far East the fuel specific gravity was about point 7.2lb per gallon so that although the tanks were filled to capacity the actual weight of fuel and therefore the calorific value was less, and this showed up on the gauges. All crew chiefs would assure us that the tanks were full, which indeed they were. However, time and time again we would find that we would be short at the end.

I remember a story of a K1 going to Akrotiri. Over France the nav radar asked if he could sit up front. Yes says Bill Palmer the captain and they changed over. "Can I adjust my seat?" says the nav. "Yes," says Bill "just move the lever to the side of the seat."

Next there was a big BANG and then nothing. He had pulled the canopy jettison and was not strapped in. The jettison had worked but the cabin pressure had prevented the jacks from rotating and then extending so the hatch stayed put. I do not know what went on in the cabin for the next ten minutes but they changed over seats and came home. Perhaps it was as well that cockpit voice recorders were not fitted in those days! As far as I know the cabin hatch stayed on the whole time, but the drill for ejecting was amended so that depressurisation was to be selected where possible prior to ejecting.

When the K1 was approaching the end of its fatigue life, all of us on the Tanker Training Flight gathered in the crew room for an important announcement. The fatigue specialists had decided to recalculate the life of the K1 so that aircraft could now go on to somewhere about 130% of the original calculated fatigue life. There's always a way.

John Jeffrey initially was a Victor K1 co-pilot and then a captain and he adds to Dick's recollections.

It was 7th May 1968 and we were in Victor K1 VA926, a new aircraft we had just collected from Radlett and it was the day we nearly lost everything. We had travelled down to Radlett by road, to collect a newly-converted tanker from 'Fred's Sheds', the Handley Page factory. Take-off seemed normal, apart from untypically brisk acceleration because we were carrying very little fuel, Radlett having a very short runway ending at a railway embankment. Almost immediately we received two very unwelcome messages – first, Radlett ATC "Something fell off just as you were getting airborne". Shortly after, the AEO reported massive electrical problems – it turned out that what had fallen off was the hatch covering the plenum chamber, a compartment usually pressurised to cool all the heavy electrical equipment in there.

We knew there was a lot of heat generated by alternators, transformers, rectifiers, you name it. Immediate drill in this emergency was to switch off every electrical load that could be spared before we had a plenum chamber fire. The AEO was reading from the emergency checklist, and I was clicking off the switches of the powered flying control units (PFCUs) on the coaming between the pilots as he read them out. Unfortunately, the captain had his own idea of what the load shed drill should be, and was doing it from memory – he, too, was switching off PFCUs. Just not the same ones that I was switching off. For a second or two there we had almost no PFCUs running at all until I persuaded the captain he might want to fly the b####y thing and let me and the AEO get on with it.

Once we settled down, with minimal electrical loads running, we found the next snag. Much of the nav gear was due to be re-installed when we got back to Marham, and the few bits that were on board had been taken off line by the load shed drill. Fortunately, it was a sunny day, so I suggested we map read our way back to Marham. (Not going to try landing back at Fred's Sheds on that titchy runway, thanks.) This went down like a lead balloon, because nobody had a topographical chart. Except me, that is, because of light aircraft flying I always carried one. So I map-read back to Marham. The nav plotter wouldn't speak to me for the rest of the week.

I remember an interesting event when the Syrian air traffic controllers offered to help us when we were taking a couple of new Lightnings to Saudi Arabia and perhaps delivering them to their air force instead, aided I well recall, with the help of BOAC.

The job was to deliver a pair of Lightnings from BAe Warton to the Royal Saudi Air Force at Riyadh. UK to Cyprus went smoothly enough, but the next day was going to be complicated. We had to take a roundabout route to avoid overflying Israel, which meant a long flight with several refuelling brackets; so, as usual, one tanker couldn't do it all, and we left Akrotiri as a large, mixed formation. We filed a flight plan with

ATC and headed east. We were soon across the narrow strip of the Lebanon and into Syrian airspace. All was OK initially but while we were heading south to the Jordanian border somebody in the Syrian equivalent of MOD obviously had a belated bright idea.

"RAFAir, your formation is too big and must split up. The Victors are clear to proceed, but the Lightnings must return to the Aleppo beacon and hold for one hour."

The Lightning didn't carry enough fuel to do *anything* for an hour. It was designed with just enough fuel capacity to go straight up, accelerate to supersonic speed, fire two missiles, and land again. It didn't take a brain the size of a planet to know that if we got separated from them, they would very soon be forced to land at the nearest – no doubt welcoming – Syrian air force base.

Big think bubbles in the cockpit. "How far to Jordanian airspace?" "Fair distance yet, just a sec, I'll check." "OK, stall Air Traffic, tell them that we don't understand."

"Er, your message is not understood, will you repeat slowly, please."

Crossly, now – "The Victors are clear to proceed, but the Lightnings must return to the Aleppo beacon and hold for one hour."

"Sorry, you are unreadable, say again please."

We were just wondering if we could keep this up long enough to slip into Jordan when BOAC played their joker. A terribly helpful chap with a terribly nice voice popped up on the RT and said with perfect clarity and correctness "Aleppo, this is Speedbird 451 (the old BOAC callsign). I can hear you perfectly well, I will relay your message, break break, RAFAir this is Speedbird 451, message from Air Traffic is that the Victors are clear to proceed, but the Lightnings must return to the Aleppo beacon and hold for one hour, RAFAir do you copy?"

With what I thought was a perfect choice of words, the AEO replied "You are weak and distorted". I don't know to this day if the BOAC captain recognised the insult lurking in this double entendre, but with no more ado the AEO went on to transmit: "All stations, RAFAir formation is experiencing communications problems, continuing as per flight plan and calling Amman Centre".

After that, the radios worked absolutely fine.

My next problem was with a VIP navigator who was replacing my normal nav plotter. I was a captain by then and we were doing a Ranger to Offutt AFB, Nebraska. The problems started on take-off from Goose Bay, when a major failure in the output of the gyro-magnetic compass meant that most of the nav plotter's equipment was unusable. Not a tragedy, because the radar could still give a picture; it couldn't be stabilised automatically, but the nav radar was smart enough to know which way was north. In any case, we had Tacan. So after we levelled off at top of climb I started coaching co-pilot Steve Biglands in how to use the Tacan for homings while allowing for wind drift and the like. The senior personage soon asked me to shut up because the chatter from the front was 'distracting'. Since he had no kit to play with and nothing to do, I wasn't sure what we were distracting him from, but you humour SPs so we continued our teach-in using conference intercomm.

However things were much more serious on our way back, a few days later. Ideally we would have waited at Offut for better weather, but there had been a fatal accident at Marham and the senior person was understandably very keen to get home. As senior crew of a two-aircraft detachment, we were following behind the other Victor in the usual 'sweeper-up' rôle. A minor snag had delayed their departure from Offut, so it was much later than planned by the time we arrived at Goose Bay. It was dark, and there was thick cloud from almost ground level to well above 30,000ft. It had been snowing, but the RCAF had been beavering away and the runway was reported as clear 'for the time being', albeit with ten or twelve foot snow banks either side. The cloud base was 400ft but expected to drop.

Before we entered cloud on our descent Steve switched on all the anti-icing – quite a Heath-Robinson mixture in the Victor 1, with warm air pipes as well as 'electric blankets' in the wings taking power directly from the engine-mounted alternators. I kept the engines at a reasonably high rpm so as to make sure the alternators turned fast enough to deliver output. There was a whine from the electrical heaters, audible on the intercom, and to my astonishment the nav plotter said, "That whine is very irritating, can't you turn the anti-icing down?" You can't, of course; it was either on or off, something I hadn't realised the senior person didn't understand. Steve looked across at me with his eyebrows disappearing into his bone dome, and looked even more amazed when I said, "OK, sorry. Steve, turn the anti-icing down a bit." I pulled No 3 throttle back two or three inches and there was a clearly audible 'winding down' noise from the engine, which apparently satisfied the picky plotter.

I hoped that would leave me free to concentrate on what was bound to be a difficult approach. The cloud base was by now reported as 200ft, which was our absolute minimum, and the windscreen was completely obscured by ice – the de-icing alcohol spray had frozen. One thing in our favour was that I had practised with Steve to use the 'split approach' technique. The pilot flying the aircraft keeps his attention locked on to the instruments while the other pilot looks ahead for the runway. That way, there is no need to keep looking up from the instruments to check if the runway is in sight yet.

The other thing helping was that on final approach there was a strong crosswind from the right, which meant pointing the aircraft to the right to counter it. So, despite the iced-up windscreen, I could get a reasonable view in the direction we were going by looking through the slightly offset direct vision (DV) panel, kept clear like a car's rear window by buried heater filaments. Once we were lined up at about nine miles I handed over to Steve to fly the final approach. He was doing a great job, nailing the centreline and glide path, when at a fairly late stage it suddenly dawned on the senior personage that I wasn't driving.

"Surely when conditions are this difficult the captain should be flying the approach?"

Hardly what you and the co-pilot need to hear, a few seconds from decision height, in thick cloud, freezing rain, and a storming crosswind. "Not now, we'll discuss this on the ground." It was very close indeed to 200ft when I saw the left half of one cross-bar of approach lights and took control, on the assumption the runway had to appear soon. It did, and once we were running straight between the snow banks I popped the dragbag and just hoped the crosswind wouldn't pull it, and our tail, round too far. It didn't.

I assume this check ride counted as satisfactory; at least, the senior personage never flew with our crew again but for some reason I later got the nickname 'Bunty'.

On 5th September 1975 in XH651 we were in Germany a long way from our usual practice areas over the North Sea. We were near Eastern Germany and the Iron Curtain allowing Lightnings from Gutersloh to practice refuelling. It was a nice sunny day and our normal oval racetrack was set up parallel to the Curtain and quite close to it. It felt odd to be looking down from 30,000ft or so over the invisible border into 'their' territory.

As usual, for obvious safety reasons, the Lightnings of 92 Squadron coming up from Gutersloh in pairs and fours were unarmed. But maybe the relatively unusual pattern of activity made the East Germans (or their Russian bosses) nervous, maybe they felt mischievous, maybe it was just a coincidence, but suddenly the atmosphere changed. The Lightnings queuing up to practise were called back to Gutersloh immediately; "We have launched Q" (the quick reaction alert Lightnings, fully armed and ready to go).

Nobody bothered to tell us what the threat was, but I could see two contrails at about our level and apparently shadowing us, just on the other side of the Iron Curtain. Civil airliners don't go around in pairs, so the chances that this was turning into a MiG/Lightning version of 'chicken' seemed quite high. Lightnings being what they are, it was no time at all before the two Q aircraft were sliding in alongside and asking for fuel. We had the wing hoses out already, of course, but were part way round the 180° turn at the northern end of the racetrack, so I cleared them to move astern the hoses but wait to make contact until we rolled wings level. The nav radar confirmed that both were sitting only a few feet from the baskets, obviously itching to get on with it.

Just as I centred the autopilot bank switch to roll the wings level, the Victor pitched nose down, hard, *very* hard. I wasn't sure if an overeager Lightning pilot had collided with us (this was only a few days after a crash caused by a Buccaneer which knocked off the tail of Keith Handscombe's Victor); or if some trigger-happy MiG jockey had twitched at the crucial moment. I didn't really care which, I was too interested in the non-standard view of the ground. It should have been below, but it was in front; we were pointing far closer to straight down than a large aircraft has any business doing. The altimeter was unwinding very fast, of course, but I knew that the worst thing to do was pull out too hard – airliners had been lost that way because they weren't built to withstand the G-stress. I closed the throttles and popped the airbrakes then eased back to check if I had any control, because if not we would have to bale out very, very soon. To my relief, the elevators did bite, so I carried on gently easing back until we levelled off.

As it happens, the explanation was not at all sinister. During the turn, the electrical pitch trim had developed a fault and was slowly feeding in more and more nose-down pitch. This would have been obvious if I had been hand-flying, but I was using the autopilot in height-hold mode. So the more the electric trim tried to push the nose down, the harder the autopilot worked to keep it up. Eventually, the autopilot could pull no harder, and tripped out. No autopilot, full nose-down trim, bingo – fierce pitch down. Talking to the Lightning pilots afterwards (in the Gutersloh bar!),

I found they were (nearly) as shocked as I was, to be presented suddenly with the underside of the Victor that had been in front of them. Apparently we registered over minus 1 G in our 'bunt', but the only damage was to our frayed nerves. And the MiGs gave up and went home. So that was all right then.

Then one night a Bear became two. It was 3rd January 1976 in XH591. Sometimes, the Cold War warmed up, especially when the players were a long way from witnesses. When I first started tanking in the 1960s, the main job was to help other aircraft fly long distances from the UK to overseas bases without having to land en route. Later on, this was extended to keeping fighters airborne for long periods to protect UK airspace, as Soviet medium and heavy bombers from the Murmansk region probed our defences. Sometimes the two missions ended up blurring together.

When a Soviet bomber was spotted heading our way, usually by the Norwegians, fighters would be launched to intercept, and a tanker would be called up as quickly as possible to provide support. This was Operation Dragonfly, called Tansor later, and if notice was too short to scramble a tanker from Marham then any tanker which happened to be airborne would be roped in from whatever he was doing – 'Dragonfly Mobile'. In January 1976, though, we had plenty of notice; some days, in fact, so this must have been intelligence-driven.

All I was told was that an 'interesting' Tu-95 (known within NATO as 'Bear') was expected on the scene quite soon, and that he would probably be anxious to avoid interception. I was pre-positioned at RAF Leuchars leading a detachment of two Victors, so that one crew would be on alert at any hour of the day or night. When the whistle finally blew, late on 3rd January, it happened to be my crew on duty, and we launched at about the same time as the 41 Squadron Phantom. Initially, the fighter controllers at Buchan sent us due north, then handed us over to the control of Saxa Vord in the Shetlands. As time went on there seemed to be some doubt about exactly where the target was – maybe he himself was taking steps to confuse matters? – and we were given a series of left turns to bring us onto a generally north-westerly heading. By the time control was taken over by Benbecula, in the Hebrides, it was obvious this Bear wasn't heading straight for UK airspace as they usually did – we were well on our way to Iceland.

Eventually, a slightly harassed-sounding controller said *"target is estimated to be* (not a happy thing to hear) *in your 12 o'clock, range approximately 30 miles, crossing right to left"*. In other words, a right royal screw up. But three cheers for the Phantom and its radar; he chipped in to tell Benbecula (and us) that not only did he have the target, but that there were two of them.

We soon turned onto a south-westerly heading to roll out behind the Bears, whom we now realised must be on their way to Cuba, with Benbecula advising us apologetically that we were beyond the limit of their radar cover. The Phantom lit his burners and started a 30-mile tail chase, leaving us to follow as best we could. I knew he would be using fuel very fast, so I didn't want to let us get too far apart. We had a handy gadget in those days, a modified version of the Tacan navigation beacon which could indicate range from a co-operating aircraft, and we used it to help us catch him up. At a little over 30,000ft, max continuous thrust gave us a fair turn of speed (though I did have to stop co-pilot Mike Jukes easing the throttles back because he thought we ought not to exceed the normal maximum speed! As I reminded him, there's a time and place . . . . .)

Even so, it took a while to catch up; the Bear may have had propellers rather than jets, but that didn't make it slow. But eventually the Tacan range ticked down to under three miles and I could make out one Bear, and the Phantom, which had been busy getting a very close look (and, I assume, photographs, despite the darkness). The Phantom pilot said he wanted to go to the other Bear, a mile or two away to starboard; would I "stay with this one?" It sounded OK to me, so I agreed. As the Phantom pulled away, he said "and watch him, he's playing tricks". Not quite so OK, so I moved in to just astern and below the Bear waiting to see what would come next. This wasn't bravado, it was more or less the same formation position we used to take fuel from another tanker, so it was familiar and therefore easier to fly. Besides, I reckoned I could see the pilot but he couldn't see me, so he would be very cautious about sudden manoeuvring. I was half right. Unlike the Victor, the Bear has a tail gunner, who has not only a turret but also a couple of side 'blisters', one each side of the fuselage, intended for visual lookout in the Bear's maritime patrol job.

There have been stories, many no doubt true, of Soviet aircrew exchanging friendly waves and even brandishing copies of 'Playboy'. This wasn't one of those times; this Bear was not about to sign up to the idea of a fellowship of the skies. After depressing the guns towards us for a while, the gunner left his turret and reappeared in a side blister holding a lamp. He lit it up and shone it down through our windscreen. It was very bright indeed, and when it shone into Mike's face he yelped in pain. It was just luck that it was aimed on his side first, because it gave me just enough time to move forward until I was directly underneath and the gunner couldn't shine the lamp down steeply enough to dazzle or blind us – though he did keep trying.

And there I stayed, in some awe of the monstrous dark hulk just a few feet above, roughly twice the size of our Victor; the deep rumble that I imagined to be from his engines was probably just slipstream, but it was a monstrous roar all the same. I was quite relieved when the Phantom called that he was complete, and I knew we could go back to Leuchars.

I can't remember whose idea it was to depart with a flourish, but I was quite happy to let navigator Kevin Toal go to the Very pistol set into the roof of the cockpit and fire off a flare. Of course, the sole purpose of this was to mark our position visually for the Phantom. It is just a coincidence that the brilliant flare shot upwards only a few yards from the aggressive tail gunner. If he would have to wear dark glasses the whole time he was in Cuba, neither Mike nor I would be too upset.

On course for Leuchars, I told the Phantom he was clear to join for refuelling, and he said "no need, thanks". His navigator had been very busy, first directing the interception and then getting all his precious pictures, so it was no surprise that he was temporarily out of touch with the navigation picture. When we told him "OK, in that case steer 137 degrees for Leuchars, range 530 miles, have a good trip", he decided to take some fuel, after all.

We finally landed at Leuchars soon after dawn. Our groundcrew must have spent a more or less tedious and uncomfortable night not knowing what was going on or when to expect us, but their first words as we opened the cabin door were *"Did you get him?"* Who could ask for a better job, or better people to do it with?

It was 28th January 1976 and we were in Victor K1 926. A new approach to 'just in time' logistics; the day we transferred enough to fill a F4 – to a F4. A typical 'Dragonfly Mobile'; we were on a ho-hum standard training sortie, flying racetracks over the North Sea for fighters to take turns to practice refuelling. Then an urgent message "How much fuel can you spare?" The usual unanswerable question – "Depends how long you want us to stay up here." Fighter controllers never seemed to quite get the hang of the fact that we didn't have two separate lots of fuel, one to fly with and one to give away.

"Well, steer north anyhow, increase speed, await further instructions." We gradually got the picture. NATO were carrying out a maritime exercise in the North Atlantic, with an allied task force ('BLUE') preparing to make an assault on the Norwegian coast to recapture it from a supposed 'RED' occupation. Phantoms from Leuchars were flying top cover for the task force when, as was not uncommon, the *real* Reds sent a Bear to watch and, more to the point, listen to our tactics, frequencies, codes and anything else they could glean. One of the Phantoms was diverted from the allied exercise to the real thing, following the usual order "intercept, identify and shadow". He intercepted his Bear and clearly had been sticking to it like glue for a long time, probably a good part of the distance back to its base around Murmansk. He was now headed home, and was quite keen for a top-up, but even if there was a tanker operating with the task force it was obviously too far away to be of help. So the Phantom headed south, we headed north, and eventually we were close enough to talk directly to one another.

We set up for a familiar 'head on' style of RV; he would use his intercept radar to offset himself to one side by a few miles, then at the optimum range start a 180 degree turn which would roll him out just a mile or so astern of us. Done it countless times before, piece of cake. Except this time he asked if we would make the turn, as he wanted to keep heading south. A wink is as good as a nod; he was obviously very short of fuel indeed, so I got the centre hose out well before arriving at the rendezvous turn. He called it, I turned, and there he was sitting inches behind the basket. Green light, first time contact, fuel flowing, all within seconds. Very high flow rate, must have plenty of space in his tanks. Co-pilot and nav plotter between them rapidly working out how much we could afford to give him and still have enough to get home to Marham. No more than 25,000lb we reckoned, but that was hardly a problem because the Phantom only needed a few thousand to get comfortably from where we were back to Leuchars. The nav radar, watching through his periscope, reported that the Phantom was fitted with a long-range tank below the fuselage.

"How much fuel can he hold in that fit, any idea?"

"Not sure, think it's about 24 thousand pounds."

"How much has he taken so far?"

"Er, 24 thousand pounds."

So when we reached the RV, he obviously was very, very low on fuel – roughly the amount he subsequently used while refuelling. No wonder he had been quite keen to keep heading south, and no wonder he kept the fuel flowing as long as possible once it started. Ever seen a really thirsty man take his first drink of water? The instinct isn't

Broken probe. Sorry Sir, it was the tanker's fault!

to take a small sip. Even so, we shut off the fuel flow and I asked him as politely as possible to call it a day. He probably landed with more fuel than we did.

In summary the common theme is the meticulous crew training that was carried out in both the normal and emergency modes. It was as a result of this work and, of course the work of the groundcrew, that the Victor Mk1 in both its bomber and tanker roles proved to be a very reliable and effective aircraft.

Chapter Four

4 Joint Services Trials Unit

When I joined Avros as a test pilot in 1956 the firm had already won the contract to produce the Blue Steel, a hydrogen peroxide[9] engined 'stand-off' missile with a range of over 100 nautical miles when launched from over 40,000ft, to be carried under the Vulcan and Victor bombers. The development of the missile was being undertaken by a design group situated on the Woodford airfield with offices on the opposite side of the airfield from flight sheds and next to new assembly. Jimmy Orrell, who was just retiring from being chief test pilot, was given the new task of managing the flight testing of the Blue Steel missiles.

The nominal range of the missile put it outside the capability of the Aberporth test range in Cardigan Bay so that it was not possible to carry out live drops, though the navigation system could be proved and dummy drops carried out there. The UK therefore arranged with the Australian government for the live testing of the missile to be carried out on the Woomera range in South Australia, with the test aircraft to be based at Edinburgh

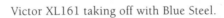

Victor XL161 taking off with Blue Steel.

---

[9] Referred to as HTP (high test peroxide).

Test Aircraft Victor XL161 and Vulcan XH539. (*John Saxon*)

Field near Adelaide. In order to waste as little time and money as possible the RAF formed 4 JSTU in 1957 at Woodford so that they would be fully aware of the missile development and would be able to provide the navigation operational support during the trials. The unit, which consisted of less than a dozen officers and NCOs of the RAF (and a number of manufacturers' personnel including John Saxon of whom more anon) was sent out to the RAAF base at Edinburgh Field to support the trials which were supervised by Ministry of Defence scientists who would give the release for the RAF to use the missile in service.

No Victors took part in the Aberporth trials, the test aircraft being Valiants and Vulcan Mk 1 XA903. In Australia Valiants were used for various 'carry-over' trials before the test aircraft arrived to check the navigational performance of the missiles and the correct communication interface with the ground control at the Woomera range. I was fortunate enough to take the Vulcan test aircraft XH539 out to Australia arriving on 12th December 1961 with the OC of 4 JSTU Wing Commander Underwood acting as navigator. The Victor test aircraft, XL161, went out in the following year.

Wason Turner, who I knew at Boscombe Down when he was B Squadron chief technical officer, was responsible for clearing Blue Steel for use by the RAF on both the Vulcan and the Victor. Initially the releases in Australia were from high altitude to achieve maximum range from the missile and to ensure that there would be maximum distance between the target and the aircraft at the moment of explosion. Half way through the programme in June 1963 the full implication was assessed of Gary Powers being shot down in 1960 by a SAM missile when flying at 80,000ft over Russia and as a result it was decided that from then on the deterrent role of the V bombers with the Blue Steel would have to be at low level. The release height of the test missiles was therefore changed to low altitude; the missile was released from 500ft and dropped down to 200ft when the engine lit and it zoomed up to approximately 75,000ft, accelerating to nearly Mach 3 and then finished by diving down twelve miles to end its forty-mile journey. Nearly fifty Blue Steels were fired during the trials and John Saxon, working for Elliotts who made the navigation system, has some illuminating comments.

I think both contractor staff and RAF personnel had a great time visiting and living in Australia. Many stayed – some went back later.

But what about the work we did? What was achieved during the missile trials? It should not be forgotten that we were developing a nuclear-armed cruise missile to be the UK's primary deterrent in the 1960s. I'm sure that we were all overwhelmingly relieved that the missiles were never used 'in anger'. And as far as I know no nuclear weapon was ever exploded at the end of a Blue Steel flight. But during the Cold War the intention to use them, if necessary, was always there.

Recently, a file of papers has turned up which were reports from Elliotts' staff in Australia back to 'Head Office', with copies to many defence department staff. These reports give brief details of some 275 flights made by all three V bomber types during the trials. I have no doubt that there were many more flights (aircraft equipment tests etc. and there are some gaps in the data) but the 275 flights that were covered reveal some interesting statistics.

These days I doubt if a project would survive after such failure rates but the UK had few options at the time, since they wanted some sort of deterrent; it has to be remembered that it was an immensely complex project for that time. The aircraft were state of the art and continuously evolving with many electronics systems using thermionic valves (vacuum tubes for our American friends) technology! A lot of the systems were electro/mechanical analogue computers. The missile itself was equally 'state of the art' in many areas, particularly the inertial navigator which must have been close to the first in the world and even the inertial navigation system used some valves! Finally the ground range systems (Woomera Range E), which had to be greatly extended for the Blue Steel trials, were also complicated with many devices spread out over several hundred kilometres. All of these systems had to work together or a 'launch' flight would be aborted prior to launch.

Probably one of the most interesting statistics is that there were a total of 124 flights where there was the intention to launch, and these resulted in 74 pre-launch aborts and 50 actual launches. Each missile cost over £1 million, so they were not launched unless everyone was satisfied that there was a reasonable likelihood of success.

One must ask how many of the launches could be regarded as completely successful; that is that they reached the target within the specified margin of error. My assessment from the data is 50% or twenty-five launches; whilst this seems like a high failure rate, there were constant changes to the hardware and to the profiles of what was expected operationally. Significantly, the rate of problems gradually decreased as the trials progressed.

A couple more statistics might be of interest. The 275 flights were divided into Valiants (various aircraft W numbers) = 149 flights, Vulcan (XH539) = 68, and Victor (XL161) = 58. As mentioned, the Valiants were often used for 'carry-over' flights some of which just tested many missile components (particularly the inertial navigation and other systems); I presume for these flights the components were mounted in the bomb bay. But the Valiants also did carry-over flights with live missiles and launched at least thirteen rounds in Australia.

John has made an analysis of all the rounds carried and fired which is available on my website www.blackmanbooks.co.uk.

A lot of the extracts that follow have been collected by David 'Ginge' Booth who was an RAF technician attached to Elliott Brothers.

GROUND STRIKE WEAPONS

In the mid-1950s two large new guided weapons began their developmental careers, under the names of Blue Water and Blue Steel. Both had the same objective: the bombardment of enemy positions up to 300 kilometres away from the point of launch, and both were intended to carry nuclear warheads. Otherwise they were entirely different. Blue Water was a ground-to-ground artillery rocket for the army, whereas Blue Steel was a large propelled bomb to be carried and launched by Britain's V bombers. The two projects co-existed for six years including a period when both were under trial at Woomera, but neither had a very long career in service. Like the majority of projects at this time they became zero factors in the rapidly changing military equation, and fell victim to the endless revisions of British defence policy....

A much more ambitious and long-lasting project was Blue Steel which had figured so prominently in the early plans for Woomera. By the mid-1950s two British firms were actively developing a cruise missile. One was Vickers-Armstrong, working on Dr Barnes Wallis's Swallow aircraft; the other was A.V.Roe with what became Blue Steel. In 1954 the Air Staff issued an operational requirement for a propelled nuclear bomb capable of being launched in any weather from a V bomber flying well clear of ground defences. Both weapons were accepted by CUKAC, Combined United Kingdom / Australian Long Range Weapons Committee, as joint project tasks, but Swallow quickly disappeared from view. The Avro proposal was accepted and a development contract was awarded to the company in March 1956.

The shape of Blue Steel was largely dictated by the bulkiness of its nuclear warhead. Still, it looked graceful enough with its sleek cylindrical body of stainless steel 10.7 metres long, tapering down from a maximum width of 1.28 metres to a pointed nose. The wings were delta-shaped, nearly four metres in span, mounted close to the rear, together with a pair of vertical stabiliser fins. The 'canard' configuration meant that there was no tailplane; instead a small fore-plane near the nose controlled the pitch angle and, together with ailerons on the rear wings, controlled the flight direction by the 'twist and steer' method. The engine was at first Armstrong Siddeley's Spectre, but was soon replaced by their more powerful Stentor. Both burnt the liquid propellants kerosene and hydrogen peroxide. The Stentor engine had two combustion chambers of different sizes mounted one above the other. Operating together from launch with a combined thrust of almost 12 tonnes weight, they acted as a booster accelerating Blue Steel to a supersonic speed approaching Mach 2.5 at 75,000ft. From this point the smaller chamber alone served as a sustainer, maintaining cruising speed to the target. The guidance and control system was produced by Elliott, the British electronics firm. Its heart was the inertial navigator which constantly measured the location of the missile in space and compared it with the programmed target position. (Data from the aircraft navigation were fed to the Blue Steel 'brain' right up to the moment of launch to fix the target position.) After launch, corrections to the flight path were passed via a computer to the autopilot, which steered the missile as well as keeping it stable in flight. A Blue Steel in flight was immune to all countermeasures short of direct attack.

The basis for trials planning and facility preparation was worked out during three visiting British missions in 1956-57. The object of the preliminary trials was to explore likely problems connected with aerodynamic stability, control and kinetic heating effects at supersonic speed. Scale models would suffice for these investigations just as in the case of Blue Water. However, since Blue Steel was an air-launched missile its trials had the complicating factor of the carrier aircraft. In fact, all three types of

Preparing the missile.

the V bomber force took part at various times. They were located at Edinburgh Field, which with WRE became the base for preparing and loading the missiles before flying to Woomera. This work was done under extreme security. The transporter parking bay at WRE was screened by a fence 5 metres high, which was still standing thirty years later.

The flight programme was ready to begin in July 1957 with the arrival of the trials team, the Valiant carrier aircraft and the first of the two-fifths scale models. This was a 'cold' missile with fixed controls and no engine, intended for use as a practice exercise. The trial was duly carried out in August. Subsequent flights were originally planned to continue at one per month, but it was February 1958 before the next scale model was launched. This time the missile was more complete; it had a solid fuel motor with a burning time of 25 seconds which would propel the model more than 60 kilometres down-range from its release point over Range E. It carried two telemetry senders, and the Valiant was fitted with bomb bay and wingtip cameras to photograph the launch. The Range had provided corresponding ground instrumentation for receiving the telemetered data, plotting the trajectories of aircraft and missile and photographing their behaviour. This was the first flight in Australia of a motored Blue Steel (albeit a scaled-down version) and its success was encouraging: the propulsion and controls worked well and the missile flew smoothly to the recovery zone, its final descent slowed by a parachute.

The following few months were occupied with carry-over trials to check the instrumentation and launching procedures again. The next scale model was launched in May with rather dismal results: neither the motor nor the autopilot operated correctly and the missile crashed before the parachute opened. However, towards the end of the year four more models were launched, two of which performed well.

Of the remainder, one suffered an impediment at launch which caused it to dive steeply, while in the other a timing failure prevented motor ignition. (Nevertheless it glided gently for over five minutes under the control of its autopilot to a landing 50 kilometres down-range.) In 1959, eight missiles were launched to complete the planned series of fifteen scale models. The results in general were satisfactory with only two outright failures caused by the solid fuel motor and the control system. Trials of the full size Blue Steel, already more than a year behind schedule, could now begin. By mid-1960 the service unit 4 JSTU had arrived, ready to take part with Avro in the combined development/acceptance programme of sixty launchings. With all the planning under way, the remainder of 1960 saw no trials except for two flights, unpowered and unguided, to prove the safety and tracking systems. Meanwhile WRE had been working on the ground instrumentation network. The main impact zone was a circle 37 kilometres across, the closest point of whose perimeter lay a few kilometres to the south of the Mirikata tracking station. This allowed a flight of some 200 kilometres down-range from the release point above Range E. Depending on the aircraft altitude at launch, the missile would first soar to 75,000ft and then continue on a plateau before diving steeply to impact, its long trajectory monitored by the FPS-16 radars at Red Lake and Mirikata supported by a succession of other range radars types AA 3 and 4 Mk 7. Additionally, the missile tracking system and two new kine-theodolite posts first put in for Bloodhound Mk 2 covered the cruise period, with a long focal length camera near the impact zone to photograph the final dive to earth. Blue Steel carried four telemetry senders to transmit data to stations at Mirikata, Mt Eba and the rangehead. In some later firings two of the senders were replaced by a special type provided by the Atomic Weapons Research Establishment to check the operation of an 'explosive test unit', which simulated the triggering of the future warhead. They required receiving stations within the impact area, remotely operated by a new control centre near McDouall Peak. Complete Blue Steels started to fly in

Loading the weapon. (*Brian Wetton*)

1961 with poor results at first but with some improvement in the next year until about one flight in two was successful. It was no better than that because of a new problem with the auxiliary power unit, a small HTP-driven turbine which supplied hydraulic power to the alternators and control surfaces. It failed repeatedly and was alone responsible for at least eight unsuccessful flights.

The future of Blue Steel had been uncertain ever since 1960 when the big ground-to-ground ballistic missile Blue Streak was cancelled. In one view Blue Steel was even more urgent than before, to give the British armoury at least one nuclear-armed missile; but in another view the fact that Blue Streak was supposedly being replaced by the advanced American air-to-ground Skybolt rendered Blue Steel superfluous. To complicate matters, the future of Skybolt was itself uncertain. Moreover, the Soviet Union's ground defences had been much improved. Blue Steel needed more range and the capacity to be launched and to fly at low altitude to avoid radar detection. The net result was that the effort which had been allocated to a Blue Steel Mk 2 was absorbed by the design problems of modifying the Mk 1. In the meantime, in September 1962, Mk 1 Blue Steels were fitted to the Vulcans of the RAF's 617 'Dam Busters' Squadron and afterwards to the aircraft of four other squadrons.

These factors disturbed the Woomera trials programme greatly, though it continued through 1963 with launchings from Vulcan and Victor aircraft until the completion of the development trials in March 1964. They were immediately followed by a short acceptance programme conducted by 4 JSTU with representatives of the British Aeroplane and Armament Experimental Establishment at Boscombe Down. Eleven missiles were launched, most of them at low level, to complete the programme with a final successful flight in October 1964. By the following January the closure of the Blue Steel programme was well in hand. Even so, its resumption was for a time not completely ruled out. WRE issued an agreed closing down specification which allowed for second thoughts:

"The Ministry of Aviation is considering the need for further Blue Steel trials. Until a decision has been made certain buildings presently allocated to the project will be preserved. The situation will be reviewed at intervals of six months and the buildings will only be held available while MOA certifies that there is a reasonable possibility of further trials taking place. The period of preservation is not expected to extend beyond the end of 1965."

But Blue Steel was not reprieved. The RAF gradually phased it out of service and with its demise British aircraft ceased altogether to carry atomic weapons. The responsibility for the British nuclear deterrent was transferred to the Royal Navy with its Polaris submarine fleet.[10]

The Blue Steel missiles were ferried out to Australia by RAF Vulcans and Victors. David Booth mentions that the ground position indicator, GPI 6, was not designed to navigate round the world. Consequently if the missile ferry aircraft flew westwards and crossed

[10]   This article written from an Australian viewpoint is reproduced in part, with thanks, by courtesy of the Commonwealth of Australia from *Fire Across the Desert* by Peter Morton (ISBN 0644060689).

the 180° meridian then the longitude counters would read over 180° and, for example, going westward to Australia the GPI 6 would show 221° 22.7' West and Latitude 34° 43.13' S arriving at Edinburgh Field. Luckily it was possible to reset the counters on the ground to 138° 37.3 E by 'flying' the aircraft eastwards back to the UK and then carrying on westwards back to Edinburgh. The only problem was that when the ferry aircraft was returning the procedure had to be reversed if the aircraft was going home crossing the Pacific.

In order for the tests to be carried out during the day so that the missile could be tracked accurately, a lot of the preparation work had to be carried out at night.

Preparing and loading the missile at night. Note the large supply of distilled water to deal with the hydrogen peroxide.

There are many tales which can be told of the adventures of the trials team, not least that of the trial on 17th August 1962 when the Victor bomber XL161 entered an uncontrolled spin from 40,000ft near Kangaroo Island and was only able to recover control by streaming the brake-landing parachute.

The trial that day was a 'carry-over' designed to test the Victor/missile/range compatibility, provide training to trials personnel and to act as a test of all of the facilities, telemetry etc. After the pilot had recovered from the spin standard emergency safety procedures were carried out and the 100A Blue Steel missile round (048) was jettisoned at the weapons proof range at Port Wakefield 2,000 yds offshore though the propellant started a localized fire. The aircraft returned to RAAF Edinburgh (shepherded by a RAAF Canberra) and circuited for 1.5hrs to release excess fuel and landed about 16.30hrs. Radio station 5DN reported on its News Bulletin at 6.15pm that 'a WRE aircraft had been in distress but it had jettisoned its load and landed safely'.

This caused a flurry of signals with the Air Ministry in London as the trials were top secret and, as the missile was designed to carry (but not carrying) a nuclear weapon, instructions were issued not to discuss 'the adventure' and the news was to be contained. But it wasn't!

An account of the incident by a reporter, Kennedy, was published in the *Adelaide Advertiser* newspaper on 23rd August and that evening the News made it its lead story. The story's theme wove the missile hazard, the inland flight path and the unstable aircraft into a scenario which caused political embarrassment in Australia. This forced a ministerial statement to be broadcast that evening on the National Radio Network on the 'PM' programme.

Fortunately for the Victor crew the tail parachute proved to be an anti-spin chute as well.

Luckily for us, if not for him, John Saxon, was in the plane and has written this vivid account.

This was going to be another Blue Steel 'carry-over' trial to test missile systems – they had almost become routine. However, flying in V bombers always got the adrenalin flowing just a little. I was a civilian working with Elliott Brothers – an English firm now part of GEC I believe. We were concluding the first development phase of one of the world's first inertial navigation systems which was used to guide the Blue Steel stand-off bomb. Our Handley Page Victor B2 aircraft was parked in the loading bay on Edinburgh airfield near Adelaide, South Australia. The 6 ton 36ft long missile was secured under the bomb bay – fully fuelled with high test peroxide and kerosene – a rather nasty mixture and so the loading bay was fairly well flooded with water – just in case.

We walked out to the aircraft in a group and climbed on board – John Baker the pilot, chief test pilot for Avros in Australia, Flt Lt Jimmy Catlin was in the right-hand seat, Flt Lt Charlie Gilbert in the rear radar navigator position, myself in the centre rear looking after the navigator systems and Flt Lt 'Glen' Glendinning in the right-hand rear air electronics officer's seat looking after the missile autopilot and other aircraft systems. Finally sitting in the 6th jump seat was Frank Longhurst – another civilian working for Avros who was there to see that Glen was doing the right things with 'their' missile. At that point in the trials the civilian crews were beginning the gradual training and hand over to RAF crews who were to complete the trials. We plugged in intercoms, oxygen, suit cooling air and began the seemingly endless pre-flight checks.

Eventually everyone was satisfied and we taxied and took off – turning to the SW to climb to our first navigational fix point over Kangaroo Island. Now, despite being an aircraft weighing around 80 tons, the Victor was no slouch in the climbing stakes. I have been from sea level to 50,000ft in around eight minutes though it was probably a lot slower rate with the Blue Steel missile loaded. Nevertheless the 10,000ft climb points were passing rapidly until we got to around 46,000ft, I believe, when all heck broke loose. Lots of rapid discussion and attempts to pull up from the front deck, the start of a real roller coaster ride (pitch ups, pull overs, etc.) with engine noise doing unimaginable things; then what seemed (from the back) to be a wingover followed by increasingly violent positive and negative G forces. John Baker activated the 'Abandon Aircraft' signs which also dumped cabin pressure. Frank (who was nominally first out of the rear door) unstrapped and hit the roof quite violently and took no further escape action. In the nominal escape plan I was next to get out; I managed to half stand and hang onto the camera bracket in front of the nav equipment. But I could get no further towards the side door as we were rotating fast and in what appeared to be a very steep dive. Then after what seemed like a long time (actually about 20 seconds), there was a loud bang from the rear of the aircraft and the rotation changed to a near vertical dive and rapid pull out, accompanied by much creaking and groaning and dust, pencils, pads, etc. flying in all directions. But we were back in semi-level flight at around 16,000ft!

Here is what I believe happened. Others, who know better than I do, can correct me if I'm wrong. When we got to 45,000ft or so the right-hand air speed indicating system had a failure causing it to indicate around Mach 1.03. This sent a 'transonic' flight signal to the auto-stabilisers which initiated a pitch-up manoeuvre as the Victors were not designed to go supersonic. The pilots however compared right and left side air speed indications and as the pitch up had started were inclined to believe the faulty right-hand system. So they too tried to reduce speed further and ended up in a violent pitch up to an almost inverted position followed by a rapid spin which was impossible to control. Very luckily for us, John Baker had done many test flights in prototype aircraft, where it had become routine to fit braking parachutes to lift the tail of the aircraft into a more stable dive position, which could be recovered relatively easily. Now this had never been attempted in an 80-ton crescent-wing Victor – but nothing much else was working. So John pulled the tail chute which lasted a few seconds before breaking away, but long enough to do the job and allow some heavy stick pulling to level out before doing a submarine imitation.

So how does one feel at a time like that? Not too great, but certainly I felt reasonably calm and I remember I had time to think about flight insurance and dependants! As usual when the adrenalin is pumping, everything seemed to go into slow motion. But it was really nice to get roughly straight and level again. It was good that we had all the records from the inertial navigator recorders and were able to analyse them later. The aircraft experienced maximums of about minus 3 and plus 5 Gs (more than airframe design limits), and the whole incident lasted about 60 secs with the descent from 46,000 to 16,000ft in about 20 secs – vertically supersonic!

Several things happened before we finally got to land. First there was a concern about the correct airspeed as the two systems were still reading differently; then possible structural damage was considered. Luckily the radio was still working so a chase plane was requested. It was decided to jettison the missile as it was full of highly explosive fuel (temperature of which was rising) and even had some TNT on board for range safety break up if it strayed outside the Woomera range limits.

Also because there was no tail parachute, if there had been undercarriage or brake problems, a wheels-up landing with a fully fuelled Blue Steel underneath would have been very spectacular! We started missile jettison procedures aiming for a military bombing range near Port Wakefield, several of the crew had 'confirm' switches for jettison and, at the last minute, the pilots called stop, and then go (I think I was the last to select my switch) and away it went. It turns out that the 'stop' calls were due to the pilots spotting a school below.

There were two guards on the range where we jettisoned and they had been told to keep a look out for a bomb drop. However, no-one thought to mention that it was 36 feet long, weighed 6 plus tons and was full of explosive mixtures, so they walked out onto the sand to take a look. Apparently they "heard it gurgling" on the way down and took off to find their hard hats when it got rapidly larger. But it crashed relatively harmlessly and burnt with only minor explosions between the high and low water marks. But they certainly got a shock.

Then the first chase plane arrived. Flt Lt Alec Hollingsworth RAF scrambled an old Meteor out of Edinburgh – it was great to see him! He flew tight formation passing on airspeed readings and confirming no apparent physical damage. There was no way we could dump the full fuel load so we had to keep flying for at least another 90 minutes or so to burn off fuel to get to an acceptable landing weight. Due to the time remaining the Meteor chase plane was replaced by a Canberra flown by Wg Cdr David Glenn which escorted us for the remainder of the flight.

In the meantime we had a nervous 70 minutes or so before the landing. During that time Charlie Gilbert introduced me to chain cigarette smoking, I think we got through at least a pack between us in the back. Took me more than 10 more years to kick the habit! Thanks Charlie! So eventually with much foaming of runways, emergency vehicles everywhere and at least one chase plane, we made a good touchdown back at Edinburgh.

A couple of aftermath items. We had a few or more drinks in the mess at the airfield with lots of toasts to our safe return. The story goes that co-pilot Jimmy Catlin was well away by the time he had to go to a church social that evening. Apparently he strode across the dance floor to tell the vicar in a loud voice, "I saw your boss today", before collapsing gently at the vicar's feet. I wasn't there but the story has been confirmed by others. A few days later the crew (plus significant others) had a celebratory dinner at a local hostelry, where the picture overleaf was taken.

Despite the large excursions outside its design limits, the aircraft turned out to be in pretty good shape and after some minor repairs went on to launch more Blue Steels for the trials – at the Woomera Range of course! Later XL161 returned to the UK and, after a refit at the Handley Page plant, went on to RAF squadron reconnaissance duties.

Needless to say news of the incident leaked to the press and, after information of the jettison near Port Wakefield got out, there were a few pointed questions in Parliament about large explosive devices being flown around populated areas. Much more fuss would be raised these days but, in the Cold War atmosphere of the times, questions soon died away.

All in all, it was an exciting few hours.

The celebration picture which hit the newspapers. Back: John Saxon, Frank Longhurst, 'Glen' Glendinning. Front: Charley Gilbert, Johnny Baker, Jimmy Catlin.

I was at Woodford when all this took place. I well remember us all trying to work out what had happened for the aircraft to go into a spin. In fact the starboard ASI system had gone wrong and was saying that the aircraft had gone supersonic. The pilots reduced speed and the aircraft stalled and then went into a spin. Peter Baker, who was a Handley Page test pilot at the time, was sent out to investigate. Here are his comments.

The spin incident in Australia was totally unnecessary and came about because of a discrepancy between ASIs and the pilots strangely believed they might be near supersonic in the climb at around 47,000ft rather than a good deal slower – so they throttled back and stalled and spun because in fact they were very slow! I was sent out to see if the aircraft was in one piece and to get the Blue Steel programme back on track; we were able to drop the first live round from a Victor shortly after arrival.

Fortunately Johnny Baker had been with us at HP getting his conversion when I entered a spin doing mach trimmer runaways at 55,000ft after we had fitted the 'hard' leading edge on the wing in place of the nose flaps to reduce weight. As a result he learned that I had recovered using the breaking parachute since normal recovery action was ineffective without an anti-spin chute.

Unfortunately for Johnny Baker the incident led to his early retirement from test flying. He was probably more criticised for letting the whole story get into the press and having a party than for getting the aircraft into a spin though I'm not sure what he could have done to prevent the press finding out what had happened. The problem was that the Australians did not like the concept of nuclear weapons being carried over their country as suggested by the press even though the stories were completely untrue. The MOD soon withdrew his approval as a test pilot.

No 4 JSTU near the end of trials.

The spinning incident was a distraction but did not prevent the programme proceeding steadily. The last flight test was flown in 1965 and a final report prepared for the Air Ministry. The personnel were returned to the UK in three groups in November 1964, March 1965 and June 1965. Many of the personnel had spent the whole eight and a half years in Australia with the unit. A very special group indeed. A plaque was constructed by 'Doughy' Baker for the unit and presented to the Edinburgh base commander by the officer commanding.

The social implications of the Blue Steel trials were enormous with 'Brits' transported to the other side of the world to carry out a highly technical trial in very demanding conditions. It is difficult to separate completely these two aspects of the trial but there is no space for elaboration here and so an account will be added to my website.

Chapter Five

Victor B2

The Victor B2 was able to be specified to meet the operational requirement at the time for higher altitude performance because the Rolls-Royce Conway engine producing 17,250lb of thrust was available, but this meant that the engine intakes had to be increased in size to accommodate the extra airflow and that the span of the aircraft had to be increased to 120ft. As well as the aerodynamic changes it was decided to improve the electrical system of the aircraft to cater for emergencies since the power controls, like the Mk1 aircraft, were electrically operated; the Mk1 relied on batteries in the event of an electrical failure which was unsatisfactory since the power only lasted for about 20 minutes. Consequently the 112V DC generators were replaced with four Sundstrand 200V 400 cycles per second constant frequency AC drives; in addition, the aircraft was fitted with a Blackburn Artouste airborne auxiliary power unit (AAPU) and, to provide power above 30,000ft when the Artouste could not be started, two emergency ram air turbines, each of which required an enormous air scoop, 'elephant ear', situated either side and in front of the fin; the scoops came out automatically when the RATs were selected. The Artouste not only provided power below 30,000ft in an electrical emergency but it could also give bleed air for engine starting and electrical power for maintenance on the ground.

The pilots' instruments were changed to introduce the Smiths military flight system which for the first time in the RAF integrated ILS information and steering commands onto the pilots' horizon and compass displays.

Thirty-four Victor B2s were built and twenty-one were converted to be able to carry Blue Steel and fitted with the higher powered Conway engines with 20,600lb thrust. Nine were converted to strategic reconnaissance aircraft, B2SR for 543 Squadron and fitted with cameras, a bomb bay radar mapping system and nuclear sniffers on the top of the wing. Later, twenty-four were converted from the bomber role to become air-to-air refuelling tankers.

The prototype Victor B2, XH668, first flew on 20th February 1959 and after being checked by the firm was sent to A&AEE for acceptance trials for the RAF. Sadly during one of the acceptance flights on 20th August 1959 the aircraft crashed into the sea off the Welsh coast and all the crew were killed. It took until November of the following year to locate and recover the wreckage and as explained in the accident appendix, it was determined that the starboard pitot head had failed which led to the loss of the aircraft. Luckily it was possible to modify the aircraft to prevent any similar failures and the first

David Shepherd's glorious painting of Victor B2 in the officer's mess at RAF Wittering.

production Victor B2s went into service in February 1962.

When the aircraft were made Blue Steel capable, chaff dispensers were fitted and the shape was chosen to minimise total drag; the concept was known as 'area ruling' an aircraft to minimise shock waves at transonic speeds and in the case of the Victor the additions were called 'Küchemann Carrots'.

Around this time the UK intended to buy the airborne rocket-propelled ballistic missile, the Douglas Skybolt, and plans were made for the Victor to carry two of these 11,000lb missiles under each wing; unlike with the Vulcan no flight trials were ever made and the project was abandoned when the Skybolt was cancelled.

The first Victor B2 was delivered in 1961 and the first B2 Squadron was 139 Squadron formed in February 1962, with the second 100 Squadron in May 1962. These were the only two B2 bomber squadrons to be formed as an order for another twenty-eight Victors was cancelled due to the end of the Skybolt project coupled with the fact that the government were unhappy with Sir Frederick Handley Page's resistance to their desire to merge his company with either Hawker Siddeley or the British Aircraft Corporation.

When the V Force nuclear deterrent went to low level in 1963 fatigue cracks were discovered at the wing fuselage join and Handley Page developed a modification to turn the Victor Mk2s into tankers. However the contract was awarded to Avros in 1970 after the firm went into liquidation.

The reconnaissance aircraft remained in service until 1974 and it was used to monitor French nuclear tests in the South Pacific. Finally the Victor Mk2 became a tanker and, as described later, was a great success being used in the Falklands to support all the aircraft operating from Ascension Island and later in the Middle East.

David Bywater, by now at Boscombe, did some testing on the B2 and confirms what a good aircraft the Victor had become.

A short ground school on the Mk2 Victor at Gaydon, followed by some familiarisation flying at Boscombe Down demonstrated the significant improvement of the Mk2 over

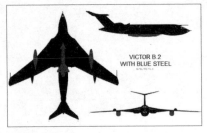

VICTOR B.2
WITH BLUE STEEL

Victor B2.

the Mk1. Changes in the cockpit layout for the pilots and in the handling qualities, made it a more pleasant aircraft to fly. An improved AC electrical system, based on constant-speed alternators, the addition of ram air turbines to provide an emergency electrical supply and the installation of an Artouste auxiliary power unit to provide standby air and electrical power on the ground and in the air, were also major improvements. However, the most dramatic advance was in the performance of the aircraft resulting from a greater wingspan and the increase in power provided by the uprated Rolls-Royce Conway engines. These were initially rated at over 17,250lb static thrust, giving a thrust to weight ratio of around 0.4 at a take-off weight of 200,000lbs, providing a significant improvement in the take-off, climb and asymmetric performance, as well as the height achieved in the cruise. A rough comparison of both aircraft with maximum internal fuel (no long-range bomb bay tanks fitted or weapons carried) illustrates this clearly. A typical Mk1/1A high level training profile would be flown at 0.84 Mach, cruise climbing from about 42,000ft to about 46,000ft at the end of five hours, giving a still air range of around 4,500nm. A similar profile in the Mk2 would be flown at Mach 0.85, cruise climbing from about 47,000ft to 52,000ft over six hours and 5,500nm.

In July 1965, I started the first of many trials flights in the strategic reconnaissance version of the Mk2 Victor. XL 165 had previously been in use with the Mk2 Intensive Flight Trials Unit at Cottesmore, but had been returned to Handley Page for extensive modifications to produce the SR version of the aircraft. It carried a fan of up to fifteen cameras in a large photographic crate and two 8,000lb, long-range fuel tanks in the bomb bay, which gave a significant further increase in the range and endurance of the aircraft. The camera fit could be varied, but included F49 cameras mounted vertically for mapping and survey work, F96 cameras mounted vertically or obliquely for day or night use and the F89 mounted obliquely for night use. Photoflashes could be carried in lieu of bomb bay fuel tanks. All the camera and photoflash controls were operated by the nav/radar. The trials requirement was to assess the performance of the photographic fit when used in the survey role and, for this purpose, a comparison was required between the product from the trials equipment and previously achieved high quality survey results from other proven aircraft systems. A trials location was therefore needed where the aircraft could be flown in daytime and clear weather for 1,500nm in a straight line over a pre-surveyed route. After much searching for a location which would meet these criteria, including the difficult to obtain correct climatic conditions, the navigation team settled on an east/west route over Canada operating from RCAF Namao, north of Edmonton, Alberta. The photographic equipment and the aircraft performed well, but huge frustration resulted from finding a build up of fair weather cumulus by the time we reached the operating area, despite bringing the take-off time forward to achieve a pre-dawn departure. It was only after the six weeks needed to achieve the necessary results had passed that it was admitted that a mistake had been made in planning when analysing the mass of climate data, and that, although the location and time of the year offered clear skies, these occurred during the night hours and not during daylight; time differences had been ignored! The trials were flown with myself or another A&AEE project pilot, Alan Fisher, as the captain and a 543 captain, Sqn Ldr Holland, as co-pilot, with an A&AEE or 543 Squadron rear crew. Unfortunately, Sqn Ldr Holland and all but one of his rear crew, who did not fly on the day, were later killed when carrying out a demonstration to the press at Wyton, when the aircraft was overstressed and broke up in flight.[11]

In December 1965, I captained XM718 and XL165 on a series of engine-handling tests with either Rolls-Royce test pilot Malcolm Muir or Handley Page test pilot Harry Rayner as co-pilot. The purpose of the trials was to investigate the engine-handling characteristics and the performance of the top temperature control system in order to give clearance advice for operations above 50,000ft. The trials involved slam deceleration and acceleration of individual engines. Problems were encountered with the top temperature controllers which required the pilots to keep a very close watch on temperatures during any engine handling at very high levels, but the major problem was the tendency for the adjacent engine in a common intake to surge and flameout when any engine was slam accelerated or decelerated, in addition to the surge and flameout of the test engine. Thus we frequently experienced a double engine flameout on one side, which halved the thrust available when at 55,000ft. Since relights could seldom be achieved until below 40,000ft, and the IAS was around 170kts (0.82 IMN), this was not a comfortable situation to find oneself in.[12]

During 1963, following improvements to the Soviet air defences, the decision was made to operate the Vulcan and the Victor in the low level role. As a result, General Dynamics terrain-following radar was fitted to both aircraft. The output was fed to the pitch demand bar in the primary flight display of the Smiths military flight system, giving pitch demands only, in both pilots' displays. The height demand could be preset from the cockpit in increments of 200ft from 200ft up to around 1,400ft. An extremely long and thorough flight test programme was devised but as it was eventually decided that the Victor 2 would replace the Victor 1 in the tanker role, the TFR programme was terminated.

During 1967, most trials work involved the development and clearance of a range of high, medium and low speed drogues on the tanker aircraft, with the assessment carried out by chase aircraft or the receiver aircraft, which included the Victor 1 and 2, the Vulcan 1 and 2, the VC 10, Belfast, Lightning, Harrier, Sea Vixen, Buccaneer, Scimitar, and Canberra. In December 1967, I carried out a series of autopilot runaway trials in Mk1A XH620 by day and night. These were designed to provide the Service with a clearance to use the autopilot in the tanker whilst the receiver was in contact, and involved the installation of trials equipment to inject runaways of varying severity, with a subjective assessment by the tanker and receiver pilots and analysis of film from a chase aircraft. It was found that the normal reaction of the receiver pilot, already highly alert using his hand and eye coordination to maintain contact,

---

[11] See Appendix I.
[12] The Olympus in the Vulcan had exactly the same problem which we had to fix. See *Vulcan Test Pilot*.

was adequate to deal with the maximum control inputs of which the autopilot was capable and a clearance was granted subject to a number of caveats.

Apart from flights to assess a new high speed drogue in 1968, there was little further Victor flying in that year and I was not to fly in the Victor again until I returned to Boscombe Down in the 1980s as the superintendent of flying. It was pleasing to see much of our earlier work on the Mk1 tanker had been carried forward to the Mk2 and that the aircraft made a significant contribution to the success of the Black Buck sorties in the Falklands war. Later, returning to A&AEE as commandant in 1988, I was pleased to see that the aircraft was continuing to soldier on in the tanker role, although by then airframe fatigue was beginning to spell the end. Just after I retired from the Royal Air Force in 1992, I attended a Guest Night at Marham to celebrate the life of the Victor and its final withdrawal from service. Many colleagues from Handley Page, the services and industry who had been involved with the aircraft throughout its lifespan were present. My recollections are of an aircraft which was perhaps not as well appreciated as it should have been, and which suffered from the politics of the day, which limited the government's commitment to its development, and yet it showed its flexibility and capability by remaining in service for longer than either the Valiant or Vulcan, providing absolutely vital support to the front line of the RAF, RN and many foreign air forces until its eventual withdrawal from service in 1992.

Norman Bonnor as previously mentioned moved from the B1 to the B2 and records his experiences on 100 Squadron.

I arrived on 100 Squadron at RAF Wittering in May 1964 as the nav radar on Terry Austin's crew. One of my first memories is of a general mess meeting when the station commander, Group Captain Lawrence, announced that he had commissioned David Shepherd to paint the Victor Mk2 and that all officers would contribute £5 on their mess bills towards the cost! I don't recall that we had any chance to vote on this, so there were a few grumbles from the more junior members as £5 bought a lot of beer in those days.

I certainly don't regret its cost, the painting looks magnificent and still hangs in the ante-room at Wittering together with a painting of a Valiant by the same renowned artist.[13] It depicts the Victor landing in the rain with the large brake parachute deployed. The aircraft is in the all-white (80 calories/square centimetre) anti-flash paint scheme designed to protect it from radiation from the Yellow Sun nuclear weapons it was designed to drop from high altitude. These were the early days of the Victor 2's service before Blue Steel was introduced and before the top of the aircraft was camouflaged for low level operations.

I had joined 100, via the Victor 2 Training Flight, after three years on XV Squadron with the Victor Mk1A at RAF Cottesmore. The Mk2 was slightly larger and heavier and all the aircraft services and systems it offered were much improved over the

---

[13]　The picture on page 81 is in black and white because the ante-room was being renovated at the time of writing.

Mk1A. But the really outstanding change was from the four Armstrong Siddeley Sapphires to four Rolls-Royce Conways. More than double the thrust available meant a dramatic change in performance. It was the first time that I had flown in an aircraft where you couldn't apply full power with the brakes on as the tyres would rotate on the wheel rims and risk bursting! Climbing out from Cottesmore in a Mk1A, we would be well out over the North Sea before reaching 40,000ft; in the Mk2 out of Wittering, we reached 40,000ft after about seven minutes and before King's Lynn!

Of course, we were subject to the famous 'four minute' warning from the BMEWS (ballistic missile early warning system) at Fylingdales and regularly practised four aircraft scrambles from the ORP (operational readiness platform) at the runway 26 end. It was a strange feeling to sit with only battery power, listening to the intercom and the Bomber Command telescramble system that beeped every minute and, perhaps with a skylark twittering above us, knowing that all hell was about to break loose. Suddenly the call would come: "This is the Bomber Controller …"; we rarely waited for more; the combustor start system fired 6,000 psi air into all four engines, and we would be moving forward in seconds with the AEO desperately trying to get all the electrics up and running as we hurtled down the runway.

My crew were often number one in the stream and I regularly timed our retracting the undercarriage in under a minute after the scramble call. Can anyone name a modern fighter that can match that from cold? Having got airborne, flying the beast was a little fraught as the compass and instruments were still erecting so going into cloud straight after take-off was a challenge. The three aircraft behind would take opposite sides of the runway to best stay out of the wake turbulence, which was the only limiting factor that prevented all four aircraft getting airborne in under two minutes. If one of the four engines failed to start, we went anyway after calling "No 1 going last" and then bringing power up on only two engines at first and adding the third when Terry had aerodynamic control on the rudder. It took a bit longer to get airborne, but there was ample power on three engines.

We regularly practised and demonstrated four-aircraft scrambles from the ORP. I do remember one unfortunate incident in the summer of 1964 when it was decided to hold a 'families day' with the object of letting the wives, girlfriends and children see what the station's role was all about. They were taken on tours of the ops block, visited the simulators, had tea and cakes in the various units and the finale was to be a four-aircraft scramble.

The families were bussed out to a roped-off area on the grass opposite the RW26 operational readiness platform. I think we were number one crew in the stream as usual. It was a lovely sunny Saturday with just the faint murmur of traffic moving on the A1. A loud speaker system was used to explain what was about to happen to all the happy families but, unfortunately, it did nothing to really prepare those poor innocent wives and children for the two minutes of mayhem that was about to occur. The scramble call was given and sixteen Conway engines burst into life; our aircraft went to full power and accelerated down the runway followed rapidly by three more. There was chaos among the families with screaming children, distraught mothers and many in a state of shock. We never again had a practice scramble on a families' day!

This picture is kindly supplied from the personal collection of Jerry Mudford, captain of Victor B1A XH617 which crashed at Diss, Norfolk in 1960. Apparently taken at a Wittering Open Day in the early 1960s it shows XL158 in anti-flash white, with a Blue Steel missile in the foreground and Vulcans in the background.

On the subject of scramble starts and the problem that some systems couldn't wake-up from cold in the time available, one bright spark of an engineering officer designed an automatic snatch-disconnect system for the power cable of a Houchin power trolley; if it worked, it would mean we could sit at two-minute readiness with ground power available and have the compass and instruments ready to go. His idea was that the power lead plug would be retained in the aircraft socket on the side of the front fuselage by a pin attached by wire to a mooring point. When the aircraft began to move forward, the pin would be pulled out and elastic ropes also attached to the plug would pull it and the cable clear of the aircraft. In taxiing trials on a single aircraft, it all worked pretty well except for the cable thrashing away rather close to the crew chief!

This was a very heavy cable some three inches thick designed to take a very high amperage. Next came the scramble take-off trial with a large number of people watching. The engines started, the aircraft moved forward, the retaining pin was extracted BUT the cable plug refused to come out of the aircraft socket.

Before the tower could call "abort", the aircraft was off down the runway towing the Houchin (about the size of a family car but probably weighing more) to a speed it was certainly not designed for. As the aircraft got airborne, the power cable severed at the trolley with a nice display of sparks, and the trolley hurtled off the end of the runway demolishing some approach lights and tumbling onward. Fortunately, the wind was from the west so this occurred at the Collyweston end; if it had been from the east, the trolley would probably have careered across the A1 and worried a few motorists.

However, this wasn't the end of the story; not knowing what was happening behind them, the crew had continued the after take-off checks and tried to raise the undercarriage. Inevitably, one main bogie wouldn't retract because the broken cable was entangled with it. Fortunately, the story ended happily as the gear locked down okay, and the aircraft landed safely after burning off some fuel down to max landing weight (we had no provision for dumping fuel in those days; this wasn't introduced until the aircraft were converted to tankers). It's a pity I wasn't in at the debrief to hear what the station commander and crew said to the 'bright' engineer.

Early in the aircraft's introduction at Wittering, a tragedy occurred when Alex Galbraith's crew took off on a night mission and had an engine fire warning immediately after take-off. Sadly, the Board of Enquiry later proved the warning was spurious. In the struggle to shut down the engine and continue to fly the heavy aircraft in poor weather, they entered a stall. Alex ordered the crew to bail out but, while the co-pilot used his ejection seat at the last moment as was the standard instruction at the time (someone needed to come back to relate what had occurred), Alex stayed trying to get his rear crew members safely clear. None of them made it, and the aircraft crashed close to Barnack village (see the accident appendix). The surviving co-pilot went on to become Air Marshal Sir Benny Jackson and a member of the Air Force Board.

This tragic incident put pressure on the MOD to improve the rear crew escape facilities. These included: quick-don parachutes, swivelling seats with an air cushion under the dinghy pack to force you to your feet under high g. The rear crew escape procedure was that the AEO released the cockpit door, the three crew would ensure their quick-don shoulder straps were in place and tight before swivelling their seats to face the door and firing their air cushions. The final touch was that a knotted nylon rope was attached to the door surround (clipped on after closing the door before engine start) and, when the door opened, the rope pulled out of its housings in the cockpit roof to form a rigid towline which you were meant to haul yourself along to escape through the open door.

One night an aircraft was climbing out of Wittering when the normally reliable door locks failed at 30,000ft. The cabin pressure blew the door open and straight off its hinges; however, it was still attached to the nylon rope which pulled down from its roof housings and went very, very taut. For the next hour before they could land, the rear crew kept their heads down while the door banged about on top of the port wing and fuselage, and the nylon rope threatened to break at any minute and decapitate the crew. A later modification introduced a weak link on the rope attachment.

With the Conway engines the Victor Mk2 aircraft climbed quickly to 45,000ft and, by what is called 'cruise climbing' (allowing the aircraft to climb very slowly in the cruise as the weight of fuel dropped), it was possible to get up to 55,000ft towards the end of a sortie, or even 60,000ft if the temperatures aloft were colder than normal. We were therefore issued and trained to use a 'pressure jerkin and anti-g leggings' which would enable us to survive a cockpit decompression at such high altitudes. Normally, the cockpit was pressurised to the equivalent of 8,000ft and was very comfortable but, if a decompression occurred above 45,000ft, we would need to breathe under pressure or the oxygen in our lungs would bubble out and we would rapidly become unconscious. Thus, wearing the extra flying clothing against the prospect of such an emergency was aimed at buying the crew the time to descend to a safer altitude; this is one of the reasons why commercial airliners, apart from Concorde, cruise at around 40,000ft or below.

One consequence of the need to wear a pressure jerkin and anti-g leggings was that you got uncomfortably hot in summer or in the tropics as soon as you kitted-up. To offset this, we wore a ventilated suit over our shreddies and under our flying suit and pressure gear. These suits were made of thin white nylon with a spider's web of tubes with holes incorporated into the fabric and a feed hose sticking out the side that you plugged into a cool air supply to stay comfortable. Each crew position in the aircraft had a plug-in point and so did the seats on the crew buses that took us to the aircraft.

We rarely bothered to use these suits in the UK as the summers weren't that hot and the crew bus systems were often unserviceable, but on Ranger flights to the tropics, we usually took them along.

On our crew's first Ranger to Singapore, we had the suits with us and decided to try them out when we realised that the outside air temperature would be approaching 100 degrees at our planned take-off time. We managed to borrow an air conditioning trolley to keep the cockpit reasonably cool while we completed the checks but, as soon as this was removed and the door closed for engine start, you can imagine how quickly the temperature in the cockpit rose, so use of the ventilated suits with the engines now providing the air input was most welcome. We taxied out with the air valves fully open and said how good we thought the system was. With clearance to take-off, Terry Austin opened the taps and we started to roll – argh!! As the engine power rose, the cold air pressure into the suits went up dramatically, and we all struggled to turn off our air valves. At the debriefing after the sortie, Terry said he nearly abandoned the take-off! On return to the UK, we recommended a change to the pre take-off checks to turn the air valves down when using air vent suits.

When Blue Steel was introduced, any sortie flown without a live or a training missile loaded was rather a waste of effort for the nav team as all our training goals involved practising operation of the missile systems. There was a readiness requirement to fly the live (or operational) missiles loaded with kerosene and HTP (high test peroxide), but I hasten to add that this was done without the Red Snow nuclear warhead installed. On those occasions when we flew without a missile, we would plan high level navigation legs using astro. On a particular winter's night, we started a 1,000-mile leg up the North Sea and then across Scotland towards Iceland.

The autopilot was in, of course, and I started taking a series of sextant shots on the stars. We cleared Scotland and relaxed as there was still some 300 miles to go to the first NTP (navigation terminal point) on the north-east coast of Iceland. I kept myself busy using the H2S radar to look out for shipping. On such a calm night, with all cockpit lighting dimmed, I noticed that the nav plotter and the AEO were fast asleep. I reported this to the two pilots with a laugh and got no reply; suddenly I realised that, if I had dozed off, we would have ended up at the North Pole very short of fuel. I raised hell and made sure that nobody on my crew ever fell asleep after that.

In 1965, our crew and others at Wittering were selected to train for the SAC bombing competition, which was to take place at Spokane in Washington State. We would have to use American JP4 fuel, a much wider cut and more inflammable kerosene than our usual Avtur. My crew was tasked with some trial flights to check the Victor's performance with this fuel. On the first sortie, all went as planned during start up and taxi. As we approached the runway, the pre take-off checks were completed, and we were cleared to roll.

One of these checks pressurized the fuel tanks; however, unknown to us, a breather valve on one of the wing-mounted slipper tanks (holding some 1,600 gallons) failed to close and, as we took off, it emptied itself along the runway. Being a wide-cut fuel, the JP4 was ignited by the heat of the Conways' exhausts and the resulting fire followed us down the runway. While we were blissfully unaware of the fire behind us, a senior controller in the tower probably saved us from a nasty incident by shouting to his colleagues "don't tell them to abort!" We rotated and climbed away and so broke our link with the advancing fire which made rather a mess of the runway surface.

Having started training for the SAC bombing competition, and getting excited about the month we would spend in the USA, our participation was suddenly withdrawn by Bomber Command. The Victor fatigue specimen at HSA Woodford had shown some cracks that could mean structural weakness; this gave serious cause for concern, particularly after the metal fatigue problems experienced a few years earlier by the

Victor B2 final configuration and camouflage for low level operation.

Valiant. Although the specimen was many cycles and hours ahead of even the highest hours flown by a Victor 2, caution was undoubtedly the sensible option. Our training targets were dramatically changed from the original ones based primarily on hours and sorties to new definitions based strictly on training value.

Notwithstanding the cancellation of participation in the SAC bombing competition, earlier in February 1965 Alan Stephenson records that he took a Blue Steel to the United States for the first time to Davis Monthan AFB in Arizona in 1965.

Norman Bonnor continues:

We were allowed no more than six sorties a month, and each one had to be packed with high value training. The senior staff at Wittering thought this would lead to a drop in morale among the crews, but far from it. We no longer flew without a missile, or had to carry unserviceabilities; we also had priority on range bookings over our colleagues in 1 Group flying the Vulcan; each sortie became a challenge to get best value. A typical example would include climbing out to the North Sea, starting an 800-mile high level nav stage including fighter affiliation with Lightnings from Coningsby or Leuchars, descending to join a low level route over Scotland, ending in a simulated Blue Steel attack at a radar bomb scoring unit over Newcastle or East Anglia which included a test of the AEO's reaction time to jam the RBSU as it attempted to lock-on to the aircraft at the start of the attack. If fuel permitted, a second Blue Steel attack would be made at the RBSU at Glasgow or Manchester before recovering for no more than a couple of ILS or GCA approaches at Wittering.

The reduced monthly training hours meant only one or at most two sorties a week per crew, which doesn't sound like hard work, but sortie planning for the rear crew would take a day while the pilots completed a simulator exercise or two, target study for our four war plan targets would take another day together with other routine ground training and, of course, there was QRA. To hold QRA, the crew had to be fully constituted (no replacements were allowed because of the secrecy associated with war plan targets) and the crew, as a whole, had to be classified to at least Combat

Ready. There were three classifications: Combat Ready, Select and Select Star, later replaced by Command.

After arriving on the Squadron from the VTF conversion course, it took several months for each individual in a crew to reach Combat Ready. You then joined the six-month training cycle involving the requirement to complete a set number of training events to prescribed standards. So it would take a minimum of eighteen months (assuming you achieved all the training goals to the high standards required) to reach the top classification if you ever made it at all. During my time on both XV and 100 Squadrons, there were never more than two crews on the squadron at Select Star standard. The V Force squadrons had an establishment of ten crews, but we rarely had more than seven or eight fully constituted crews available because of leave, sickness, postings etc. and at least one of these would not yet be Combat Ready and thus available for QRA; as a result, most crews would be on fifteen-minute standby for twenty-four hours each week.

During the day, QRA crews could undertake some ground training and target study, but the five members had to stay together and ready to react to the 'hooter'. Fortunately, unlike some other V Force bases, the officers' mess at Wittering was reasonably close to the QRA pans, so we slept in the mess and took our meals in the aircrew feeder. Fifteen-minute readiness meant you had to be able to reach the aircraft, undertake last-minute loading actions on the weapon and be ready with the cockpit door closed in under ten minutes; you were now at five-minute readiness. The Bomber Controller might then advance you to two minutes or stand you down; two minutes meant starting up and taxiing out to the threshold in no more than three minutes. It was a rare 24-hour duty, if you were not called out on a practice readiness 'Exercise Edom' during either day or night. At weekends, apart from the daily aircraft checks and the usual practice call out, we would relax in the mess playing bridge or mah-jong.

However, if the weather was good, my crew would head for the garden at the front of the mess to take up our passion for competitions with favourite toys of the mid-60s plastic rockets. These were just over a foot long and were launched using very strong elastic bands. The body of the rocket contained a parachute for safe recovery; however, you could adjust the delay on the parachute opening. Our competitions involved setting the delay so that, after the rocket started its descent, the parachute opened at the lowest possible height and maximum descent speed. The winning margin was usually less than three feet; optimistic losers spent time gluing the broken parts of their rocket back together.

One sunny Saturday, we were indulging our usual passion and had achieved some very low openings around six feet or so off the lawn. We set up again and one bystander called the count-down; a cheer went up as the rockets soared away, but one picked up the wind and headed over to the car park in front of the mess. Concern rose as it looked like a serious repair job would be needed if the parachute didn't open; concern rose further when the station commander's car with his standard flying swept round the front of the mess and our rocket looked to be on a precise interception course.

The chute opened six feet off the ground and the rocket fluttered down bouncing off the boot of the car. We all hid behind a hedge and awaited our fate but, fortunately,

Victor B2 XL512 carrying a Blue Steel stand-off missile. (*Philip Goodall*)

either he didn't notice or chose to ignore our children's games and strode straight into the mess. From then on, we took more care when launching our toy rockets.

One of the limiting factors on making best use of a training sortie was the time it took in the air to align the inertial navigation system (INS) of the Blue Steel missile. Ground alignments took twenty minutes but were totally unrealistic for a force designed to scramble in less than four minutes and so were abandoned at an early stage. The standard operating procedure (SOP) to align the INS was climb out and not attempt to start up the missile until you were straight and level at 45,000ft. One day, we were looking at an aircraft with a missile loaded, when Jeff Morgan, our co-pilot, said, "We align that missile when we are in level flight, but the missile isn't!" What he meant was that to fit Blue Steel on the Victor, unlike the Vulcan, it was hung in a nose-down attitude of some ten degrees.

"Why don't we align it in the climb when it's closer to level?" The nav team, being typically dismissive of what co-pilots say, replied as one "Cos the SOP says you do it when you are level in the cruise!" But he had started Gordon Hagel and me thinking; we could save up to twenty minutes by starting the alignment immediately after take-off. We got out our Blue Steel course notes again and then went to see the missile technicians.

We soon realised that the SOP had been written during the trials programme in Australia and nobody had considered revising it since the system had entered operational service. In the INS bay, we persuaded the technicians to let us experiment with an INS on a test bench and found that we could easily complete the alignment process in less than five minutes.

Just to be sure, we contacted Dr Roberts at RAE Farnborough who had been deeply involved in the design of the navigation and guidance system of the Blue Steel. When

The crew of Victor XL190 are seen with the station commander who is pouring some celebratory refreshment; they are all smiles after completing their successful mission. The personalities are from left to right: Wing Commander John Curtis (OC Operations Wing retired as Air Marshal Sir John Curtis), Flight Lieutenant John Charlton (air electronics officer retired as squadron leader), Group Captain John Lawrence (station commander RAF Wittering retired as air vice-marshal), Flight Lieutenant Jeff Morgan (co-pilot retired as group captain), Flight Lieutenant Terry Austin (captain retired as squadron leader), Flight Lieutenant Norman Bonnor (navigator radar).

we explained our thoughts about aligning the INS in about five minutes during the climb, he said he couldn't see any reason why not. Of course, we kept all this 'under our hats', but it soon became rather obvious that we were completing many more Blue Steel practice attacks than any other crew on the station.

First it was the wing weapons staff who questioned us, but we easily sold them a story, but then the boss, Wing Commander John Herrington wanted to know what we were up to, so we came clean. He said we could keep going, but we had to let the other 100 Squadron crews "in on the plot"; however, "Don't tell 139 Squadron!" That didn't work for long; 100 Squadron were soon completing twice as many practice attacks as 139, so the station commander had to know. Group Captain Lawrence said it was okay, "But don't tell anyone on those flatirons (Vulcans) at Scampton!"

It was soon after this that we were chosen to be the first fully operational crew to launch a Blue Steel missile as part of the 'post-acceptance checks'. The missile we launched and fired that day nearly didn't make it because of an incident a few days earlier on one of the carry-over sorties we had to complete at Aberporth before we were allowed to fire it.

We had completed the sortie and fly-through at Aberporth very successfully and climbed away to recover to Wittering. As we approached the airfield, the undercarriage was selected down, but one of the main legs refused to go 'green'.

We had about thirty minutes fuel remaining, so we entered the circuit, reported the problem and considered our options. Raising and lowering the undercarriage again had no effect; we still got two greens and a red. Using the secondary hydraulic system produced the same result.

The Victor had experienced undercarriage problems in the past, and one of the modifications to solve possible problems was the addition of a compressed air bottle that blew the undercarriage down, but once used the hydraulic lock on the undercarriage would be lost and reliance placed on mechanical locks only; so this was a last resort.

By this stage, the duty pilot had informed the senior staff who rapidly assembled in the tower. Why so much high powered interest? Well, if we did attempt to land with dodgy gear, we would have to jettison the missile first. Remember this was a fully operational round, full of kerosene and high test peroxide, which when mixed in measured quantities in the rocket motor was a pretty explosive combination. Crushed together all at once under an aircraft with a collapsing undercarriage doesn't bear thinking about.

Dumping a million-pound missile (at 1966 prices!) in a farmer's field wasn't a very good idea either. Our options were narrowing with every minute, and our decision was that we should head for The Wash to jettison the missile but make one last-minute attempt to blow the gear down with the compressed air system. If we got three greens, we would not jettison but, either way, we would have to divert to Marham because of our expected fuel state when we reached The Wash.

When Terry related our intentions to the tower, you could sense that they were going through the same drama as we were. But, I must hand it to the station commander and his team, they made no attempt to interfere with our decision; they just wished us the best of luck and said they'd warn Marham of our emergency. About half way to The Wash, for no accountable reason, three greens suddenly appeared and we quickly turned about and landed safely at Wittering with much relief all round.

The aircraft for Operation Fresno was XL190; it was originally delivered to 139 (Jamaica) Squadron at RAF Wittering as a B2 but was returned to Handley Page for modifications to carry the Blue Steel missile (more powerful Conway engines, modified bomb doors, nav computer GPI Mk6 and Blue Steel control panel in the rear cockpit, Blue Steel cooling pack in the bomb bay etc. etc.) and returned to Wittering as a B Mk2 (BS), by which time the station was operating as a wing so all the aircraft were held within the wing rather than being individually assigned to the two squadrons.

The highlight of my time in the V Force, and my abiding memory, was the launch of that Blue Steel missile at the RAE range in Aberporth Bay on 27th May 1966. We had to achieve at least three successful carry-over sorties on the low level route specially arranged for Operation Fresno before we would be authorised to make the launch. Throughout April and early May we struggled to achieve successful carry overs, but it seemed that either the weather, the aircraft or the range were against us.

Finally we were airborne on the Friday before the Whitsun weekend with authority to launch. The flight went like clockwork and we approached the range overland from the south at about 400ft accelerating to 350 knots; our release point was just off the coast abeam the range head. I remember starting the countdown and hoping that the range would be free of shipping so that we could be cleared to continue but, at this critical stage with just a few seconds to go, the range had not managed to lock their tracking radars on to us despite knowing our track, height, speed and timing very precisely.

On top of this, we were transmitting on VHF, UHF, telemetry and with a C band tracking transponder in the missile. With less than five seconds to launch, the range finally got us and we were cleared to launch. The missile dropped away and the aircraft gave a noticeable upward lurch having lost such a large load, and we started a two-and-a-half g escape manoeuvre; doesn't sound much but it's a lot for a big aeroplane at 350 knots.

We knew the missile would free fall for some fifteen seconds before its 16,000lbs was hit up the rear by a rocket motor giving 24,000lb of thrust. By that stage, the foreplane would have made its nose point up so it was aiming at us!! The pilots confirmed that it didn't miss us by much, and the Hunter chase plane that had joined us a few minutes before launch as we coasted out had no chance of keeping up with the missile's amazing acceleration to Mach 3.

Blue Steel dropping away before ignition.

One thing I didn't say was that, having completed all the preparation sorties as a constituted crew of five, on the day, Wing Commander John Curtis (OC Operations at Wittering) was down to fly with us. Our obvious thought was they don't trust us to do this as flight lieutenants so they've sent a senior officer to check us out. We needn't have worried, the WingCo just wanted to be in on the action; as I counted down to the drop, I looked round to eyeball him as he sat in the sixth seat expecting to get the nod to go ahead; instead, he very deliberately looked away.

Besides Norman Bonnor's vivid account of using the Victor B2 on 100 Squadron he also comments on the maximum altitudes which Victors reached.

It is right that the Victor B Mk2 was only cleared to 57,000ft in normal operations and, I believe, this was not an airframe or systems limit but a crew limit with the flying clothing and oxygen equipment we used on the bomber version.

We used a P or Q oxygen mask (depending on the size of your face) connected to a Mk21 oxygen regulator. We also wore a pressure jerkin – with integral Mae West – and anti-g leggings, that were also connected to the Mk21. The anti-g leggings were not to help at high g – the old bird was hardly an F16 or Hawk, but for pressure breathing of which more below.

Normally, we operated at a cabin pressure of between 8,000 and 12,000ft depending on our operating height, so we breathed either cabin air or a mix of air and oxygen with our masks on. If we had a failure of cabin pressurisation or an explosive decompression below 40,000ft, we would breathe the 100% oxygen automatically provided by the Mk21 without any major problem. However, above 40,000ft, the ambient pressure is so low that – even with 100% oxygen – your lungs would not absorb enough oxygen to keep you awake for more than a very few minutes or eventually even alive.

However, for an explosive decompression above 40,000ft, the Mk21 filled the bladders in the jerkin and leggings and delivered 100% oxygen under pressure to the mask. We now had to breathe in reverse, fighting against the pressure in the mask on the intake of oxygen and forcing against the pressure to breathe out; it's difficult to talk while doing this, so we practised it regularly in pressure chambers at the Aero-Medical School. Clearly, we would descend below 40,000ft as soon as possible should this occur but the combination of Mk21, P or Q mask, jerkin and leggings bought us the time to do so.

With this combination, our cleared operating limit was 57,000ft or 52,000ft without the leggings. That said we regularly broke that limit to 60,000 but not too much beyond; at that height, the stalling speed (IAS) was close to our max flying speed anyway so turning had to be gentle or we rapidly lost height. I think everybody did this at least once during their tour at Wittering and my crew were a particularly gung-ho lot so we regularly did it mainly to take three-star astro fixes in the daytime and annoy the station and group navigation officers who didn't believe it was possible – the sky goes dark blue at above 55,000ish and the brightest stars show.

I also recall that, at Wyton, 543 Squadron were cleared to 60,000ft and maybe more as they wore a Taylor helmet with a neck-seal that gave added protection. It was also very easy to go supersonic in a Mk1 at altitude, and I believe most crews did this occasionally over the North Sea. Despite the more powerful engines, this was not so easy on the Mk2 because of the extra drag of the big wing tanks and the fact that the Mk1 had variable rather than fixed nose flaps so was a very slippery aircraft. Without the airbrakes, it didn't want to descend from 45,000ft when you throttled back!

As a 'died in the wool' Vulcan operator with its enormous wings I was always amazed that the Victor could get as high as we could, that is 60,000ft. I never went above that height and I don't think anyone else did. Maybe the Conway engines were more suited to high altitude than the Olympus but I can't help feeling that it must have been a lot safer in a Vulcan than a Victor since the Vulcan had virtually no spin tendencies.

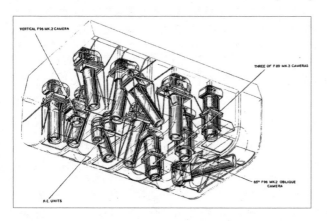

Alan Brooks was a radar reconnaissance operator on the Victor SR2 543 Squadron and in a few paragraphs demonstrates how effective the aircraft was. The Squadron undertook reconnaissance mission sorties far and wide. It also carried out high-level survey photography for various governments, Norway, Denmark, Thailand, East Africa, Atlantic Islands, Borneo and many more locations. It was said that one Victor SR2 could photograph the whole of the UK in a single two-hour sortie. There have also been claims that three aircraft operating from Wyton could photograph the whole of the Mediterranean and see surface shipping during a single seven-hour mission from its home base, Wyton. There was a single camera for surveying and a bank of cameras for intelligence work.

I was on Squadron 543 for four years until 1st January 1970 and at that time I had already done three and a half years on Valiants. I became the wing radar leader, the guy responsible for the operational tasking of the Squadron. I actually went to the Vulcan in 1976 and so played the same role on all three V bombers. We had another role which was monitoring radiation from nuclear explosions. We used to operate from Lima, Peru to monitor the French nuclear tests on Moruroa and Fangataufa, two atolls in the south-eastern area of the Tuamotu Archipelago, French Polynesia. I did three of the detachments from Lima basically at maximum altitude so we were knocking around at 55,000ft. Unfortunately we had to keep the slipper tanks on because we needed the

Top and above: Victor SR2 with cameras in the bomb crate.

fuel; there was a penalty to pay for the weight and drag but we needed the fuel for searching for radioactive fallout bearing in mind the distance from Lima to the atolls was about 3,600 nautical miles, not that we went anywhere near overhead since the

Left: Victor B1 XA936 at Farnborough in 1958.

Middle: RAF Tengah, Singapore, Operation Chamfrom 1964.

Bottom: Phantoms to Cyprus with Victor K1. (*T.Cottingham*)

Top: Victor K1A in appropriate camouflage when deterrent went low level early 1960s.

Above: Lightnings being refuelled by Victor K1A of 57 Squadron.

Left: Victor K1 refuelling Phantom.

Above: Picture through the periscope of a Lightning 6 being refuelled from the Victor. *(Barry Neal)*

Left: Harrier being refuelled from Victor K1.

Below: Norman Bonnor has kindly supplied this splendid picture of 100 Squadron probably taken in 1966.

Top left: Victor B2s on exercise at Goose Bay with lone Andover Mk2.

Top right: Unusual formation of Comet R Mk2, Victor K2 and two Canberras on the occasion of the Duke of Edinburgh's visit to Wyton on 13th June 1969.

Above: Victor K2 jettisoning fuel from five ports. Rare picture as the procedure was later stopped. (*John Brown*)

Left: Standard procedure Victor K2 refuelling another K2.

Top: F4 and Lightning being refuelled by Victor K2. (*Dick Russell*)

Above: Victor K2 refuelling Buccaneers returning from the Middle East before the Gulf War.

Top: Victor K2 refuelling Nimrod. This was a flight before the Falklands operation.

Above: Victor on Wideawake runway with South Gannet Hill behind.

Top: Wideawake Airfield with Victor on runway, C5 on ramp and C141 behind C5.

Above: Wideawake with Victors. (*Dick Russell*)

Left: Black Buck planning meeting. (*Barry Neal*)

Middle: Black Buck briefing. (*Bob Tuxford*)

Bottom: Transferring fuel to Vulcan on Black Buck raid. Note Westinghouse jammer. (*Bob Tuxford*)

fallout was carried eastward by the winds. The French exploded weapons there from 1966 to 1974 and I was there in 1968, 1971 and 1974.

Ray Williams was our flight commander the first time we went to Peru. We were sitting there as high as we could get, very heavy doing 20-mile radius turns on the pre stall buffet the whole way. The next test pilot we had on the squadron was a chap called Gordon Harper and he stopped that straight away because it appears we were operating in dead man's corner between the stall and maximum permitted mach number; but being a navigator the actual delicacy of it I can't explain to you but I was very glad that we were out of the buffet.

We did a lot of work with the navy on various things. Most of our tasking came from Northwood via wherever the maritime HQ was up in Scotland. We worked with submarines and with surface vessels, all our own of course. We used to track their really fast small boats which we couldn't see on radar but we could see the wakes very clearly. I think the Nimrod also did similar sorties but their Searchwater radar would be more effective than ours. In fact I liaised with Kelvin Hughes, I think it was, about the possibility of fitting a Searchwater radar into the Victor but when I asked them how big it was, because at that time no one had seen one, they said about the size of a domestic gas oven so we abandoned the idea at that point.

We were using basically the same radar as the Vulcan, H2S but tweaked to Mark 9. We also had a side scan facility which was quite useful on occasions. In fact when the first Kresta, which is a Russian warship came out we were sent off to find it and of course they could 'hear' you coming from 300 miles away by listening to our radar. So as we got near and saw where it was with side scan, we stopped the scanner pointing out to one side of the aeroplane and flew on. When we saw the radar light up with the ship on it we steered the scanner and kept the ship on the screen which effectively gave them a lock-on indication. In response the ship came out with all the radar he had got on board and we managed to record all the bits and pieces he was pushing out.

Peter 'Nobby' Clark also had a go monitoring the nuclear explosions of our ally France.

I served on 543 SR Squadron for six years from December 1965 until April 1971. In 1968 a flight was detached to Lima, Peru to locate and take samples of the French nuclear tests being carried out in the Tahiti area of the Pacific. On 10th August on one such flight we had fuel problems, which meant that we could not return to our base in Lima. We put out a PAN call and even though it was 3am we luckily got an answer from the control tower at Mendoza, Argentina. The person in the tower passed the message on and eventually we could see traffic on the road from the city and shortly afterwards we were given landing clearance. I was questioned for sometime, which bordered on a wartime interrogation and when I mentioned this the questions stopped and I was allowed to go to bed.

The next morning we were obliged to open the bomb doors to prove that we were not carrying a Nuke. Our engineering officer flew down from Lima and checked the aircraft, sorted out the fuel problem and we were cleared to return to Lima on 14th having been regally entertained by the Argentine air force for three days. We were attached again to Peru in 1970.

As I read Nobby's words the Falklands situation is boiling up again since unfortunately oil has been discovered in the area. One wonders whether today Alan and the crew would have been allowed to have such a splendid stay as they clearly did in Mendoza.

The *Daily Mail* Atlantic Air Race took place in 1969 and there were prizes for the fastest person starting from the top of the New York Empire State building finishing at the top of the London Post Office Tower and vice-versa. Derek Aldred was the navigator of the Victor B2 reconnaissance aircraft XH672 which took part in the race going eastwards using Floyd Bennett Field in Brooklyn, New York (now a park) and BAC's Wisley airfield just south of London; the aircraft had two large bomb-bay fuel tanks fitted. Their passenger was a 58 Squadron navigator, Derek Aldous, and he just beat the Harrier pilot by 28 seconds. The Victor flying time was only 5hr 25min but the flight nearly ended in disaster as there was a misunderstanding on the time to start the descent by the captain. In the event by positioning the end of the let down just three miles on the approach to Wisley's runway they managed to land without running out of fuel but with only 1,400lb left at touchdown. Looking at the accounts on the internet, a Royal Navy Phantom received all the publicity for flying non-stop New York to London in 5hr 11min; however, winning from a standing start, in my view, was a much more impressive performance.

For the record, on the way out to New York the Harrier beat a Phantom and also a runner in a Victor; the fighter aircraft, both ways, were refuelled by Victor K1s. This anonymous excerpt came from the Vectric Forum.

A couple of weeks back, while in the south of France, I met an elderly couple who had moved over there a number of years ago. During a conversation over Sunday lunch the gentleman told me he was once in 1 Fighter Squadron in the RAF. In fact he was a squadron leader. He told me a few tales about the days when he was flying. Here is a brief description of one of the best he told.

During the *Daily Mail* race to commemorate the first transatlantic crossing my new friend, Sqn Ldr Tom Lecky-Thompson was going to fly his Harrier. He told me that on the day of his attempt he set off from the GPO Tower and went down in the lift, jumped on a motorcycle and drove to St. Pancras railway station, where he had parked his Harrier the previous day. After taking off vertically he met up with two Victor refuelling planes from one of which he refuelled. Later he caught up with a further four which had set off from the UK earlier. Finally he met another which had left the US and, after refuelling a total of four times, he finally arrived in New York. Not at an airport but at a demolished 'convent' that the RAF had acquired for the event. Finally having reached the top of the Empire State building he won the event.

Summing up the Victor B2, it is quite clear that with a dedicated crew the aircraft performed well as a deterrent both as a free fall nuclear bomber and with Blue Steel. However Blue Steel was a tricky weapon with hydrogen peroxide as a fuel and the weapon was designed for high altitude release. When the attack role went from high level to low level the effectiveness of the V Force began to deteriorate and the Victor was affected more than the Vulcan because of its restricted fatigue life. This was in no way due to the flight and groundcrews who performed in an absolutely first class manner but the writing was on the wall signalling the end of an era. However for the Victor, unlike the Vulcan, there was a second life as a tanker and perhaps it was at its most effective in this final role.

Chapter Six

Victor K2
Development and Operation

In 1970 Handley Page Ltd was forced to stop operating due to financial difficulties and my first job when I became chief test pilot at Avros was to bring all the Victor Mk2s on Handley Page's airfield at Radlett up to Woodford to be converted into flight refuelling tankers. I could almost sense Sir Frederick Handley Page turning in his grave since up to that time Avros and Handley Page had been in continual competition starting between the two world wars. The Lancaster and the Halifax, the Tudor and the Hermes, the Avro 748 and the Herald and, of course, the Vulcan and the Victor, were typical examples of competing aircraft. I first got involved in the contest at Boscombe Down in 1956 when the Vulcan and Victor were having their RAF acceptance trials; both manufacturers were trying to prove that their aircraft was the better. Purely by chance I was on the Vulcan acceptance team which is perhaps why Avros asked me to join them as a test pilot and I left the RAF.

Johnny Allam was Handley Page's chief test pilot and he helped us bring the twenty-four airframes up to Woodford, starting by checking me out on the Victor. It must have been a great sadness for Johnny to see the development of his splendid aircraft, on which he had spent so much time and expertise, handed over to his erstwhile competitors but he never complained or showed any sign of bitterness. We brought the first aircraft up on 9th April 1970, XL188 followed by the other twenty-three. The aircraft were parked all over the airfield and they stayed there until they were brought into the assembly sheds, one by one, to be converted to tankers.

The object of the programme was not only to convert the Victor Mk2 into a tanker but also to restart its fatigue life. The noses of the aircraft were rebuilt at both Bitteswell and Chadderton and a completely new fuel management panel was needed between the pilots' seats.

The ailerons were rigged upwards by three inches from their previous neutral position to further reduce the wing bending moment in flight – a concept not adopted by Boeing or Airbus on their civil airliners until some twenty-five years later. Fuselage barrels were placed into a jig to enable the wing box main spar to be replaced as part of the overall programme of providing the aircraft with an 'as new' fatigue life starting from zero. This would ensure a minimum of fourteen years of concentrated heavyweight tanker flying. In addition to all the design changes to the crew compartment, two very large bomb bay tanks were designed which, together with the Mk 17B centreline hose drum unit, filled the whole of the vast Victor bomb bay. Outer wing pylons were also produced to carry the two Mk 20 flight refuelling drogue units with their associated fuel piping and wiring as this was to be the RAF's first ever 'three-hose' tanker. The whole programme from commencement of the strip down to aircraft roll out, in a gleaming new paint scheme, took about three years per aircraft. The pilots' panels had to be changed to accommodate the new central fuel panel which controlled the refuelling and which tanks were being filled and emptied.

Victor K2 pilots' panels. (*Graham Buckle*)

The aircraft selected to become the Victor K2 flight trials aircraft, XL231, underwent a somewhat abbreviated redesign and modification programme which took just two years to first flight instead of the three for the production aircraft. This plan was adopted to allow time for any necessary changes resulting from the flight trials to be incorporated in the remainder of the aircraft before they were too far advanced in their rebuild.

For the flight trials XL231 incorporated the aerodynamic changes of reduced wing span, upward rigged ailerons and the wing pylons with their pods. Also included were the massive underwing fuel tanks so fundamental to the aircraft's future capability as a tanker. Full flight trials instrumentation was fitted including internal cameras and television equipment and also an anti-spin tail chute which would be required for the slow speed handling.

I sent Johnny Cruse, Harry Fisher and Charles Masefield on a two-week RAF Victor K2 pilot conversion ground school course at the RAF OCU at Wittering. This was very important because the fuel system and its management was inevitably the most complex of the aircraft's systems consisting, in its forthcoming tanker role, of no less than thirty-two different tanks with an ability to pump fuel from any one of them to any other. The total fuel capacity of the tanker was to be 128,000lbs (57 tons). More than half of this, 67,000lbs (30 tons), was to be contained in sixteen separate fuselage tanks crammed into every available space from nose to tail – including the two massive tanks in the former cavernous bomb bay. The fuselage would, indeed, become a flying fuel bowser with the crew perched in front. The wings contained another 32,000lbs (14 tons) housed in twelve different tanks and the large underwing tanks contained a further 27,000lbs (12 tons). To complete the picture each wingtip pod would provide an additional 1,000lbs of fuel capacity. The system was fitted with a 'proportioner' which, in normal operations, automatically fed fuel from each group of tanks in the proportion necessary to maintain the aircraft's centre of gravity within the mid range. During handling flight trials, however, we were constantly pumping fuel all around the aircraft to position the centre of gravity either at its extreme forward or aft limits – often shifting the c of g from one of these extremes in the envelope to the other on the same flight. All this had to be managed by using the new fuel panel positioned between the two ejection seats. This panel contained a formidable mass of no less than fifty-four switches, contents gauges, flow indicators and push buttons which, for ease of operation, were arranged into three neat groups – the fuselage, port and starboard wing groups. Luckily we had a working model of this panel in the pilot's office so that we could practise fuel management drills at our leisure well ahead of the aircraft's first flight. Thanks to this useful practical aid, we all felt very well prepared to handle any fuel management challenge that might be thrown at us in the air.

Syd Buxton who was a co-pilot on 55 Squadron in the Middle East describes the practical problem of controlling the fuel and also gives a flavour of being on a front-line squadron. He also describes very well why I preferred the Vulcan way of stopping on the runway, lots of drag and no chute!!

It required a bit of an adjustment to get used to the size and general speed of the Victor K2. I was also initially a bit overawed by the fuel panel located centrally between the pilots' seats, that was at the heart of the K2's role. Whilst most of the training was necessarily run in-house on the Tanker Training Flight of 55 Squadron, Fg Off Al Mann and I did have to go down to RAF Brize Norton to attend a short course on the principles and capabilities of air-to-air refuelling within the RAF and our wider NATO allies. Something I did find very surprising was that the AAR school at Brize Norton had a Victor K2 fuel panel training console, which I am sure would have been of much more value (to me, certainly)

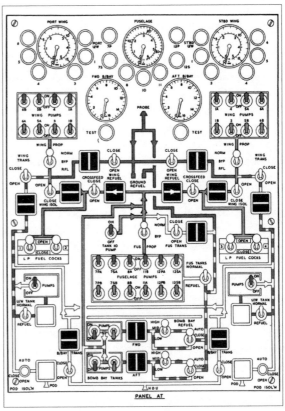

Victor K2 pilots' fuel panel.

as a regular training tool had it been with the TTF at RAF Marham. After all, there were no other Victor squadrons anywhere else. It was the only such training device for the fuel panel, outside of the full Victor K2 flight simulator, that I ever saw. I guess the AAR school was jealously guarding its 'empire' but this console must have barely been used sat down at Brize Norton!

Nevertheless, with practice, it all came together and I began to enjoy the AAR and 'force projection' role of the old jet. When on the ground refuelling the Victor K2, away from RAF Marham, the fuel panel was generally the responsibility of the co-pilot. He would sit in the cockpit ensuring that the incoming fuel went in to the correct tanks, in the correct quantities, by manipulating the multitude of valves and pumps via their respective switches, and monitoring the gauges on the panel. A minor distraction, or miscalculation of fuel specific gravity, and you could quickly find yourself with a geyser of fuel gushing out of the ram-air pressurisation intake on the front of the underwing fuel tanks.

Being largely responsible in this way for the fuel panel had its pros and cons. If you had just arrived at a very cold or wet airfield, it was no bad thing to be sat inside a relatively warm, dry cockpit looking after the incoming fuel. Your colleagues would be outside, in the cold and/or wet, trying to load a replacement braking parachute in to the hopper at the rear of the vertical fin. Conversely, if you arrived somewhere hot and/or humid, you really just wanted to get out of the cockpit for a while as there was no cockpit air conditioning once the engines were shut down. This could be exacerbated if time was tight for an aircraft turn-around and you might have to remain dressed in your immersion suit coverall, with rubber seals at neck and wrists, which could quickly become your personal mobile sauna.

The chute hopper was just over nine feet above the ground, so some sort of steps or ladder was needed to gain access. The height-adjustable platform commonly used in the RAF, often termed a 'giraffe', was adequate for the job but similar devices were not always available when landing elsewhere in the world. A set of airline steps was a very good substitute as it gave plenty of room to manoeuvre the heavy length of main ring-sail parachute (within its bag), drogue chute, associated rigging lines and chunky attachment shackle, up to the hopper. However, when it came to it, we took what we could get and it wasn't unknown to be trying to drag a repacked chute up some rickety ladder or from the back of a truck.

The chute hopper itself just didn't seem big enough for the voluminous 32-foot diameter brake chute. It would usually take three of you, in a line, to walk the whole gubbins on your shoulders up to the hopper, attach the shackle, and then carefully start s-folding it all into the compact space. Between each fold there was some judicious prodding with aircrew boots to make best use of that limited space in the hopper. Trying to maintain a secure footing whilst doing all this, usually by standing just inside the upper strakes of the air brake, was a feat in itself as you were also concentrating on avoiding splitting your face in half on the steeply raked trailing edge of the rudder! By the time the last of the chute was going in, the prodding and stamping had usually graduated to full scale Olympic stomping, accompanied by equally Olympic cursing. It is amazing we didn't have plenty of falls from this precarious spot.

Even if you were fortunate enough to get the whole kit and caboodle to fit into the hopper first time, there was still a pièce de résistance to perform – holding down the spring-loaded drogue chute, shutting the hopper doors, extracting the tie-cord and chute tag, and not trapping your fingers whilst doing so. This sleight of hand was often left to the experienced crew chief, if you had one accompanying the crew.

The fuel panel itself was a large and heavy piece of equipment that was attached, at its forward end, by a hinge to the lower centre edge of the cockpit instrument panel. When not in use the rear end of the panel was raised up between the pilots' seats so that it latched on to the cockpit roof. This then allowed the pilots to gain access to their ejection seats via the low floor space between them. This floor space also extended forward, like a tunnel, under the instrument panel, to what was once the visual bomb aimer's prone position, looking out through three small windows near the tip of the Victor's nose. We generally used this compact space to store baggage when travelling away from base. It was also occasionally used as a 'snooze spot' for the crew chief when he became bored with his position on the centre fifth seat on a long trip.

The floor of the rear part of the cockpit, where the other three seats were mounted (nav, AEO and fifth), was much higher than the floor where the pilots' seats were situated. If I remember correctly it was roughly level with the seat pan of the pilots' ejection seats. These seats in the Victor K2, Martin-Baker Mk 3, were the same as those in the Jet Provost 5 but were raked back at a noticeably steeper angle. This, together with the additional retractable arm rests, made them a bit more comfortable. Being strapped to a 'bang' seat, wearing a helmet, oxygen mask, life jacket and, often, an immersion suit, probably couldn't be *completely* classified as 'comfortable' but we got used to it.

On 1st March 1972 the great day arrived for the first flight of the Victor K2. With Stu Grieve as my co-pilot we roared into the air and happily there were no immediate problems. The flight lasted only thirty-five minutes and then we flew again six days later to start the serious work of finding out how the aircraft behaved in its new configuration. We began by looking at the aircraft behaviour at aft centre of gravity followed quickly by some flutter tests. By October the aircraft was ready for A&AEE to have their first look at it and they agreed with us that there did not seem to be any major problems though it had been necessary to make the elevators 'heavier' by adjusting the artificial feel to avoid pilot-induced oscillations at high indicated airspeeds.

The aircraft flew seventy-four development flight tests until 21st July 1973 when it was delivered to Boscombe Down for the RAF test pilots to determine whether they agreed with us that the type was now ready for squadron service. These flights consisted of measurements of directional, lateral and longitudinal stability, rate of roll, handling at high speeds and heavy weights, mach trim runaways, establishment of the aircraft's buffet boundary envelope at varying weights and low speed handling approaching the stall; stalling was not permitted on the Victor since, due to its high tailplane, the aircraft would go into a spin which was not recoverable without a tail parachute. During the development I gradually handed over the work to Charles Masefield who by then had become my deputy. Charles describes his involvement and the rest of the programme.

My first Victor flight was very similar to my first Vulcan flight when Tony put his head around the office door: "I have the paperwork – let's go". First stop was the pilots' changing room where we each had a locker for our flying kit. Within minutes shoes, suits, ties and shirts had been replaced by standard RAF green flying overalls, life jackets, leg restraint straps, heavy duty boots and white kid gloves. We picked up our inner helmets with their attached oxygen masks and our PECs (personal equipment connectors) and headed out to the aircraft. The AEO for this flight was our master of all trades, Bob Pogson, who was also our senior Nimrod flight engineer and Vulcan AEO whenever there was one to be crewed. Bob would also double up as our navigator today – not too demanding a task as we always remained under military radar control throughout test flights of military aircraft. The two flight test observers were Alan Vincent and Dick Muir – both of whom were massively experienced on the Victor having joined us from Radlett where they had performed the same task. As the rear crew had parachutes to carry they were usually driven out to the aircraft in the airfield ambulance – a mode of transport I always considered somewhat bizarre and inappropriate. Tony and I walked out, if the word 'walk' could ever be used to describe the pace at which Tony moved when there was an aircraft to be flown.

There stood the sleek and purposeful form of the Victor and I followed Tony's rapidly disappearing heels up the ten-rung metal ladder hooked to the sill of the open fuselage side door containing a large metal wind deflector to shield the rear crew from the airflow in the event of a bale out. On entering the aircraft the first difference between the Victor and Vulcan was immediately apparent. When entering the Vulcan you climbed a ladder resting upon the rear crew escape chute leading up into the belly of the aircraft, a dark almost windowless 'well' in which the three tall backed rear-facing crew seats were located. From there, mounting a second ladder, you squeezed through the very tight gap between the two ejector seats to take your place in the narrow cockpit. One's initial impression on first exposure to the Vulcan was of the very limited forward view with a curved high topped instrument panel ahead of which were three very small windscreen panels. It wasn't quite like looking out from the inside of a letter box – but initially it appeared not far off. The extraordinary fact that the large bubble canopy over the pilots' heads was constructed entirely of metal, containing just two port holes, was clearly the cause of this restricted view. I always felt that the compact Vulcan's cockpit with its fighter-like control stick, and the aircraft's spectacular manoeuvrability, made it feel much more like a large fighter than a bomber – indeed this proved to be one of its great advantages over all other bombers, including the Victor, when the operational requirement was switched from high level to low level interdiction.

By way of contrast with the Vulcan, the Victor's rear crew sat at the same level as the pilots with plenty of daylight streaming back from the cockpit to their positions – a rather more sociable arrangement altogether. With the two pilots' ejection seats spaced well apart I slipped easily into the one on the right. Normally it takes two or three flights to feel totally comfortable in an aircraft that you have never flown before but, very occasionally, you feel completely at home from the very outset and, for me, this was one of those occasions. The original prototype Victor Mk1 did, like the Vulcan, have a solid metal roof but, following early flight trials, this had been rapidly replaced by four large strip windows spanning the complete width of the cockpit roof. Thanks to the generous amount of transparency to the front, to the side and above the pilots' heads – twelve window panels in all – the cockpit felt light and roomy while, at the same time, fitting snugly around you with everything at your finger tips without having to strain against your harness – even when trussed up into your ejection seat like a turkey ready for the oven. This impression of space was enhanced by the conventional black instrument panels and cockpit surroundings having now been changed to a pale grey of the same colour as in the Nimrod flight deck – and what a huge difference this made. The instrument panel was positioned closely in front of you and, once I had folded down the fuel management panel, this neatly filled the space between the two seats. The operation of this panel was to be one of my tasks during the flight.

The engine starting panel was in the roof and in a matter of minutes all four were running smoothly. Next came our own functioning of the controls to their full deflection so that Alan Vincent, in the back, could check that the control surface position instrumentation was behaving correctly throughout its full range. With the groundcrew chief's intercom plugged into the underside of the aircraft he gleefully chanted to us "elevator up, elevator down" and so on around the aircraft. This external chant was unnecessary in the Vulcan which had the position of all control surfaces clearly displayed at the top of the pilot's instrument panel – no doubt to the disappointment of the crew chief on ground intercom. Next came the manual functioning of the two ram air turbines producing another chant from the ground "RATs out – RATS in". This was the moment for Tony to instruct "clear the aircraft" producing the response "have a nice flight" – and the crew chief was gone. Within seconds so were we.

There was only just time to race through the pre take-off checks as Tony backtracked at his normal breakneck speed. Once turned on the end of the runway I called "Avro One ready for take-off" to initiate our normal Woodford delay as we waited for Ken Cook to synchronise our departure with Ringway's (now Manchester International Airport's) airline departures from their runway, which was parallel to ours and only three miles distant. At last "Avro One you are clear for take-off, heading 120, climb to 3,500ft until clear of Amber One" and we were away. With 80,000lb of thrust pressing us back into our seats, within seconds I was calling "V1" as we shot through 120 knots and then "Vr" as we reached 145 knots and rocketed up into the sky. My immediate task was to initiate the transfer of 1,000lb of fuel into each wingtip pod providing additional wing bending relief to protect the aircraft's fatigue life. While I was occupied thus Tony had retracted the undercarriage and flaps and turned left onto our south-easterly departure heading. In less than 60 seconds we were level at 3,500ft and throttled well back to cruise out below the UK's main north/south airway. "Time for you to get a feel of the aircraft – you have control", came across the intercom and for the first time the Victor was mine.

As we slid along at 320 knots IAS the aircraft felt smooth, stable and rock solid and within minutes we were past Amber One and cleared to climb to 35,000ft. In the Victor, each pilot had his own set of throttles outboard of his seat and I pushed mine fully forward with TGTs (turbine gas temperatures) protected from exceeding their

Spin chute fitted for slow speed testing.

limits by temperature limiters on each engine. At full power we shot up into cloud and seconds later popped out on top like a cork out of a bottle. Six minutes later we were level at Flight Level 350 at which altitude the test schedule called for stall approaches in all three configurations – clean, take-off flap and landing configuration with undercarriage down and full flap. Tony indicated that he would demonstrate the safe limits on the first two stall approaches leaving the final one to me. Stall approaches required a certain amount of caution in the Victor to avoid the non-recoverable 'deep stall' – particularly with the aircraft at aft c of g. Trimmed in the clean configuration Tony gradually reduced speed at a rate of one knot per second as the aircraft assumed a steadily increasing nose-up attitude. Eventually we began to feel a mild pre-stall buffet rather like driving a car along a cobbled street. "First stage buffet" announced Tony. With speed continuing to decrease the shaking suddenly increased with a marked step change in amplitude – onset of second stage – this is as far as service pilots will be allowed to go. "Now you need to be careful", Tony said as he eased the control column further rearwards to keep the speed decaying. I was left in no doubt whatsoever when the onset of the third and final stage of buffet was reached – suddenly we started bouncing up and down in our seats as though driving a Range Rover off road over a series of closely spaced potholes. Tony released rearward pressure and applied power to accelerate back to smooth level flight, the instrumentation having accurately recorded the speed of onset of each clearly recognisable stage of buffet.

A repeat in take-off configuration produced identical characteristics although the onset of each stage of buffet did, of course, occur at lower speeds – then it was my turn. With full flap and undercarriage down I closed all four throttles and blipped the electric trim switch on top of the control column to trim out the resultant nose-down trim change. Once satisfied that the aircraft was fully in trim I concentrated upon making sure that speed reduced at exactly one knot per second – any faster or slower rate of speed decay would render the recordings of buffet onset meaningless.

One thousand, two thousand, three thousand....I counted to myself until the distinct airframe 'burbling' occurred which could be very clearly felt through the control column. "First stage" I identified and kept going. Once past second stage onset I resisted the temptation to reduce the rate of speed decay and kept the control column moving steadily rearwards. Yet again there was no missing the onset of third-stage buffet and I initiated an immediate recovery. It seemed to me impossible for anyone to miss the extremely marked vertical bouncing of the third stage – or so I thought until a little over three years later in July 1975 when I was conducting heavyweight trials operating from Bedford in Victor XL232 especially instrumented for this purpose. In the right-hand seat was an RAF wing commander who wished to experience the aircraft's handling at heavy weight for himself. I briefed that he should recover at the onset of third-stage buffet but, to my surprise, having reached this very obvious point he continued to reduce speed. I quickly pushed the wheel forward with my heart thumping somewhat harder than usual. Upon subsequent analysis of the instrumentation recordings back at Woodford, chief aerodynamicist Laurie Raffle told me that we had reached within two degrees of the wing angle of incidence (Alpha) of a deep stall. I later learnt that the brave wing commander had not flown a Victor for a very long time and I kicked myself for not establishing this before the flight.

Back in XL231, and with the slow speed handling complete it was time to descend to low level for our PE runs. Tony had re-assumed control and I called Northern Radar to request descent clearance and radar vectors to Waddington for a radar handover to their approach controller. Tony selected airbrakes out and we plummeted down like a high speed lift. Having been handed over from Northern Radar to Waddington Approach Control and eventually to Waddington Tower we arrived overhead and were cleared downwind. We called our ground team on the standby radio and received confirmation that everything was ready for our first run. There was little or no turbulence and all seemed very sedate as we sailed smoothly past the cameras at 200ft with Tony nailing the speed precisely at 250 knots before applying power to climb back onto the left-hand downwind leg. After the next run at 290 knots Tony handed over to me saying "you have a go at the next one". One of the great things about flying with Tony was that he always shared things. As I was in the right-hand seat with no view of the runway when downwind and turning onto base leg, Tony positioned the aircraft onto finals and handed it back to me. Tony had positioned me perfectly and as I descended towards 200ft I focussed upon stabilising the speed at 310 knots for the run past the cameras. I was surprised that at that speed the elevators felt rather lighter than the ailerons because the normal convention for well co-ordinated controls is for the ailerons to be lightest, elevators somewhat heavier and rudder heaviest of all – a ratio of 2, 4, 8 often considered to be optimum for the three different control forces. I think I had been a couple of knots above 310 as we swept past the cameras but I was confident that the speed had been stable with no acceleration or deceleration which was the really important thing. Tony's next run at 340 knots was uneventful but when running down the runway on the penultimate run at 370 knots we suddenly hit some turbulence. Instead of the resultant slight aircraft nose-up pitch damping out, as would be expected, it pitched down and then rapidly up again. Tony immediately closed the throttles and selected the airbrakes out and we climbed away decelerating

Full testing on drogues.

rapidly. "I didn't enjoy that much – I think we will go home and look at the recordings to see what happened", Tony said and I rapidly agreed.

Upon reaching the Sheffield area Tony handed control back to me for my first experience of landing the Victor. We headed towards Woodford and were cleared down to 3,500ft, the minimum safe altitude over that part of the Peak District. Kinder Scout, which is directly in line with runway 27 at Woodford, was 2,300ft above sea level and always seemed rather close as you skimmed over it. There is a waterfall at that point which, in a very strong westerly wind, blows vertically upwards in a spectacular plume. Today the wind was moderately calm and as soon as we had passed Kinder Scout with the runway already in sight I called for take-off flap and undercarriage down. For the approach my target airspeed was 150 knots which, with my right hand resting upon my own set of throttles, was easy to maintain. In line with, and to the inboard of the four throttles, was the selector lever for the clamshell airbrakes opening like huge rear-facing jaws on either side of the tail cone. This airbrake selector was almost like a fifth throttle. As I became more familiar with the aircraft I discovered that, once set up at this stage of the approach at a steady airspeed, you could then use the airbrake alone to control the speed extremely accurately – almost like flying a single-engine aircraft.

At this airspeed both the elevators and ailerons felt extremely light as their power controls were now operating well below the point at which the artificial Q feel system cut in to increase the control forces in proportion to increasing airspeed. Without any artificial feel the ailerons, in particular, felt almost as though they weren't actually connected to anything. Indeed, on this my first Victor approach, I couldn't resist applying a little bank every now and then just to reassure myself that the ailerons were actually connected! Perhaps I was influenced by the fact that I had flown a Shackleton the week before which required two hands to apply aileron. Both the

Nimrod and the Vulcan had an aileron self-centring spring instead of aileron Q feel which at least gave some feel in the circuit. It took me several Victor flights to get used to having a nice firm feel to the ailerons when manoeuvring at normal operating speed but then no resistance whatsoever to aileron movements in the circuit. I couldn't help thinking that a light self-centring spring to provide some aileron feel at slow speed would have been an improvement.

The forward view of the runway was excellent as we came ever closer and I called for full flap and reduced the airspeed to 140 knots. With its extremely light and precise controls the aircraft slid smoothly downwards towards the runway with none of the shaking and rumbling of a Nimrod with full flap. On short finals I selected airbrakes fully open and, at the threshold, closed the throttles and flared at 135 knots. Caught by surprise by the lightness of the elevator and the tendency I had read about of the Victor to initiate the flare by itself once in ground effect, we ballooned slightly upwards – I had undoubtedly been guilty of a 'Nimrod flare'. Having realised my mistake I allowed the aircraft to sink back towards the ground to execute a reasonably smooth touchdown in the end. Tony selected the airbrake closed and the flaps to take-off and said "off you go". I pushed the throttles fully forward and this time with a cautious rotation we roared back into the air. Throttling back I turned left onto the downwind leg. I was now really beginning to enjoy this as the strange feeling of a new type was rapidly wearing off and the ability to position the aircraft exactly as you wished with minimum effort engendered confidence that this was proving to be an easy and very pleasant aircraft to fly.

I turned onto base leg and, a few seconds later, onto finals calling for full flap. I was much happier with my second landing as, this time, I was ready for the flare and did very little other than select airbrakes fully out, close the throttles and apply the gentlest of rearward pressure. We rumbled smoothly onto the runway and Tony again cleaned up the airframe and said "go". A smooth landing at the end of a flight always leaves you with a warm feeling and as I got to know the aircraft better I discovered a way to achieve that almost every time. I found that if you cheated a little and purposely arrived at the threshold 5 knots above the correct target speed this inevitably resulted in the aircraft beginning to float down the runway in its strong self-induced ground effect. Instead of continuing the hold off with rearward pressure, I would then very gently push the control column forward to ease the aircraft softly into the runway at a very low rate of descent to deliver a 'greaser' nearly every time. Indeed the only three aircraft I have ever flown in which one could be very confident of almost always producing a smooth touchdown were the Victor, our company Dove with its soft and 'squashy' undercarriage and the Meteor 7 which I had flown a few times at Farnborough's Aero Flight during a one-week stay for a Canberra familiarisation before undergoing my very first master green instrument rating test on that aircraft. The Canberra was to become very familiar as we all had to submit ourselves to Boscombe Down once a year for an instrument rating renewal test on that aircraft.

As we climbed away from the second landing Tony said "I have control" and round we went. Tony executed a rather tighter circuit than I had on my first time out and once back on the runway reached forward to select the braking parachute. Within a couple of seconds we were thrown forward against our shoulder straps and experienced a very rapid deceleration. From then onwards I always enjoyed this unusual and exhilarating way of stopping the aircraft. Indeed its effectiveness can be gauged by the fact that in six years of Victor flying I never once had to touch the brakes after landing until I had cleared the runway at the intersection only some 2,000 yards from the threshold. To stop an aircraft weighing about 70 tons and touching down at around 160 mph in less than 2,000 yards – without using brakes – speaks for the effectiveness of the parachute. If the tower warned that the chute had for some reason not fully deployed the drill was to jettison it, apply full power, and divert to a longer runway. In six years of Victor flying from Woodford that never happened. Tony always considered a parachute to be a somewhat ignorant way to slow an aircraft and much preferred the subtlety of the Vulcan in which the nose could be held skywards after touchdown to achieve an amazing amount of aerodynamic braking from the huge surface area of the delta wing thus presented to the airflow. So ended my first Victor familiarisation flight and the beginning of a deep and lasting affection for the aircraft. It seemed to have everything – a comfortable cockpit environment, spectacular performance and extremely pleasant and precise handling characteristics once you got used to its little quirks.

Tony called a debrief and explained to John McDaniel, head of the flight test department, and his team that at 370 knots IAS quite minor turbulence had caused the aircraft to start 'porpoising' which, had he not immediately closed the throttles and selected airbrakes out, he felt might have developed into a divergent PIO (pilot induced oscillation). No one had any bright ideas as to the cause and it was agreed to wait until the flight recordings had been examined. These subsequently indicated that there had been a significant amount of 'play' in the elevator power control system and that the effect of this had almost certainly been exacerbated by the very light elevator stick force – play in the system and light controls being a fairly lethal combination at high speed. The immediate fix was clearly to make the necessary adjustments to the power controls to eliminate the play before the next flight – but it would be impossible to guarantee that this level of play would not develop in the future on aircraft in service. The obvious longer-term solution would be to increase the elevator stick force sufficiently to eliminate the potential for PIOs even with play in the system. We all agreed that a slightly heavier elevator would also improve the aircraft's handling by giving it a more 'solid' feel in pitch as befitted its future role as a flight refuelling tanker – this was not a fighter.

Our brilliant resident design engineer, Bill Stableford, was called for to provide his views upon how to achieve this solution. Bill was the only person I, or I think any of us, had ever met who was not only an outstanding mechanical engineer but equally outstanding in the design of both electrical and hydraulic systems. Bill decided that he could relatively simply re-gear the elevator system to deliver the required result and immediately set about doing so. His eventual modification was incorporated during the next maintenance grounding of XL231 and thereafter the aircraft did, indeed, feel much more solid in pitch.

Flight development trials continued apace and it was upon my sixth flight with Tony that he decided that it was my turn to occupy the left-hand seat. The main difference was that with the throttles in your left hand, almost uniquely for an aircraft of this size, you were able to fly it with your right hand. As most of us are right-handed, this made a very pleasant change. The only other largish aircraft I had flown with left-hand throttles was the Shackleton – which was just as well as you needed your strong right hand for the controls. The other two differences when flying from the Victor left seat were that you had control of the braking parachute selector on the extreme left of the instrument panel, and the nosewheel steering comfortably placed to your right hand.

This flight was to be for autopilot development and called for a series of approaches with the autopilot coupled to the ILS (instrument landing system).We carried out five coupled ILS approaches for this aft c of g loading with me executing touch and go landings after each one – many more such flights would be required to check the gearings at other c of g positions and weights. When turning downwind after the fifth touch and go Tony throttled back numbers three and four engines and asked me to carry out a two-engine approach and overshoot from 200ft followed by a two-engine full-stop landing. In truth at this light weight it was hard to tell the difference between flying the aircraft on two engines or four – with all this power I suspect one could even get around the circuit on one without too much trouble. On lowering the nosewheel after landing I placed my right hand on the nosewheel steering and, for the first time of many, reached forward to select the tail chute. As though catching unseen runway arrestor wires we rapidly decelerated and I released the chute once we had turned off onto the short runway. "That's fine," said Tony, "I will call John Ratcliff, (MoD PE staff officer flying) to mail your Victor captain's approval." Only then did it dawn upon me that this had been my captain's check ride.

Two weeks later I made my first flight in command of this magnificent machine with Johnny Cruse as my co-pilot in the right-hand seat. The test plan for this flight called for buffet boundary measurements at 50,000ft, then working down in stages to 40,000ft. At the end of the runway we received the welcome message "Avro 5 clear for take-off with a 120 departure. Amber One is currently clear of traffic so you are cleared for an unrestricted climb." Only rarely were we excused the necessity to remain below the airway until clear of it to the east and I needed no second invitation. With my usual feeling of exhilaration heightened by being in command we roared off down the runway and, with the aircraft's nose pointing steeply skywards,

Centre retractable hose drum unit.

turned onto our south-easterly departure heading. In the solid grey overcast at some 10,000ft I noticed a small blue hole at an angle of some 45 degrees above us. Our rate of climb needle was off the clock but surely there was no chance of us climbing steeply enough to pass through that tempting opening – but we did – and rocketed through it to burst out on top into bright sunshine. In the 1970s no civil aircraft flew above 35,000ft so once through that level the sky was ours with Northern Radar occasionally advising of the position of any other high level military aircraft in our vicinity. Level at 50,000 I looked at my stopwatch which indicated just nine minutes and thirty seconds from brakes off – not bad for a flying fuel bowser! At this altitude the horizon was noticeably curved and the sky above was of a distinctly deeper azure blue. Indeed even the cockpit was significantly darker than at lower levels.

The purpose of buffet boundary measurements is to establish, for the whole spectrum of aircraft weights and altitudes, the maximum mach number at which the aircraft can be flown without encountering high mach number 'compressibility' buffet. From these measurements the operational flight envelope can be established and available to RAF squadron crews in the form of graphical 'flight envelope charts' which show the limits of height and mach number at which they will be cleared to operate at any given weight. The end objective is to clear a flight envelope at the upper limits of which the aircraft can be flown – and gently manoeuvred – while remaining clear of buffet.

Our first test point was at 50,000ft where we established that, at our particular weight, 0.9 IMN (indicated mach number) was just 'buffet free' and that 0.88 IMN enabled buffet free gentle turns to be made. We recorded cruise fuel flow measurements at 0.88, 0.86, and 0.84 IMN from which, after many more test points, operational range charts would also be established. This procedure was repeated at 45,000 and 40,000ft at which level the aircraft could be flown and manoeuvred clear of buffet at 0.95 IMN – or 95% of the speed of sound. This represented the 'never exceed' mach number for squadron service although on development we were cleared to fly at 0.96 IMN which was the highest mach number at which the Victor K2 remained clear of buffet. Although the achievement of 96% of the speed of sound in level flight required much less than full power, sadly not for us was the supersonic flying of the Victor B1 which had no massive underwing fuel tanks and also had much slimmer and lower drag engine intakes for its considerably smaller Sapphire engines. I suspect that, if pushed, the Victor K2 probably could have gone supersonic – but it would have been a very buffety ride which would certainly have done the structure no good at all. Further buffet boundary measurements would need to be made for a whole series of weights before the aircraft ODM (operating data manual) could be established. Indeed the vast majority of development test flying consists of hours and hours of such routine measurements which may sound rather mundane and boring – but none of us ever found flying the Victor either mundane or boring.

Indeed I recorded in my log book that on 26th February, about a year into the K2 flight development programme, I had been flying with Tony on a test which required pulling 3g at 0.96 IMN. I cannot recall what such a test was meant to prove – perhaps other than to demonstrate that there was this safety margin in the event that someone inadvertently got themselves into that situation in service. As the test called for 3g to be achieved in level flight at 0.96 IMN the only way to achieve this was to establish the aircraft in a gentle descent and at a lower speed and, as it accelerated towards the target speed, pull up at a rate that would achieve exactly 3g as 0.96 IMN was reached with the nose coming through the horizon. On the first attempt at this rather demanding task Tony was accelerating through 0.94 IMN and 2.5g when we felt a jolt accompanied by a bang. Once back on the ground Mike Taylor, by then head of flight test, met us as always at the aircraft as we climbed out. "Your inboard starboard flap seems to have disappeared", he informed us. The aerodynamics department subsequently told us the rather disconcerting news that, upon breaking away from the aircraft, this 26-foot-long piece of structure could only have passed upwards and 'over' our T tailplane at the top of the fin. We had clearly been fortunate that it had not hit the tail on its way past as that would certainly have spoilt our whole day. The ever-alert Bob Pogson had made an instant note of our position at the time of the jolt and two weeks later a farmer found the offending flap lying in the middle of a field precisely where Bob had forecast it to be. Once the failure mode had been analysed a modification was produced – so perhaps there had been some point to this test after all.

With the exception of the Victor and Valiant, all other flight refuelling tankers were, and are, developments of civil airliners. As a result of this the Victor K2 remains the highest performance large tanker ever to have entered service. When refuelling from the civil aircraft derivatives it is inevitably necessary for fighter aircraft to have to slow down and descend from their operational level to conform with the performance capability of whatever tanker they were about to formate upon. Uniquely with the Victor, however, we merely had to ask fighter pilots at what speed and altitude they would like to take on fuel – in the certain knowledge that we would be able to comply with their wishes. Indeed we had cleared the hose to stream at 320 knots and at Mach 0.9 IMN. This capability did, however, necessitate a large number of sorties while Lightnings, Phantoms, Harriers, Victors and other aircraft assessed the limits of refuelling speed and altitude that felt comfortably manageable for each type.

With the May 1974 scheduled date for the first delivery of a K2 to RAF Marham rapidly approaching, we worked flat out to complete the refuelling clearances of all these RAF types. Eventually only the Buccaneer remained to 'consummate' its union with the Victor K2. On 22nd January 1974 I therefore flew newly completed XV232 to Boscombe Down for a pre flight briefing with the Buccaneer pilot. We agreed that after take-off he would formate upon me until we reached the altitude of 35,000ft for our first scheduled refuelling run. As we climbed through 20,000ft a somewhat embarrassed call came from the Buccaneer: "could you reduce your rate of climb please we can't keep up". Once level at 35,000 we still had some distance to run to our nominated 'tow-line' location. Now that I had appreciated that we were operating way outside the Buccaneer's low level comfort zone I could not resist a further demonstration of the K2's remarkable performance. Knowing that at this altitude the Buccaneer's two 10,000lb thrust Rolls-Royce Speys would be no match for our four 20,000lb thrust Conways I opened up to full power which immediately produced another strangled cry from our rapidly disappearing charge.

Finally the two-year flight-development programme was successfully completed and, on 7th May 1974, I had the privilege of delivering the first production Victor K2, XL233, to 232 Operational Conversion Unit at RAF Marham. In the right-hand seat was Squadron Leader Don MacDougall who had been the liaison officer between

Marham and Woodford for the last few months and would now become one of the OCU QFIs. Once on the ground we were greeted by the station commander Group Captain Caillard to whom I formally handed the aircraft log book and who then christened the aircraft by, somewhat to my surprise, emptying an entire bottle of champagne over its nose. This rather expansive gesture was more than matched by the subsequent celebration of the aircraft's arrival in the officer's mess. It was some hours later that myself, Bob Pogson, Alan Vincent and Dick Muir were helped aboard the Dove which was standing, engines running, waiting to take us back to Woodford.

By 1975, with the K2 now in service, the squadrons were increasingly making the point that, even when loaded to the Victor K2's maximum ramp weight of 224,500lb (100 tons), there was still plenty of unfilled capacity in the aircraft's voluminous tanks – indeed enough capacity to take on another 13,500lb (6 tons) of fuel. Accordingly Hawker Siddeley was asked by the MoD whether an increase to the maximum ramp weight of this magnitude would be feasible for 'operationally essential' use? Geoff Heath and his Woodford stress department did the calculations and responded that the structure could indeed accept such a weight increase – but with a significant increase in the fatigue count during any such flights. In the early summer of 1975 we received an MoD contract to undertake the necessary flight trials to clear the aircraft for operations at a new maximum take-off weight of 238,000lb (106 tons) – six tons heavier than the Victor had previously flown.

The Woodford runway at 7,500ft was far too short for operations at such a heavy weight so we positioned the second fully instrumented K2 development aircraft, XL232, at Bedford from mid June to mid August 1975 for the two-month duration of these trials. Bedford's runway was one of the longest in the country at 10,500ft and so was ideal for this task. The trial was to include all the normal flight development items of general handling, heavyweight climb and cruise performance, heavyweight stalls at forward and aft c of g, directional, lateral and longitudinal stabilities and the establishment of a buffet boundary envelope. But the most interesting tests at this heavy weight were likely to be the accelerate/stop aborted take-off, and the max weight take-off with one engine shut down at the decision speed V1 – and so it proved. The only issue we ran into during general handling was that – although aft c of g stall approaches behaved normally with the expected three stages of buffet, albeit at higher speeds – at the forward c of g limit I found myself with the control column fully back into my stomach and with full up elevator against its stop with the aircraft descending at a stable speed still a good 30 knots above the forecast stalling speed. Clearly this inability to control aircraft pitch at slow speed and forward c of g meant that, in service, fuel usage would need to be very carefully managed to maintain a mid-to-aft c of g until the aircraft was down to the normal max take-off weight. On 1st August Boscombe Down test pilot Flt Lt Stangroom came to Bedford to fly with me to examine this issue and expressed himself satisfied that our proposed operating procedures would be acceptable for service operations.

For the max weight accelerate stop Johnny Cruse and I flew together – although of course we didn't actually fly. The requirement for this test was to accelerate the aircraft up to a 'stop or go' V1 decision speed of 135 knots, close the throttles and apply maximum braking until the aircraft came to a halt. The distance achieved would be recorded on cameras beside the runway. For this test you were not allowed to deploy either the braking parachute or the airbrakes so as to simulate the worst case. As there was a distinct possibility that the brakes might catch fire, three fire engines would be positioned beside the runway at our forecast stopping point. With the aircraft loaded to its maximum 'overload' weight we turned onto the end of the runway with the fire engines visible in the distance. A call to the tower for clearance to go and to the camera crew to confirm that they were ready, engines up to 80%, and a count down over the radio "Three, two, one, go".

After two months of flying at this weight we were beginning to become conditioned to the slow but steady acceleration. At last we reached 135 knots – the throttles were closed and maximum braking applied. Without the familiar braking parachute the lack of deceleration felt extremely strange. Eventually we ground to a juddering halt with the brakes beginning to 'grab', and exactly level with the fire engines. Our performance department's prediction had been spot on. As we shut down the engines a series of popping noises could be heard as, one by one, the fusible plugs on each of the eight main-wheel tyres blew out and we felt the aircraft sink onto the wheel rims. The fusible plugs were clearly doing their job of preventing overheated tyres exploding. A marked smell of burning rubber coincided with a call on the radio "brakes on fire". At this point it occurred to us that it might be better to be somewhere else and to watch developments from outside rather than being part of them. Bob Pogson opened the door, hooked the ladder onto the sill, and within seconds all five of us were strolling nonchalantly away to a safe distance from where we viewed the impressively glowing eight wheels and the burning rubber. The certification rules state that in this situation the fire engines had to wait for a certain number of minutes before they were allowed to take action to douse the flames. This was to simulate the realistic in-service case. The fire engines were eventually cleared to spray their foam and we returned to dispersal by car.

Next was the final test – the continued take-off with engine cut at V1. For this we had to wait for a day with both calm winds and a warm temperature to simulate the most demanding conditions likely to be encountered during a British summer. At last, on 30th June 1975, the wind and temperature were considered to be ideal. XL232 was fuelled up with every tank full to the gunnels giving us a total of 57 tons of fuel on board. With Harry Fisher in the right-hand seat, I taxied out to the runway threshold where we were required to remain with engines running for a 30-minute 'hot soak'. As we sat trussed up in all our gear the cabin temperature became ever warmer and Harry opened all four engine bleed valves to provide us with air conditioning during our wait. Eventually 30 minutes was up, we ran through the pre take-off check list one more time and were ready to go. The test required us to shut down number four engine at a V1 of 125 knots and then continue the take-off on the remaining three to rotate at a Vr of 165 knots and a V2 (take-off safety speed) of 185 knots.

I checked that the cameras were ready, the crew were ready, and called "Avro 2 ready for take-off". Having received affirmative responses from all directions my next transmission was "Three, two, one, brakes off" and we were away. As usual each successive acceleration seemed slower than the last – and this was no exception. Eventually Harry transmitted to the ground camera crew beside the runway "125 knots cutting number four" and pulled the throttle rearwards through its idling gate to cut off the HP (high pressure) fuel cock. We now faced an acceleration of 40 knots on three engines to reach rotation speed. If the acceleration had been unimpressive before it now became positively painful as the airspeed crept past 140 knots. At 150 knots we seemed to be eating up the long runway at a rate that was beginning to cause me some concern as we were well past the point at which we would have had any chance of stopping. "We don't seem to be accelerating very fast", commented Harry helpfully. At 155 knots with still another 10 knots to accelerate and the end of the runway beginning to appear alarmingly close as we hurtled towards it – a 106-ton fuel bowser carrying 57 tons of kerosene travelling at 180 mph – I decided that I couldn't afford to wait any longer and pulled back on the control column. The nose lifted but the rest of the aircraft was clearly still reluctant to leave the ground. Gradually, however, at 160 knots we 'mushed' into the air and began a ponderous ascent as the end of the runway flashed past not too far below. "Avro 2 is everything all right?" called the tower. "Yes we are fine", I responded, to be contradicted on the intercom by one of our resident wits in the back "speak for yourself!"

We climbed thoughtfully towards our prearranged rendezvous with a Victor K1 flown by Wing Commander John Lomas – the CO of 214 Squadron. John plugged in and took on 74,000lb (33 tons) of fuel establishing, in the process, a new British record for the volume of fuel transferred from one aircraft to another. John then broke away to take up his prearranged tow-line holding pattern to wait for any thirsty fighters in the vicinity. As we descended towards Bedford I reflected that if the MoD accounts department charged fuel to the end user what a nightmare today would have been. Fuel that we took on board at Bedford had now been transferred to 214 Squadron which would, in turn, transfer it on to a whole series of different fighter squadrons. Once back on the ground an investigation found that all four engine bleed valves which had been opened on the ground to provide cabin conditioning before take-off had, for some reason, stuck in that open position. We had, therefore, unwittingly attempted a max weight three-engine take-off with engine bleed very significantly reducing the power available to us – a practice not to be recommended. The test was successfully repeated on 8th August, this time with bleed valves very securely closed, and the aircraft landed back at Woodford with our heavyweight clearance successfully completed.

On 23rd May 1978 I delivered XH672, the 24th and final Victor K2 to Marham. By this time I had become chief test pilot as Tony had accepted an offer to become technical director on the Aerospace Board of Smiths Industries. Accompanying me in the right-hand seat was Robby Robinson, former chief flying instructor at the Empire Test Pilots' School and now my deputy at Woodford. As I climbed out of the aircraft for the very last time it was a sad moment – but I was able to look back with enormous pleasure upon six years of fascinating and highly enjoyable flying in this magnificent aircraft. Indeed, I still do.

So what of my own personal opinion of the comparison between the Victor and the Vulcan? In truth I believe that the capabilities and characteristics of the two aircraft were so different that any attempt to compare them would be unfair to both. In the role for which they were originally designed, that of high altitude bombers,

Victor K2s at Marham. (*Nick Weight*)

the Victor was clearly superior with its 15% greater load-carrying capability and a bomb bay that was 50% larger. The Vulcan was, however, the more versatile of the two with its ability to operate at both high altitude and at low level, where its superior manoeuvrability and its low airframe stress levels in turbulence due to the multiple structural load paths in its massive delta wing, provided excellent fatigue life, unlike the Victor's more conventional structure which would have made low level operations far too damaging to its fatigue life. As things turned out the former Air Ministry's originally bizarre decision to order both aircraft had, by force of circumstances, proved to have been remarkably prescient. The Victor became an outstanding tanker and the Vulcan a highly versatile and effective high/low bomber. By sheer luck they had got it right.

From an aircrew point of view the Victor undoubtedly had the superior environment with everyone in the same cabin and on the same level and, for the pilots, with more space and better visibility. Both aircraft were delightful to handle with the Victor flying like a very high performance transport aircraft and the Vulcan flying more like a large fighter – certainly in Tony Blackman's hands. The Victor had particularly excellent control and stability on the approach not least due to its extremely precise and effective airbrakes. I recall that in the Vulcan it was quite important to reduce speed earlier in the approach as, without flaps and its less effective airbrakes, it was difficult to reduce speed at the last moment which could then result in an extended float down the runway. It also took a couple of Vulcan flights to get used to having to employ the rudder in turns to counter aileron-induced yaw. All very minor points on two wonderful aircraft.

Jettisoning was tested and it was particularly important for the Victor with its very high fuel weighing more than the empty weight of the aircraft; landing immediately after take-off would be very undesirable. There were five ports, two under each wing from the underwing tank and the drogue units and one centre port. John Brown who was a captain and instructor on the Victor adds a comment.

> I moved to the K2 as a captain on the first operational course (after the instructor course) and became an air-to-air refuelling instructor, the squadron display pilot, and a supervisory captain on 55 Squadron. After ETPS, on B Squadron at Boscombe, I flew four sets of flight tests following Victor K2 modifications (radar warning receiver – handling and system performance; performance testing of reduced thrust take-offs; aileron up-rig trials – handling and structural testing). I also flew the K2 as a tame receiver for testing the Vulcan, Hercules and VC-10 tankers.
>
> The centre jettison point was available when the aircraft came into service. Sometime in 1976 or 1977, an aircraft climbing out at the beginning of a sortie suffered an uncommanded opening of the centre point jettison valve. Around 17,000lb of fuel was lost before the problem was spotted and the valve cycle closed. I believe the captain of the aircraft was Dave Parker. Immediately thereafter, the centre point jettison valves were wire locked closed and electrically isolated, and we lost a valuable capability. In October 1977, I had an engine fire during a maximum weight take-off, flew an emergency instrument circuit jettisoning from underwings and through the pods all the way around and down to 300ft agl, and still landed (safely) overweight. The event in the picture (in the colour plate section) was the only time I saw the centre point used.

What Charles did not relate is some flight testing involving by chance Dick Russell who tells what happened.

> In the early 1970s the Mk1 Victor was having fatigue problems. A large spar component in the wing was being replaced and it was apparent that a replacement aircraft would be needed. The Mk2 Victor was about the only aircraft available; several had been taken out of bomber service and could be used. The first K2 was delivered to Marham and 232 OCU in 1974. The training staffs were a mixture of Mk 2 and Mk1 personnel, giving a combination of type and role.
>
> It was harder work to make the approach and contact to take fuel in the K2 from another K2 tanker. Initially, all receiver training was done by the K1 AAR instructors. It became apparent that the exhaust of the bypass engines of the K2 affected the high tailplane of the K2 receiver. Taking fuel became quite a struggle after the rather benign characteristics of the K1. On the other hand operating out of the Mediterranean meant that we could take off with a full fuel load, something not always possible in the K1.
>
> In August 1977 I was the instructor on a formation training flight. Ordinarily it would consist of formation RVs and a demonstration receiver contact. Prior to take-off I was asked to rendezvous with XL233 flown out of Woodford with a Hawker Siddeley test crew. They wanted me to take fuel from them as part of their profile. I refused because it would upset my student sortie and I would be overweight on return to Marham. However I was ordered to comply. I rendezvoused with XL233 on completion of my student sortie and commenced taking fuel. In a turn half way through the transfer XL233 suddenly veered violently up. There was a loud bang and

my probe broke off not, as occasionally happened, just the tip, but the whole probe disappeared. After landing back it showed the probe minus the tip bent back flush with the fuselage.

With all these happenings it was nearly always the receiver pilot at fault but I knew it was not my fault since my aeroplane was in trim all the way through. I met the test crew after landing and they or rather the captain said that they had done nothing, but a member of my crew a few minutes earlier heard the co-pilot of the test aircraft say to the captain something about the autopilot.

A unit enquiry was set up. I was in luck. The test crew were flying XL233 which was the only K2 fitted with a recorder and a lot of strain gauges, the purpose being to try and assess K2 fatigue life. The measurements showed quite clearly that the manual control of the autopilot had been operated whilst the height lock was engaged during the turn and the sudden override of the height lock caused a strong nose-up trim change on XL233. I was exonerated but it took nearly a year before it was done formally.

I mentioned Dick's experiences to Charles and he remembered the situation.

This event certainly does ring a bell almost exactly as Dick Russell describes it. I delivered XL233 to Marham as the first K2 on 7th May 1974 and it certainly never came back to Woodford. However at some point XL233, as the first K2 into service, was strain gauged as part of an airframe fatigue measurement exercise. I recall that some three years after entry into service, which would make it the summer of 1977, an exercise was initiated to undertake two flights separated by approximately one year. During each flight high g manoeuvres would be performed and the difference in strain gauge readings a year apart would be established. As the g to be pulled was above service limits both sets of test points had to be flown by manufacturer's test pilots. The test plan called for these strain gauge measurements to be carried out at a high all-up weight which meant that, upon their completion, fuel would need to be transferred to another Victor to bring XL233 down to its maximum landing weight.

Both of these flights were operated from Marham, the first in the summer of 1977 by a Woodford captain test crew and the second by myself some fifteen months later on 30th November 1978. The reason I recall the first of these two flights is that I do well remember there being quite a subsequent row about it over the snapped probe.

All very embarrassing for us at Woodford but this was one of only two incidents that occurred during six years of Victor K2 development and production test flying which I guess was not too bad a record. Ironically the other incident also happened to the same pilot when he went off the side of the runway when landing at Woodford with the aircraft ending up sunk up to its axles in the grass. By sheer coincidence I watched this happen with Tony out of his office window (it was a 09 landing). It was subsequently found that the starboard wheel brakes were grabbing severely causing the aircraft to veer to the right. I always wondered why the brakes had been applied at high speed anyway as the chute had already been streamed so there was no need to touch them at all until taxiing.

Charles added that he couldn't recall the K2 autopilot ever being cleared for refuelling. He thought it would have been unlikely since there was no way that it would be possible to protect against an autopilot runaway. Certainly Charles never used the autopilot during fuel transfer, however Dick Russell maintained that they always used the autopilot in level flight and turns.

Pilots' and rear crew hose controls.

The co-pilot and the rear crew had very important roles when taking on and dispensing fuel using the fuel panel in the front and the fuel controllers in the rear. Barry Neal, who flew a Victor K2 in the Black Buck 1 bombing mission during the Falklands war, recalls the fuel-management procedure involved when carrying out regular AAR exercises in the Victor K2.

The co-pilot had slightly different roles when the Victor was acting as a tanker from the aircraft being a receiver. In the tanker role the co-pilot had to manage the fuel through the centre fuel panel to ensure that the maximum volume of fuel was available to transfer. That would ensure that the best possible fuel flow rate could be obtained from the centre hose. To achieve this meant that the planned fuel to be transferred would be in the bomb bay tanks which each held 15,000lbs of fuel. A transfer of larger than 30,000lbs would mean topping up the bomb bay tanks from elsewhere in the fuel system as soon as the transfer started. In the receiver role, the co-pilot needed to get the bomb bay tanks almost empty, ie down to the min setting of the bomb bay float switches prior to the transfer so that the largest space was available to take advantage of the maximum fuel flow rate from the tanker and minimise the time the aircraft captain would have to be in contact. For the aircraft to be filled full of fuel would also mean taking some fuel into remaining 'spaces' in both the wing and fuselage fuel tanks.

The navigator radar, later the AEO after the crew was reduced to four with only one navigator, was the AAR 'whiz-kid' – the expert. In addition to assisting the navigator plotter in routine navigation he was responsible for the AAR equipment, their control panels and for monitoring all aspects of the AAR. He had two control panels for the underwing pods and one for the centre hose which could be operated either automatically or manually – from trailing the hoses all the way through to finishing the planned fuel transfer. The actual amount of fuel to be transferred was set at the control panels and if more fuel was needed at the end of the transfer then it would have to be controlled manually. The navigator radar had also to troubleshoot and resolve any problems with the AAR equipment. He had a downwards-facing rear-view periscope which he used to monitor a receiver aircraft on an individual hose to make sure everything was going smoothly – extremely important when refuelling a young, inexperienced, first-tour single-seat fast-jet pilot on his first AAR sortie!

Summarising the Victor K2 in its design, it is quite clear what a good decision it was by the Ministry of Defence to convert the Victor Mk2s into tankers. In the end it was the Victor that stayed the course and performed its designated task many years after the Vulcan had gone out of service.

Chapter Seven

The Falklands Campaign

On 1st April 1982 the Argentinians landed troops on the Falkland Islands and the decision was taken to recapture the islands a day or so later by the UK Government under the Prime Minister, Mrs Thatcher, and given the name Operation Corporate. The distances were enormous and it was quite clear that if our ships were to be guarded in transit and if reconnaissance was to be carried out, not only of the islands themselves but also of South Georgia in the Sandwich Islands and of Argentina, then the use of the volcanic island of Ascension with its capital Georgetown, 7° south of the equator and in the middle of the Atlantic, would be necessary.

The island is a British Overseas Territory and has one airfield, Wideawake, which is jointly operated by the Royal Air Force and the United States Air Force. There is a European Space Agency rocket-tracking station, relay antennas for the BBC World Service and a control facility for GPS. At the time, the USAF was the main user with a relatively small apron for parking aircraft; the ramp and refuelling facilities were operated by Pan American Airways.

The RAF had five long-range aircraft at the time that could be used and operated from Ascension; the Victor, the Vulcan, the Nimrod and the C130 plus the VC10 transport aircraft. The Victor was no longer a bomber but now had been converted into a very effective tanker for refuelling other aircraft. However, it was used in its first few sorties from the island as a reconnaissance aircraft flying down to South Georgia. The Vulcan was primarily a nuclear bomber, right at the end of its life but still capable of dropping up to twenty-one 1,000lb bombs; it was to be used to drop these bombs and attack radar in the famous Black Buck attacks on Port Stanley. The Nimrod maritime reconnaissance aircraft was in regular service, used in anti-submarine warfare, in search and rescue and in intelligence gathering; it not only flew along the coast of Argentina during the campaign but was also used in a search and rescue role during the Black Buck operations. The C130 was the invaluable workhorse transport aircraft; however, because of the large distances involved neither it, the Nimrod nor the Vulcan could operate from Ascension without enormous tanker support from the Victors.

In an incredibly short time all the crews had to be trained for night as well as day air-to-air refuelling and, in the case of the Vulcan and the Nimrod, the aircraft had to be modified. The Vulcan had to be configured to carry bombs and equipment under the wing from long forgotten underwing attachment points and the Nimrod had to be configured for air-to-air refuelling. Only the Victor was immediately ready for operations though it had to undergo a trial fit of a Martel anti-radar weapon.

In this chapter there are related personal accounts of the Victor flights starting with Barry Neal, who was at the time a squadron leader/flight commander on 57 Squadron at RAF Marham flying Victor K2 aircraft in the air-to-air refuelling (AAR) role. He sets the scene and gives a first-hand account of the Victor operation. Bob Tuxford who was the captain of the final Victor which refuelled the first Black Buck Vulcan before it set course to bomb the airfield at Port Stanley gives his personal account in the next chapter.

Trial fit of Martel.

Our first reaction when we were told in late March that we were deploying to Ascension Island was "Ascension where??" So we first had to find out exactly where Ascension Island was, and how we were going to get there. The second hurdle came when we were told that our initial operations – maritime radar reconnaissance (MRR) – would be carried out at night and would require multiple tanker/tanker air-to-air

refuellings. To cut a long story short, Victor K2 aircraft captains were not trained in night receiver techniques (taking on fuel from another tanker). But former Victor K1 captains had been, as I had been, and the ten crews initially selected to deploy to Ascension Island each had a former K1 captain, senior and very experienced. So before deployment, myself and the other nine captains flew at night with an air-to-air refuelling instructor to complete one night receiver contact to gain instant qualification! All of us were qualified over two nights. Preparations complete, nine crews and aircraft deployed on the 18th and 19th April; my crew went on the 19th. Each aircraft required air refuelling over SW England to give it enough fuel to complete the trip to Ascension where diversions were in serious short supply so 'island holding' in the event of bad weather was in order. Each

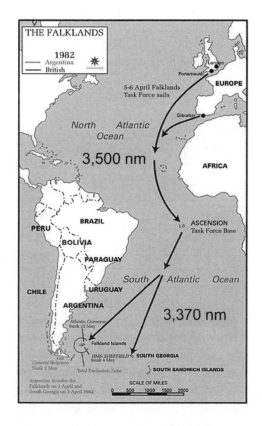

aircraft carried its own dedicated crew chief. The tenth crew, ground support party, and engineers deployed using RAF air transport support.

Prior to the Victor deployment some AAR training had been given to Vulcan aircraft crews who were to take over a UK standing AAR commitment with modified aircraft, and also to Nimrod maritime patrol aircraft (MPA) crews whose aircraft had just been fitted with refuelling capability. The latter also carried out trials to see how effective the Nimrod Searchwater radar would be if used to assist in air rendezvous between aircraft in the South Atlantic since there were no navigation or radar aids there at all. Qualification of new Victor K2 captains and crews had been speeded up in order to give a back-up capability and because Victor crew training in the UK would necessarily slow down due to lack of training resources.

Facilities on Ascension were pretty good. Wideawake Airfield was a well equipped US base used then primarily as an alternative recovery location for the NASA Space Shuttle. Initially, our facilities were a bit limited, especially the personal accommodation – three or four people to what was a single room – with mattresses on the floor! However, the base personnel looked after us very well; the food was good and plentiful, and soon the profits at the base exchange, clubs/bars and cinema rocketed. The island was routinely re-supplied by a USAF C141 weekly, but that soon proved insufficient and re-supply flights quickly increased, supplemented by extra supplies from the UK. At one stage, the main bar on the base was in serious danger of running out of beer. Additional accommodation was sourced in Georgetown, the island's 'capital', and the Exiles Club began to see its profits rise.

The USAF were a great help in accommodation as they flew in 'concertina' type rooms in their C5s. Barry resumes:

Accommodation on Wideawake, some weren't so lucky.

Operating by night and sleeping by day while the island went about its normal business, plus a lot of additional activity from the transiting UK task force, caused major problems with crew fatigue. We had to continually monitor crew welfare and morale, sleep being critical in ensuring safe and successful operations. Tried and tested AAR procedures, refined over many years, ensured consistency and success. The main MRR task was around South Georgia to assess whether or not Argentine forces had been deployed to the area prior to the re-taking of the territory. A Vulcan squadron had had the role of MRR until its disbandment in late 1981 when the role ceased. We were not trained to carry out MRR, but the navigation and radar equipment was almost identical between the two aircraft, so one former Vulcan MRR experienced navigator was attached to each Victor crew. The Victor had had a sixth (spare) seat, but because of the absence of navigational aids in the South Atlantic that seat had been removed in each aircraft and replaced by a twin inertial navigation system enclosed in a large plywood box. The former Vulcan navigators, wearing their back parachutes and survival packs, had to endure the 'comforts' of the INS box for hours on end to and from the search area, swapping seats with a Victor navigator for the on-task time for MRR. Twelve to thirteen-hour sorties were not unusual, supported by several Victor/Victor air refuellings. Each aircraft had to return to Ascension with enough fuel for island holding; fortunately, any poor weather usually passed through the island relatively quickly and aircraft rarely had to hold off.

As mentioned in a previous chapter, Alan Brooks was a very experienced maritime radar reconnaissance operator and he and some others were sent to support the South Georgia operation.

What actually happened was that the Strike 3 force was leaving the UK and the MOD were worried about the aircraft carrier *Belgrano* and where it might be operating. The Vulcans of 27 Squadron, which had been on maritime radar reconnaissance up to a fortnight before, weren't available so five of the radar operators from 27 Squadron went down and actually flew in Victor K2s between Ascension towards South Georgia looking for any signs of battleships. We were flown down in a VC10 – nothing else had arrived at that stage. Then a Nimrod came in, then a Hercules and gradually the tankers started coming. We did the reconnaissance in the Victor tankers because to get that far you had to have aircraft refuelling, rather like the Vulcan sorties, to go down to the Falklands. We were a sixth crew member and had to transit sitting on the Carousel inertial navigator which had replaced the normal sixth seat.

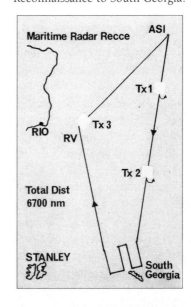

Reconnaissance to South Georgia.

The ramp became very crowded with up to eleven

Victors, two Nimrods and two Vulcans not to mention frequent visits from VC10s, USAF C5s, RAF C130s, and various fighters as the fleet went by.

Barry continues:

While these sorties were continuing, we were tasked with enabling a Vulcan bombing raid on Port Stanley airfield on the Falklands. The reason for the mission was not only to bomb the runway and thus deny its use to the Argentinian fighters but also to demonstrate to the Argentinians that the UK had the ability to carry out long-range bombing missions over Argentina given the political will. Disabling any runway with medium or high altitude 'iron bomb' missions is an imprecise science with unreliable results. All the planning was carried out on Ascension, by which time Vulcan aircraft and crews, ground support and engineers had arrived. This would be a unique operation as nothing like it had ever been conducted before – thirteen aircraft at maximum weights taking off at night at forty-five second intervals, in radio silence, to get together in formation at some point south of Ascension. Vulcans had never before operated in anger with full bombloads, let alone in such a large formation and air refuelled at night. We took the planning back to basics – old fashioned graphical data from aircraft operating data manuals which, as tends to be the norm, contained original performance data. In view of the unique operational circumstances some sort of a performance contingency factor was needed, particularly in respect of fuel consumption, and the best that we could come up with was to add 10% to everything. The critical factor in AAR operations of this kind is that at the end of each refuelling sector, each receiver aircraft must end up with a full fuel load; that criteria is then used to plan the next stage of the mission. A Victor AAR instructor was attached to each Vulcan crew to assist with the air refuellings. The plan was for a fifteen-aircraft outbound formation (including the primary and reserve Vulcans), and a separate four-Victor aircraft recovery formation, which I would lead, to meet the Vulcan at a pre-planned rendezvous point on its return from its mission to refuel it to enable recovery to Ascension.

The mission was codenamed 'Black Buck 1' and flown on the night of 30th April/1st May. The final plan was to split the outbound main formation into two elements each operating independently, the first at a slightly higher altitude and slower speed than the second which flew lower and a little faster. AAR could then take place in each element until the number of aircraft was reduced to a more easily managed formation and the second element had caught up with the first. The first hurdle came on take-off when the primary Vulcan was unable to pressurise the flight deck, so the airborne reserve Vulcan had to fill the primary role. One of the check procedures that we used was to trail and test the centre refuelling hose when passing through 10,000ft in the climb; there was no point in being scheduled to use the centre hose for the first time some four or five hours into the mission to find it wouldn't work! Our 10,000ft check worked well but was no ultimate guarantee that the hose would work again later. One Victor's centre hose did not check out as planned so the airborne reserve had to take over; ironically it was the aircraft planned to give the Vulcan its last refuelling before starting its bombing run, which failed the hose check.

The first test of our planning and the contingency factors came at the first Victor/

Victor AAR – four tankers and four receivers – where we passed a lot more fuel to each receiver (to ensure it was full on completion) than we had planned; I was Red 3 as a tanker at the time. Radio silence was in force until the time that the Vulcan transmitted a codeword on HF radio that the mission was complete, so the tankers and receivers were not aware of what was happening with their colleagues' fuel states. On the return flight to Ascension each of the four tanker crews independently realised that they were going to be critically short of fuel on recovery. I was seriously considering breaking radio silence to find out how the others were faring when, to the relief of all, one of the others called up with his concerns and notes were compared. There was only one safe direction to approach the runway at Ascension and on landing aircraft had to backtrack the runway to exit to the ramp. That took time and an added complication was the need to use a brake parachute on landing which had to be jettisoned and cleared off the runway by ground personnel before an aircraft could taxy back up the runway to exit. Detailed airborne re-planning between the four of us revealted that there would not be enough time for each of three aircraft independently to land and clear the runway before the fourth aircraft would likely run out of fuel. For this particular operation there was not enough total fuel available to plan for diversion or island-holding fuel on recovery. The decision was made in the air, and the authorities on Ascension told, that each aircraft would land in turn and pull to the end of the runway and wait while their colleagues landed after them. Fortunately, all went well. While all this was going on the rest of the mission was proceeding according to plan, fuel consumption had settled down, and that need to have each receiver aircraft full at the end of each air refuelling had meant, after the first AAR, that fewer contingency factors were coming into play.

Barry makes the rescheduling of the planned Victors sound relatively straightforward but I was very impressed by David Emmerson's remarks; he was Nimrod Squadron commander and in the monitoring Nimrod on Black Buck 1's outward flight to the Falklands:

My most vivid lasting memory is listening to the radio communication during the first Vulcan Black Buck sortie when the Victor tanker crews totally reorganised the complex refuelling programme as unserviceabilities and other potential disasters occurred. An incredible performance and one so complex that it would have confused any eavesdropper.

Barry once more:

Meanwhile, I changed aircraft and took off again with three other tankers for the recovery mission. The plan had been to put two tankers at the rendezvous point – geographically abeam Rio de Janeiro well out over the South Atlantic – to give as much redundancy as possible should the primary tanker's hose not work properly, or the refuelling not go to plan. Diversion to South America was not an option that night for political reasons. Unfortunately, at the 10,000ft check, one aircraft's hose did not work and it had to return to Ascension. More airborne re-planning had to be done for me as the primary Victor to take on as much fuel from the other two aircraft to get to the rendezvous, with enough fuel for the Vulcan and ourselves so that both aircraft would recover to Ascension successfully. We arrived at the rendezvous in good time and with plenty of fuel.

While this was going on, things were taking an unfortunate turn as the outbound mission reached its final stages. Some unexpected bad weather had been encountered as the final Victor/Victor AAR was taking place. Forecasting the weather in the whole of the South Atlantic was extremely difficult as weather stations and reporting of weather were almost non-existent. As fuel was being transferred between Victors some severe air turbulence was encountered. Those conditions mean it is extremely difficult for a receiver aircraft to remain in contact with a tanker's hose as both aircraft are being buffeted by the turbulence. The inevitable happened and the receiver aircraft's refuelling probe broke. Fortunately, the probe tip did not remain in the tanker's hose as that would have rendered the hose unusable, and it is doubtful that enough fuel would have been available from the receiver aircraft – which had now become a tanker in a reversal of roles – to enable the mission to proceed as planned. That said, the directive had been that the mission to bomb Port Stanley airfield was to succeed even if it meant the loss of aircraft and/or crews.

The two Victors reversed roles and the aircraft whose probe had broken started to transfer fuel to the other. But the transfer had to start with giving back to the other aircraft the fuel that had already been transferred to the original receiver, before the planned fuel transfer could start. There was insufficient time available to complete the full transfer between Victors before the Vulcan refuelling point was reached, after which the Vulcan would begin its descent into its bombing profile. So the transfer was stopped leaving the Victor due to refuel the Vulcan with less fuel that it should have had, and unable to transfer the planned amount of fuel to it before the Vulcan had to depart. Radio silence was still in force so the actual situation could not be communicated between aircraft. Nonetheless everyone did the best they could; the Vulcan set off alone towards its target; and the final Victor turned to recover to Ascension in the knowledge that it had only enough fuel left to reach a point some two hours flying time south of Ascension. The Vulcan's attack went ahead successfully, the Port Stanley runway was cratered and, on completion, the appropriate codeword was transmitted. At that point the final Victor recovering to Ascension made HF radio contact with the island to request emergency help to recover. A Victor was launched from Ascension and met the one struggling home to transfer the necessary fuel for a successful recovery.

We were waiting patiently abeam Rio and heard some of this on HF radio but we were not able to understand exactly what had happened. A Nimrod MPA had been assigned to provide search and rescue cover for the whole operation, but also to assist with the Victor/Vulcan rendezvous using its Searchwater radar. The Vulcan was running late and by the time the Nimrod crew picked up the aircraft at the very maximum range of its radar, the Nimrod was running low on fuel and had to return to Ascension. We reverted to old-fashioned UHF direction-finding techniques with the Vulcan to establish a 'head-on' profile for a well-tried rendezvous procedure. Dawn had broken, the weather was good, the sun was up, and a very smooth, successful

Left: Dick Russell being congratulated after completing Black Buck 1.

Below: Martin Withers and Dick Russell immediately after landing from Black Buck 1.

Bottom: Bob Tuxford's crew. From left, Sqn Ldr Ernie Wallis (nav radar), Sqn Ldr Mike Beer (AEO), Sqn Ldr Bob Tuxford (captain), Flt Lt Glyn Rees (co-pilot), Flt Lt John Keable (nav plotter).

Top: Vulcan 558 in formation with Victor K2, taken after the Falklands campaign.

Above: Jaguars in the Middle East taken from a Tornado. (*Stuart Osborne*)

Left: Victor K2 in Middle East colours.

Above: Victor K2 in the moonlight. (*John Brown*)

Left: Victor K2s at Punta Raisi airport 1989.

Below: Buccaneer during a Middle East sortie. (*Stuart Osborne*)

Top: Tornado about to refuel during Middle East operations. (*Stuart Osborne*)

Above: Tornados refuelling on the way to the Middle East. (*Dick Russell*)

Left: Unique airborne picture of Saucy Sal taken by Stuart Osborne from a Tornado.

rendezvous was accomplished. As the Vulcan had already been short of fuel and with its late arrival at the rendezvous, it required quite a bit more fuel than we had planned to ensure a safe recovery to Ascension. We were, once again, on minimum fuel and had to land at Ascension before the Vulcan which had fuel to spare. For my crew a total of fourteen hours and ten minutes of flying on the two sorties that night.

An eventful but, fortunately, successful operation was made safe by dint of experience, flexibility, and sticking to well established AAR procedures and techniques. There were many lessons from Black Buck 1, and all were learned and applied to the subsequent six Black Buck operations with Victors supporting Vulcans carrying a mix of iron and anti-personnel bombs, and anti-radar air-to-ground missiles. Two of those subsequent missions were aborted for various reasons.

With two Vulcans, thirteen Victors, one Nimrod, nineteen separate in-flight refuellings, forty take-offs and landings, forty-two 1,000lb bombs, ninety aircrew, and over 1½ million pounds of aviation fuel, Black Buck 1 was "the most ambitious and complex offensive operation the RAF had mounted since the end of the Second World War".

After Black Buck 1 and during the subsequent Black Buck missions, Victor AAR support continued for Nimrod maritime patrol and surveillance missions, and for Hercules C130 transport sorties re-supplying the task force with supplies and, in some cases, key personnel. During the whole period of the war Victor aircraft serviceability was excellent and the Victor ground engineers on Ascension deserved a huge amount of credit for that. Equipment-wise, notably the AAR equipment proved exceptionally robust and occurrences of centre hose problems were minimal – without that centre hose none of these operations would have been possible.

Chris Morffew was posted to 57 Squadron as nav leader in early 1981 after three flying tours on Vulcans, a tour in Germany and then the Victor OCU. He was Barry Neal's navigator and complements very well Barry's description of Ascension and the Black Buck sorties.

The first year was fairly uneventful; we took fighters to the US and Cyprus and we were scrambled a few times in support of the QRA fighters to intercept and shadow the Soviets – usually Russian Bears.

Of course it all changed when Argentina invaded the Falklands. Initially, there didn't seem as if there would be much for us to do, since so few aircraft were capable of receiving fuel from a tanker. Indeed, Easter fell on Sunday 14th April that year and although there were a lot of contingency plans being looked at we were allowed to take the long weekend providing we left contact details. I and my family went down to stay with my parents in Berkshire, but we were not there long before we were recalled to Marham.

Most of our crews were no longer qualified to receive fuel at night so currency had to be regained. At the same time, the Vulcans were having their AAR probes brought back into operation and work was going on that eventually led to Nimrods being fitted with them. On the Victor it was decided to re-activate the old F-95 camera system and three crews, captained by Sqn Ldr Martin Todd, one of our flight commanders, and Sqn Ldrs Bob Tuxford and John Elliott from 55 Squadron, were told to start training for photographic-reconnaissance missions. However, it was clear that if we were to operate the Victor in the South Atlantic we would have to do something about its navigation system; we had the old GPS 6 which was kept updated through the radar system and astro navigation (sun and star shots). Clearly, operating in the South Atlantic would mean that we would have to rely on astro navigation which really wasn't that accurate. We trialled two fits, the Carousel inertial navigation system and an Omega VLF fit. Both worked quite well and both fits were subsequently used on operations.

On 14th April Marham started to qualify the Vulcan pilots for AAR. On 17th April RAF will forms were handed out – I had never thought of writing a will despite the fact that Jane and I now had three children. On 18th April the first Victors were sent to Ascension Island; a secret destination that even our wives were not allowed to know. Our crew refuelled the outbound aircraft before returning to Marham and then heading south ourselves the next day.

Ascension Island was really interesting. Tanker ops was basic but functional; it consisted of a couple of tents on the airfield. But domestic accommodation was something of a problem; we had the use of a single block and it was a case of squeezing in a complete crew to a room initially. I remember one of the guys decided he would rather sleep in the corridor; at one end he erected a sort of barricade to create a room that he then had to himself. He was happy and it seemed to work well. A much bigger problem was the navigator radar who snored so loudly he kept getting thrown out of rooms!

Initially the flying was fairly straightforward. Victors went out on reconnaissance sorties and they would need AAR to give them the necessary range. Some were doing maritime radar reconnaissance and of course some had been training for photo reconnaissance. On 22nd April we flew in support of one particular MRR sortie; it was the mission that resulted in a Victor taking evasive action when one of the RN Task Force ships locked on to the aircraft with its fire-control radar. We flew again on 24th and 28th April and on 29th April the Vulcans arrived.

Our squadron commander, Wing Commander Alan Bowman, had been made the Victor detachment commander and as his squadron navigation leader I took on the role for the detachment. We had a full tanker operations team that did all the fuel planning, run by Squadron Leader Trevor Sitch so there really wasn't that much for me to do until it came to Operation Black Buck. One of the problems we had been wrestling with was how to get thirteen aircraft (eleven Victors and two Vulcans) that took off at one-minute intervals together in the same piece of sky. Normally there would only be three or four aircraft, and we would conduct a snake climb where the leading aircraft would make slow, partial turns to right and left to let the chasers catch up. This couldn't work with a formation of thirteen large aircraft. We resorted to world war two procedures by establishing a rendezvous (RV) point where aircraft could join up before setting off on route. The first two waves, Red and White Sections, each consisted of four Victors and the third wave, Blue Section consisted of three Victors and two Vulcans. Two Victors and one Vulcan were acting as reserves in case another aircraft became unserviceable. Red Section was to RV at F360, White at F340 and Blue at F320. The ops team briefed the refuelling plan and I briefed the RV and join procedures; it was amazing; some seventy aircrew packed into a large briefing tent with paper cups, charts etc scattered everywhere.

Problems started on the ground when one of the Victors had difficulty on start-up and we had to use the first reserve. But, twelve aircraft got airborne before the next problem revealed itself; John Reeve, captain of the primary Vulcan, and thus planned to actually drop 21 x 1,000lb bombs on the runway at Port Stanley, was unable to close his DV (direct vision) window. This meant the aircraft could not pressurise properly and John had no choice but to abort and hand over to the in-flight reserve flown by Martin Withers.

Next, all the tankers had to check the hose drum unit to ensure that the refuelling equipment was working properly; Wg Cdr Alan Bowman was in White 4, planned to accompany the Vulcan all the way to the final transfer point. Imagine his disappointment when his navigator radar discovered he could not trail the hose; another aircraft aborted and returned to Ascension. We were now down to the minimum required to achieve success.

The first transfer point was at 19°30'S 21°41'W and was due to last just 11 minutes. We were in Red 3 and planned to transfer 47,000lbs of fuel to Red 4 before returning to Ascension for a couple of hours rest and then getting airborne again to meet the Vulcan on its way back. The fuel transfer was fine although we had to transfer a little more than planned but as we headed back toward Ascension it became clear that the fuel plan had been optimistic; we were short of fuel. We had enough to get back but only just. More to the point, there were another three Victors on their way back and they were probably just as short of fuel. What made this a problem was the fact that at Ascension there was only one runway and no parallel taxiways.

Since we had the most fuel we were to come in last; if anything went wrong with the brake chute or the aircraft brakes there could be a potential disaster as we crossed the hump in the middle of the Wideawake runway and bore down on the other three Victors. Our captain, Sqn Ldr Barry Neal flew a great night approach and touched down right on the markers. In those final few feet he completely lost sight of the other three aircraft, lights blinking at the end of the runway, as they became hidden by the infamous hump. The rear crew, with no ejection seats, held our breath as the brake parachute was streamed and Barry tried the brakes. As we came over the hump the lights of the three Victors at the end of the runway came back into view and the brakes started to slow us down. A huge sigh of relief as the speed came off; Barry did a 180 as soon as we had reduced to taxi speed and as he turned he released the brake chute and applied a burst of power to the engines to try and ensure the parachute did not block the runway. We were all back safely but for our crew there was just a couple of hours before we were due to get airborne again.

This time we were going all the way to the RV with the Vulcan to give him the fuel he needed to get back to Ascension. Four aircraft were to take off; two of us would be refuelled by the other two and then proceed to the RV. The intention was to provide redundancy at the RV and double the chances of a successful refuel. The primary tanker was Sqn Ldr Frank Milligan's crew, with Wg Cdr Bowman as the navigator and Flt Lt Harper as the nav radar. They were flying the same aircraft that had failed them earlier and despite the efforts of the groundcrew it failed them again – the hose still wouldn't trail. We took over as primary but it also meant that we could no longer get two tankers to the RV. We either made the RV, and met up with Martin Withers and crew, or they would have to divert to Rio with all the political ramifications that would go with it.

At this stage of the conflict we had a couple of Nimrods based at Ascension. Although they were not yet capable of in-flight refuelling they still had good endurance and one was positioned off Rio to assist with the RV. Without him we would have to rely on air-to-air Tacan and radio bearings; an RV procedure that worked but was quite time consuming – a luxury the Vulcan didn't have. We got to the RV on time and the Nimrod identified us, but there was no sign of the Vulcan. We knew the raid had been successful because it had been released on the BBC World Service but where were they?

Almost an hour passed and the Nimrod was getting close to minimum fuel; he would soon need to turn for Ascension. We had enough fuel to loiter quite a bit longer but we would have no way of knowing the Vulcan was near unless air-to-air Tacan worked and it was notoriously unreliable. As the Nimrod turned for home he picked up the Vulcan and was able to put us on converging headings but I needed range to be able to tell Barry Neal when to turn so that the Vulcan ended up behind us. With a lot of help from the fast disappearing Nimrod I gave Barry the instruction to turn and hoped that just for a change it would be spot on; all too often it didn't quite work and only by getting a succession of radio bearings and using the air-to-air Tacan would you eventually find yourselves in the right relative positions. This time it worked perfectly but when the Vulcan told us they were visual we couldn't see them, and they couldn't be cleared in to the hose until we could. I asked for another radio transmission for bearing and it showed us they were right behind. A rather exasperated Flt Lt Dick Russell, the air-to-air refuelling instructor (AARI) flying with the Withers crew, came up on the radio and said they were right behind us at a range of three or four miles. Our nav radar, Sqn Ldr Del Padbury, finally picked them up in his rear-view periscope and cleared them in.

It took three attempts but finally they made contact and fuel was flowing. We could see that it was a wet contact with fuel leaking around the probe and onto the Vulcan but they were short of fuel and were not going to risk breaking contact again. To us it seemed as if the fuel was gushing in but because of the leak around the probe it was a little slower going into the Vulcan's tanks. Eventually they had enough and dropped back. They broke contact and then positioned themselves on our starboard side while I took the formation back to Ascension.

The scenes after landing, the Vulcan went first of course, were amazing; I am not even sure if we managed to speak to them. And then of course there was the post-mortem, why was the fuel planning so wrong. It was essential to find out before another raid could be mounted; fortunately the crews keep records and it was possible to work out which aircraft used how much fuel. Also, the Vulcan had been heavy throughout its trip south and was therefore using more fuel; finally, nobody had really been able to take into account the effect of formation flying on fuel consumption. Lessons were learnt and of the rest of the Black Buck missions, six were flown but one was aborted after take-off because of AAR failure (an HDU would not trail). Three were bombing missions and the other two anti-radar strike missions.

The most interesting sortie we flew after Black Buck 1 was in support of a Nimrod, now fitted with a refuelling probe; a fit that was to lead, many years later, to the loss of an aircraft and its complete crew. The Nimrod was tasked to confirm the position of the Argentinian fleet. It was believed that after the sinking of the *Belgrano* the fleet had retreated to port but since final preparations were now being made for the amphibious assault on 21st May, the Nimrod was tasked to carry out a reconnaissance of the Argentinian ports by effectively flying along the Argentinian coast. We took off on 14th May and landed back next day. Our sortie was relatively short, about 11 hours, but the Nimrod flew for over 19 hours[14]. The only danger was the risk of intercept by Argentinian air defence aircraft but there was no evidence they had a realistic night-intercept capability. I can't remember if the Nimrod was fitted with Sidewinder at that stage but we only had ECM. Although the danger was minimal the crew was very quiet until we were well out of range of the Argentinian bases and I asked the pilots to turn on to a northerly heading; all of a sudden everyone became talkative.

On 28th May we became the first crew to rotate back to Marham, primarily for an aircraft change. We were very lucky because we ended up staying for two weeks although we still had flying to do at Marham. While we were away, the accommodation problem had been finally solved with the delivery of more collapsible cabins. They were erected very quickly and the site was christened Concertina City! Compared with the rooms we had all been squeezed into up until then they were pure luxury.

We were to do two further detachments to Ascension, one from 11th June to 20th July and another one in August. By then the flying had become routine, refuelling the Hercules aircraft that were operating the airbridge to Port Stanley, but in a very demanding five-day cycle. The first day we would get up at 0300 and do a 5hr 30min flight, the next day up at 0400 for a 3hr 30min flight, the third day up at 0430 for a 7hr 30 min flight, the fourth day 0530 for an 11 hour flight and then finally 0530 again but to act as a ground reserve.

We returned to Marham at the beginning of September to be told that we would be leading the Victory Flypast on 12th October. This was quite a bit trickier than it probably sounds because we had to be on track, or we would miss the Mansion House and on time so that we passed over the saluting base at the precise time of 1205. We carried an extra navigator, from PR Canberras, whose job was to lie in the nose of our aircraft and tell us our precise position in relation to a number of fixed points that had previously been photographed by a PR Canberra. I established two final timing points, at 35nm and 17.3nm and worked out a table to adjust our groundspeed to ensure a timely arrival. It worked a treat and we passed over the saluting base about two seconds late. Somewhere I still have a copy of the signal we received after landing that congratulated us on our 'timely arrival'.

I was to enjoy one more year on the Victor before being posted to RAF Brize Norton in connection with the arrival of the VC10 Tanker – a ground tour unfortunately. However, I was to complete one more task; the organisation of the RAF Marham

---

[14] See *Nimrod Rise and Fall* by same author.

Open Day on 9th April 1983 to celebrate 25 years of in-flight refuelling.

Dick Russell was a very experienced Victor tanker operator as mentioned earlier. He was a QFI and air-to-air refuelling instructor on both the K1 and K2 so not surprisingly he was chosen to be in Martin Withers' Vulcan for Black Buck 1 and was awarded a Mention in Dispatches. He has added some comments on the operation and also some observations on flying from Ascension after the war had ended.

When I came back from an eighteen-month tour in Germany (missiles) the Victor scenario had changed. The Victor was suffering from fatigue and it was decreed that air-to-air refuelling was to be curtailed. As a general rule pilots would not train in the air-to-air role but each squadron would maintain AAR instructors, one per squadron. So when I got back in 1981 although I had been an AAR instructor for about ten years I was not needed.

Suddenly Operation Corporate was on and AAR training started in earnest. All the pilots on the squadrons had to be converted; for quite a few it was just a case of refreshing for day and for night; however, for some who were very new it must have been a little traumatic. I was back on the OCU and we seemed to be left out until I had a call from Jeremy Price the station commander when I was on my patio one evening with a beer. He said get in tomorrow morning and do the two sorties to get your currency as an AAR instructor back. One day and one night later I landed on 13th April to find a Canberra had been booked to take me to Waddington at 0900 on the 14th. I met Martin for the first time and we flew our first training sortie at about 1400 on the 14th. We flew together seven times but I was in the back for one trip when we practised a low level bombing run.

The Vulcan was much easier to handle than the Victor when refuelling from another Victor due to the high set tail of the Victor being in the downwash of the Conways, making the Victor a handful even at the best of times. The Victor tanker overcame this to some extent by having markings on the HDU which, when lined up by the receiver, gave a line of approach which would result in a contact, assuming of course that the basket stayed still which it didn't most of the time. After having done it for more years than I care to remember I lined up on the markings initially and then ignored them as I made the approach. (Not what I taught!)

The Vulcan was totally different. First the probe was below the windscreens and out of sight for both pilots in the front; therefore the markings on the HDU had no relevance. I remember my first flight with Martin; on our first go I took my bone dome off, loosened my straps and stuck my head over the coaming so that I could see the probe. I flew the Vulcan into the basket while Martin started to take his reference points on the Victor. We did several like this and Martin started to get the hang of it, and in fact at the end he was as good as I was in making contact but not quite so good when in contact, particularly at night. This was hardly surprising since I had over the years done a great deal of it, and we taught it on the OCU conversion.

The way we worked, always at night and mostly by day, was that I flew the aeroplane for the join and put the aeroplane astern, Martin did the approach and contact and then I took over and flew in contact taking the fuel; close formation is a matter of

Refuelling view from inside the Vulcan. Note very different pilot's view since, unlike the Nimrod and Victor, the probe is below the windscreen.

confidence and not something learned overnight.

From the beginning I sat in the co-pilot's seat and poor old Pete Taylor sat in the sixth seat. We went out to Ascension like that but during the actual attack he sat in the co-pilot's seat from the top of the descent to Stanley to the level out at 37,000ft going home. Having me in the co-pilot's seat was ok until I broke the probe on withdrawal coming back to the UK and we lost two engines (see later).

So, after what was an abbreviated conversion in the UK due to the limited time available, getting used to the fuel leakage from the probe obscuring the windscreen and putting the probe lights out at night, we prepared to set off for Ascension. At the pre-flight briefing I asked for the fuel plan as the fuel consumption was given as 10,000lb per hour; this caused pandemonium as they couldn't find it though they had had it for some days. When they finally produced it we went off to plan with an hour and a half to go before take-off. I discovered that we would run out of fuel just before our let down at Ascension. Pete Standing, the other AAR instructor confirmed the calculations.

I went to see the station commander and told him and he had to tell the AOC and C-in-C; it was a fiasco. The whole thing went back to 1 Group and we delayed until the next day 29th April as another tanker was now needed in addition to those planned. Incidentally it must be borne in mind that all the tankers out of Marham were going to be flown by student crews who were only part way through their course and had never done a maximum weight take-off, much less a refuelling trail like this.

The next day, after detailed planning, Black Buck 1 finally got under way and we suddenly found ourselves catapulted into the lead position. Some seven hours later and after three transfers of fuel we watched the heroic efforts of Bob Tuxford as he took fuel from Steve Biglands in tremendous turbulence. As a result it was hardly surprising that he was not able to give us all the fuel that had been planned.

I swapped seats with Pete, who took over for the bombing run, but climbed back up the ladder again as we headed for Ascension knowing that we had less fuel than expected and hoping that we would meet our tanker on time as planned. The RV was off the coast of Brazil about 400 miles out. About 20 minutes from the RV and whilst we were in contact with the Victor, the Nimrod piped up as apparently it had us on its Searchwater radar. It did not make a great deal of difference since we were already in contact with the Victor and we were direction finding each other, called an RV Bravo, but it was a nice feeling that there was someone else looking.

We had practised RV Bravos out in the North Sea; usually we would see the other aircraft long before it turned in front of us but this time although talking to the Victor we did not see it until he rolled out half a mile ahead of us. It was brilliant. The top up was about 35,000lbs total and since I could not see the HDU and only a vague outline of the hose because the windscreen was covered in fuel with our nav radar giving a bit of a commentary from what he could see standing on the ladder between Martin and me, it seemed to take forever but I guess was about 10-11 minutes.

This is probably a bit obtuse but this is how an RV Bravo went. The two aircraft with an RV time would navigate to be about 100 miles apart, any heading it did not matter. One would transmit to the other and the other would look at the bearing and then give heading corrections to get head on. Air-to-air Tacan would give us the distance. At about 12-15 mile range the tanker would start a turn to the left through 180° plus an intercept heading, probably 45 degrees. One other direction-finding call on the inbound leg to check the receiver's position was required and then an on-time roll out on the receiver's heading. We practised this technique frequently being based on the OCU.

My problem with the probe was on 6th May on the return from Ascension. Our last top up was behind Colin Seymour of 57 Squadron. We were approximately west of Lisbon and it was dark. Martin plugged in and I took over and we were probably topping up with about 10,000lbs. We went into cloud but generally that is not a problem. We were just coming to the end of the transfer when Seymour said "break". Well I was just a little too hurried and came out at a bit of an angle and the probe broke; it was the only one I ever broke. I don't count the one that your fellows did on me in XL233.[15]

When the bit of the probe at the end comes off there is nothing to stop the fuel pouring out until the tanker shuts the refuel valve. This is what happened and the fuel went into the port intake and both engines went out; they just got drowned in fuel. Luckily the probe tip did not seem to hit anything.

After dropping out we completed the drills and not being a proper co-pilot I just did as I was told which was very little. I was as much use as a wet rag but luckily the engines relit quite nicely. There had been at least one similar incident in a Vulcan where the loss of a probe end had caused a double engine failure.

We landed back at Waddington at about midnight to be met by the station commander, John Laycock, and Simon Baldwin, officer commanding operations.

On 13th May we tried to go back to Ascension along with the other Vulcan but we failed because our tanker could not trail its hose and we had to return to Waddington. Pete Standing, the other AARI, went on in his Vulcan but it got short of fuel and had to jettison its bomb to make it; incidentally not all his bombs jettisoned which is not an ideal situation with real bombs! We did manage to go out the following day and we got ready for Black Buck 2.

Pete's fuel shortage was almost certainly due to the fact that besides a Westinghouse AN/ALQ-101D piece of ECM equipment which had been fitted to the Vulcan under the port wing Skybolt pylon attachment point for Black Buck 1, a Shrike missile had been fitted under the other wing. Understandably the hastily manufactured mountings were not at all streamlined; they looked like pieces of old railway lines and were very 'draggy'. We were hampered with forecast headwinds for Black Buck 2

---

[15] Reference the previous chapter when a Hawker Siddeley test pilot crew caused an abrupt break when Dick was taking fuel.

View from the C130 Hercules. Note the superb view compared
with the Vulcan and Victor. (*Adrian Balch*)

while I moaned away about the extra drag. Amazingly while we were waiting for the
weather someone authorised cutting the Shrike off, though it was refitted for another
sortie later on.

I returned to the UK in a VC10 and, apart from refuelling Martin on another of his
trips out, my part in the active Falkands campaign was over. However, after the war
there was a daily C130 Hercules to Port Stanley to deliver mail and other 'less essential'
items. I did a stint for 14 days refuelling the Hercules. It took four Victors plus a
reserve to get the aircraft down there so that it had enough reserve fuel since there were
no diversions at the time. The way it worked was that one Victor took off an hour and
a half after the Hercules and refuelled it about 700 miles out from Ascension. Then
about three hours after the Hercules took off three Victors took off; one Victor would
refuel the other two after about an hour and return to base. Next, one of the remaining
two would refuel the other and go back after about three hours. The last Victor would
transit at 35,000ft and RV with the Hercules some five and a half hours later.

However there was a problem refuelling the C130 because of its very different
aerodynamic characteristics with its turboprops contrasting with the crescent-
winged jet-engined Victor; the maximum height for refuelling the Hercules was
about 25,000ft and the max speed was about 235kts while the minimum speed for
the Victor at that height was roughly the same so a procedure had to be evolved. The
Victor descended to 25,000ft overtaking the Hercules with its hose trailed. It then
slowed down to 230kts allowing it to make contact. As the weight of the Hercules
increased the Victor started to 'toboggan', that is it descended at about 300ft per
minute so the Hercules could remain in contact. On the two occasions I did this we
ended at about 4,000ft. On completion both aircraft climbed, the Victor to 41,000ft
and cruise climbed for five to six hours back to Ascension. It was just as well the
weather at Ascension was invariably good as we had precious little fuel left and no
diversion; our average flight time was eleven hours thirty minutes. Later the Hercules
were modified so that four of them became tankers and took part in the refuelling.

The living conditions on Ascension were not ideal. The American marine tents were air conditioned, supplied by a jet engine running day and night about fifty yards from those unfortunate enough to be the closest but even those furthest away were only 100 yards off. It was very difficult to sleep particularly as it was at the time of the Hercules resupply and crews were getting up at about 0330 hrs for a take-off time of about 0545 hrs. Each crew had their own tent, but found it very difficult to sleep; some took sleeping tablets but my navigator and I would go to the Exiles Club and have about three pints; we, or maybe just I, reasoned that if we stopped drinking at about 2300 we would get rid of the alcohol in the time prior to take-off. Maybe?

Another task after the war was getting F4s down to Stanley and I did one trip just before Christmas. We took two down to Ascension on 23rd December; we refuelled our Victor over Cornwall and then refuelled the two F4s off Dakar; the F4s went on to Ascension meeting a Victor from there to refuel. We landed to refuel at Dakar and went on to Ascension. The next day some Victors took off, not sure how many, to get the F4s to Stanley but my aircraft went unserviceable. On Christmas day we took a spare F4 back to the UK; we were refuelled by another Victor and then refuelled the F4 before going on to Marham. As bad luck would have it for the F4s, Coningsby was closed and they had to divert to Wattisham.

One way to spend Christmas I suppose!

Though the Victors and their crews performed almost flawlessly, it was extremely hard work and not without considerable risks. Gary Weightman was a co-pilot at the time and he describes what could have been a disaster, only saved by the expertise of the crew of the aircraft.

The Night of the Exploding HDU

It was the night of 24th May 1982. It had already been a busy day for the Victor detachment on Ascension with a five-tanker wave launching at 0205Z to recover a Nimrod MR2(P) 'Tuppence' mission and another four Victors in two pairs at 0842Z and 0944Z to support a C130 Hercules airdrop codenamed 'Lara'.

The Task Force had started landing troops on the Falklands a couple of days earlier and Nimrods were urgently needed to provide intelligence and early warning, so another 'Tuppence' Nimrod mission was launched that night and the complex AAR support plan swung into action at 2245Z, when Andy Tomalin's crew in XL160 led a two-ship wave to refuel the Nimrod at about 1600 nm south of Ascension. Shortly after take-off the second Victor confirmed that its centreline HDU was u/s and Martin Todd's crew launched to replace it. At 2301 the primary wave of five Victors, which would support the second Nimrod refuelling, led by Neil 'Badger' Brooks in XL232, began a one minute stream take-off and I was in the second of these, co-piloting for Dave Foulger in XL188 following right behind Badger at 2302Z. Last off was Bob Tuxford in XH512 at 2306Z as airborne reserve.

All this took place in the dark of a completely moonless night and in total radio silence! It was my fourth trip out of Ascension and my second mission in two nights and frankly I was still in the dark myself, struggling just to cope with the very complex fuel plans. The previous day we had flown a short slot of fours hours and thirty minutes but tonight we were a long slot, meaning we would refuel from Badger's tanker about two hours out and then pass fuel on to the primary tanker, flown by John Elliott, two hours after that.

The formation's track was clear of cloud and the air silky smooth, perfect for AAR. Dave Foulger, 'the Young Master' as he was known, made a nice steady approach and contact and the fuel started to flow. I was heads down, hands flashing over the pump and valve controls on the fuel system tray between the pilots' ejection seats, to ensure it all went into the right tanks.

Suddenly there was a dull thump and I looked up to see we had dropped out of contact in what looked like thick cloud. As Dave slipped back into echelon I could then see that the 'cloud' was in fact fuel pouring out of the back end of Badger's jet. Seeing that XL232's crew were clearly busy, Dave just opted to slide over to Bob Tuxford's spare Victor and proceeded to tank all over again.

In Badger's aircraft the first indication that something was amiss came from the nav radar who told Badger that he had lost all indications on the HDU panel. Co-pilot Andy Bray then confirmed that fuel still appeared to be flowing out of the tanks but then we told them that it was venting to atmosphere instead of into us! Badger glanced at the panel and saw that the aft bomb bay tank quantity was dropping like a stone. There had been no physical indication of any explosion and at first he hoped they might recover the situation and continue with the mission. However, it quickly became apparent that the fuel leak was catastrophic and the issue was whether they would even have enough to reach base at Wideawake airfield, Ascension.

Badger briefly considered flying toward the nearest land, the island of St Helena 700 nm south east of Ascension, but opted to push for recovery to Ascension. He told Andy to salvage as much fuel out of the ruptured tanks as possible and hoped they could keep the Victor's c of g inside safe limits. Breaking away to port and leaving the formation, Badger set maximum power and climbed hoping to use the fuel from the bomb bay tanks before it was lost. As weight decreased they climbed higher to get the best fuel efficiency but the 80ft long centre hose was still attached and dragging behind. Attempts to jettison it failed as all electrical power to the HDU had been severed by the explosion. The navigators and co-pilot checked the figures and it now looked like they would make it back to base, but only just. With hindsight Badger realised that he should have considered shutting down two of the Victor's four Conway engines. The two remaining would probably have provided plenty of power to get them back at their lighter weight and fuel consumption would have been almost halved.

With only a few thousand pounds of fuel remaining Badger set them up for a straight-in approach to land on Wideawake's 10,000ft runway at 0322Z on 25th May. Just after touchdown came the call from ATC "You are on fire!" The sparks from the hose basket scraping down the runway had ignited the residual fuel still pouring out of the holes in XL232's fuselage! Badger had to let the Victor run on to the very end of the runway as to stop any sooner would have blocked it for all the other returning tankers. Once at a standstill the crew made an orderly evacuation and fortunately the small fuel fire was quickly extinguished by the Pan Am contract fire crews.

Bob Tuxford's Victor was the next to return and after the debrief he went out into the pouring rain to inspect the damage to Brooks's XL232. He couldn't believe what he saw.

The HDU fuel pump flywheel had shattered at high RPM and fragments of steel had punctured fist-sized holes all around the rear fuselage of XL232. A little more damage and the airframe might have broken in two. Further inspection revealed that electrical wiring looms had been severed and shorted, starting a small fire. Such was the scale of the fuel leak from the ruptured bomb bay tank that the flow of cold Avtur actually extinguished the flames and stopped a potential fireball of 80,000lb of fuel that could have consumed both Victors and killed all ten aircrew. Tuxford took a few pictures of the damage that stand testimony to everyone's lucky escape that night. Fortunately the shrapnel from the explosion missed the control rods and most of the main load-bearing structure on XL232 but how we in XL188, just 50 feet behind the explosion, escaped any damage from what must have flown past us is nothing short of a miracle.

As for my crew, we pressed on to the second refuelling bracket and tanked the primary Victor, but shortly afterward we got the codeword for mission cancelled so made our way back to Ascension, landing at 0740Z after eight hours and forty minutes flying time. I went over to XL232 to look at the damage in daylight and it made quite an impression on me. That day, 25th May, was Argentine National Day and the day both HMS *Coventry* and *Atlantic Conveyor* were sunk, so there was plenty of distraction to take our minds of the 'what might have beens' of the previous night. There was certainly no rest for the tanker fleet and Badger's crew would fly again that day, taking off at 2248Z in XH512 on another Nimrod short slot tanker sortie. As we had done a long slot our crew were rested, but flew the long slot on the four-Victor recovery wave for the same Nimrod, taking off at 0653Z on the morning of the 26th May, clocking nine hours and twenty-five minutes. Over eighteen hours flying in less than forty-two hours for a mostly rookie tanker crew.

Such was a typical couple of days for the hard pressed Victor crews on Ascension, and not a single Vulcan in sight! Sadly XL232, after being repaired, met its end a few months later when a turbine disk in one of her Conway engines broke free as she was taking off with a full load of fuel on an operational scramble from Marham. Despite all the efforts of the RAF and Norfolk fire services she burned out completely with just her nose tip and right wing remaining.[16]

In April 2012 I met Badger and Bob at a V Force reunion and we discussed the events that day. It was proposed that on the 30th anniversary we should all pop a bottle of good champagne and toast to the fact that we both remain in the vertical and to that robust old lady, XL232.

Clearly Badger Brooks and his crew did a brilliant job dealing with the emergency so professionally. In my view he did exactly the right thing using all four engines since it was impossible to tell what else might go wrong and the fuel saving on two engines would probably not have been all that great.

The other thing that Gary explains so well is the pressure the crews were under, refuelling not only Vulcans and Nimrods but C130s and itinerant fighters. One only has to look at pictures of the Wideawake ramp to know that the key aircraft there was the

[16] See Appendix I.

Some of the damage caused by the exploding hose drum unit of XL232. (*Bob Tuxford*)

Victor, giving support to all the other aircraft. In fact, the ramp was so crowded that, apart from the Victors, there was only room for two Vulcans and two Nimrods. As Gary mentions, the Nimrods went on even longer flights than the Vulcans.

There can be little doubt that the Victor, the aircrews and the groundcrews performed flawlessly throughout the Falklands war and afterwards in their support of the Vulcan, Nimrod, C130 and the different types of fighters. They were the workhorses of the whole airborne campaign, they made things possible; yet somehow the Victor did not then, and does not now, get the plaudits it deserves. Hopefully these chapters will help to put things right.

The briefing – it needed the men as well as the aircraft to make it all happen.

Chapter Eight

Black Buck 1

'He either fears his fate too much, Or his deserts are small,
That dares not put it to the touch, To gain or lose it all.'
Shakespeare, *Julius Caesar*

Bob Tuxford was flying the final Victor in the refuelling plan for the Vulcan, a plan which started with eleven Victors. His aircraft gave the final top up to the Vulcan and just reading his write-up thirty years later filled me with alarm; how he, Martin Withers and their crews must have felt at the time belies imagination. In this chapter he narrates an extraordinary story which, if it had been fictional, nobody would have thought credible.

Bob spent five years at the beginning of his RAF career on Mk 1 Victor tankers, two years as a co-pilot and then three as a captain on 214 Squadron. After an exchange officer appointment on a KC135A tanker squadron with the USAF at Mather AFB in California he returned to the UK tanker force in 1980 after a spell at Central Flying School instructing on Jet Provosts. Initially he was pilot leader on 57 Squadron but was then transferred across to 55 Squadron on 1st April 1982 as flight commander. Apparently part of the reason for the transfer was to balance an otherwise lack of tanker experience on 55 Squadron because of the influx of ex-Vulcan pilots as the aged Vulcan squadrons were being disbanded. He was immediately picked by the station commander Group Captain Jerry Price to

With special thanks to Gary Weightman.

undertake the low level and subsequent photo-recce exploratory flights in the K2 during the busy pre-deployment phase of the Falklands campaign. He flew to Ascension Island on 18th April 1982 on the first wave of tankers as part of Operation Corporate, with Barry Neal flying out the next day.

Barry has set the scene very well in the previous chapter and Bob Tuxford follows by writing a fascinating personal account of the operation. Operation Corporate was really the pinnacle for the Victor showing what a wonderful aircraft it was and, of course, also the climax for the Vulcan carrying out the longest bombing run ever made.

Bob has given many written accounts describing his and the Victor's contribution to Black Buck 1 and he takes great pride in getting the flight details and statistics as accurate as possible. This time when he was finalising his account he added a few comments which I have included at the beginning. Here is his almost unbelievable story.

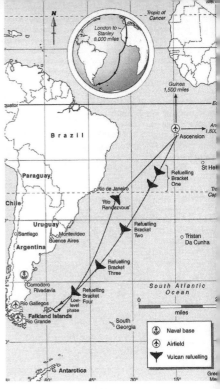

Black Buck sorties. (*Barry Neal*)

On 18th April 1982, the first wave of five Victor tankers of 55 and 57 Squadrons deployed to Ascension Island in the South Atlantic. The following day, four more aircraft and crews arrived forming the nucleus of the only available forward operating base in support of Operation Corporate. Airfield facilities at the ironically named 'Wideawake' Auxiliary Airfield were minimal, to say the least. Aircrews and groundcrews worked together in the searing heat to erect the 160-pounder tents on the lava-strewn landscape next to the single dispersal. Within 48 hours of the first aircraft's arrival, this tented complex was serving as our operations centre, complete with engineering and supporting units. Adjacent to it was sited a Tactical Communications Wing, which linked the newly established air head to the air commander to CTF 317 at Northwood in the UK.

The aircraft and crews were combined to form one tanker unit, colloquially known as '112 Multi-Role Victors', derived from the addition of the two squadron numbers (57+55), and a reference to the recently acquired roles of maritime radar reconnaissance (MRR) and photo reconnaissance (PR). With the Conways of the second wave of aircraft barely spooled-down, the 1st MRR mission was mounted on the night of 20/21st April. Its aim was to provide intelligence of the disposition of Argentinian naval forces, for the Task Group led by HMS *Antrim* engaged on the re-capture of South Georgia. Lessons were learned quickly in terms of generating and manoeuvring large formations of aircraft within the confined ramp area, and their sequencing to the single, albeit long runway. From an air-to-air refuelling (AAR) point of view however, the launch, rendezvous (RV) and subsequent airborne fuel transfers necessitated in that first mission were relatively straightforward. The expertise of 1 Group's tanker planning cell, coupled with the finely honed skills of its tanker squadrons in worldwide refuelling operations, were well recognised. Standard operating procedures (SOPs) developed from numerous fighter trails and deployments were an ideal base upon which to launch the operation from Ascension Island – that is so long as only the Victor K2 was involved! The problems were to arrive with the advent of its unfamiliar and somewhat incompatible stablemate, the Vulcan.

As the only suitable aircraft capable of flying a round-trip mission of almost 8,000 nautical miles, whilst being able to deliver an effective bombload, the venerable Vulcan was hurriedly prepared for the first offensive air action: the bombing of the runway at Port Stanley in the Falkland Islands. The air-to-air refuelling capability within 1 Group's bomber force however had long since been obsolescent. Not only had refuelling probes to be found and retro-fitted to the airframes as a priority, but also their pilots required formation training and, even more importantly, receiver training for in-flight refuelling. This was virtually impossible within the short time frame available. Each tasked Vulcan crew therefore would carry a Victor AAR instructor to assist during the fuel transfers. Only four tankers were needed on the outbound wave to get the MRR sweep aircraft (known as the primary) to its operating area in the vicinity of South Georgia. A similar number were then launched on the inbound wave to enable two tankers, and therefore the choice of two serviceable hoses, to meet the returning primary aircraft at a pre-determined RV. Eight tanker sorties (plus one reserve) were thus needed to satisfy the MRR task. However, the predicament was that a heavily laden Vulcan bomber would need considerably more refuelling support to achieve the profile for a variety of reasons; more frequent refuellings (to enable all aircraft to return to Ascension at any stage of the flight), incompatibility between Victor and Vulcan optimum cruising altitudes and speeds, the need to descend to lower altitude and speed during refuellings and considerably more complicated departure and RV join-up procedures not catered for in the SOPs. All these factors combined to make the refuelling support of such an operation several degrees more difficult than that of the earlier MRR tasking. In reality, it was calculated that eleven tankers would be required on the outbound wave alone, with a further five supporting the inbound recovery wave. At least, that was the plan.

At the time of launching Black Buck 1, to my certain recollection, we had amassed no less than fifteen Victors on Ascension (which is why that number appears in various articles). The fuel plan shown in this chapter is indeed the original article, even adjusted for winds at noon (which implies the second edition!) The outbound wave of tankers supporting the Vulcan does correctly show the eleven K2s planned in company with the two Vulcans, essentially each type having one reserve. Not shown is an additional K2 acting as a ground reserve for Red and White sections[17], which went belly up on starting, necessitating one of Blue Section's tankers to stand in as airborne reserve. In the event as we now know, both reserves were needed and used, Martin Withers vice John Reeve, and Steve Biglands vice Frank Milligan. By the time these events were taking place, our exasperated ops team overseen by Jeremy Price, Marham's station commander, were putting in place modifications to the plan by the minute – all unknown to us of course because of the necessity for radio transmission black out.

---

[17] See the main write-up following.

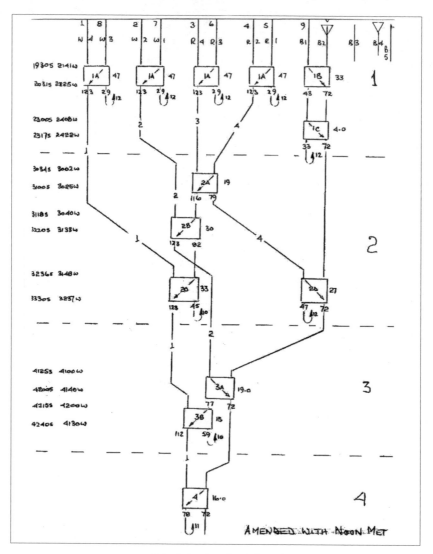

Black Buck 1 fuel plan.

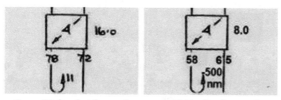

Steve Biglands planned   Bob Tuxford actual

The plan in the left-hand illustration shows that for the final refuel outbound the Victor was to deliver 16,000lb to the Vulcan giving it full tanks of 72,000lb leaving the Victor 78,000lb to get back to Ascension with 11,000lb fuel.

As Bob explains in this chapter, in spite of severe problems he managed to be able to deliver approximately 8,000lb but leaving the Victor with only 58,000lb, relying on an unplanned inbound refuel or they would have had to bail out or ditch 500 nautical miles short of Ascension. The right-hand diagram shows that the Vulcan only had 65,000lb.

The night of 30 April/1st May provided the opportunity to put to the test the most ambitious bombing mission since the Second World War. It would signal the commencement of offensive air operations in support of the South Atlantic Fleet. Upon it would rest the RAF's capability or otherwise of striking the enemy at extreme range, and helping establish an air superiority situation for the South Atlantic Fleet's own offensive aircraft. The buzz of excitement in the briefing tent was intense as the scene was set for Operation Black Buck. Victor and Vulcan crews listened shoulder to shoulder as the scenario unfolded. Three sections, comprising Red, White and Blue would form the outbound wave. Four tankers would make up each of Red and White sections, whilst a further three would support the primary Vulcan and its airborne reserve in Blue section. Five tankers including an airborne reserve would comprise the recovery wave, intended to enable two Victors to meet the post-attack Vulcan at an RV, situated some distance off the coast abeam Rio de Janeiro. The offer of two refuelling hoses at the bracket for the Vulcan's final refuelling, permitting its return to Ascension, would reduce the potential for refuelling equipment failure within a single tanker. With the exception of this critical fuel transfer, and in keeping with normal fuel planning criteria, all tankers in the formation should have been able to return to Wideawake Airfield, with operationally acceptable fuel reserves. It had to be borne in mind that there was no alternate landing airfield available to the tanker force operating from this remote island base. Just as formidable were the demands placed upon the detachment engineering wing. They would be called upon that night to produce all available airframes, several of which would be required to fly a second sortie on the recovery wave following immediate turn-rounds.

After the short walk across the cinder track to our aircraft, the operation began to pick up momentum. One by one, and in the pre-briefed sequence, call signs checked in with the minimum of chatter. As the night air was charged with the sound of 52 Rolls-Royce Conway and Olympus engines, the aircraft clawed their way to Runway 14, jostling for position on the crowded pan. Red One, commanded by Sqn Ldr Todd, then led the thirteen-ship snake climb between the volcanoes into the black South Atlantic skies. Two days later, I was to witness a similar spectacle, as Black Buck 2 was launched. The deafening sound of a dozen 4-jets littered with anti-collision lights, dodging and weaving between the jagged volcanoes either side of the runway, was a spectacular sight never envisioned in this previously peaceful outcrop close to the Equator. Without delay, the next priority for each airborne tanker was to prove the integrity of its hose drum unit by trailing the hose. Although no guarantee that a subsequent trailing would be assured, at least the early detection of a fault might avoid complications later. To White 4's horror, this turned out to be the case as his nav radar frantically tried everything possible to achieve a fully trailed hose without success. So soon into the mission, the first of a catalogue of surprises surfaced to test the flexibility of the crews and the feasibility of this ambitious plan. With text-book ease however Flt Lt Biglands having launched as Blue 3, slid across to White section and assumed White 4's position, which coincidently elevated his role from that of airborne reserve to primary outbound tanker. The task would fall upon him therefore to anticipate being the last tanker to refuel the Vulcan prior to casting him off some seven hours later!

A more sinister situation was beginning to develop however, as the formation continued its planned trombone pattern designed to let all sections join as one formation. Blue 2, the primary Vulcan was unable to pressurise properly. Shortly afterwards, he had to declare his unserviceability also. Flt Lt Withers as No 4 in Blue section, and designated as the Vulcan airborne reserve, was now faced with the opportunity of taking over the primary Vulcan's task. In the new role as Blue 2, Martin Withers took his place in Blue section as the eleven remaining aircraft climbed to their allocated flight levels. At least the weather factor at Ascension's latitude presented no problems at this stage of the mission. The skies were clear and visibility in the star-lit night sky was unlimited. Indeed, the only problem was trying to identify which set of lights represented your own section leader. As White 2, and only sixth in the stream, I was able to settle in echelon starboard to my leader without too much difficulty. Nevertheless, it seemed as though the whole sky was awash with flashing red beacons, amidst a clutter of red, white and green navigation lights. On more than one occasion during subsequent missions, section leaders would have to resort to the faithful Very pistol to assist join-up. Before long however, Red, White and Blue sections were heading just to the west of south, staggered at their respective flight levels of 360, 340 and 320. The engines settled into their familiar drone as a comfortable formation position was achieved. There was now time to relax a little after the anxieties of the less than ideal start to what was shaping up to be a night to remember.

Transfer 1 was to take place after approximately 1hr 45mins, some 700nm down track. On reaching the refuelling bracket, the four pairs of tankers in Red and White sections prepared to offload to their respective receivers sufficient fuel so that at the end of the bracket, the latter would be full to the gunnels. The huge transfer of around 50,000lbs left each of the fully laden Victors with 123,000lbs of Avtur. The depleted tankers, Red 1 & 3, and White 1 & 3 then turned for Ascension Island with a 'chicken' load of fuel sufficient for their recovery and a small reserve. In the event, the four returning aircraft were all stretched to the limit, and found very little remaining fuel on arrival at Wideawake. There was not even time for the first landing aircraft to backtrack the length of the prevailing runway to vacate it for the following Victor. The first three aircraft were thus faced with no option but to land in sequence, and position as close to the end of the landing strip as possible. By the time that Martin Todd was on finals, he was faced with the prospect of completing his landing rollout with his three colleagues blocking the end of the runway. The potential for a major pile-up did not need to be spelled out! In the event, all was well, and the four aircraft were able to taxi back to dispersal where time was of the essence to prepare the airframes for the recovery wave. However, the initial signs were beginning to appear that the refuelling plan was not going quite according to expectation. The air commander on Ascension, Gp Capt Price, himself a very experienced tanker pilot, was quick to realise that not only must the aircraft be regenerated as quickly as possible, but any aircraft additional to the original plan that might become available must be offered up for use as terminal airborne tankers. This reserve refuelling capability in the form of back-up tankers would normally have been built into the overall plot, had the numbers of available aircraft not been so limited.

Meanwhile, the remaining tanker with the Vulcan in Blue section had refuelled the bomber, and was staying with the formation prior to offering it a final top up before departing northbound. This done, the five-ship formation continued to the next bracket, situated 1,900nm south of Ascension. Into the early hours of the morning, the physical exertion of upwards of twenty minutes in contact during the first refuelling, and over three hours of concentrated formation flying were beginning to show. At one stage, as No 3 to Red 2 & 4, Steve Biglands on my right alerted me as an undetected slow and potentially dangerous roll to port was beginning to develop. Shaking off the momentary drowsiness, I regained my position, and vowed not to let my attention wander again.

More changes of position were to take place during Transfer 2. Having refuelled Red 4, Red 2 moved across to take the lead of the formation on the starboard side where the Vulcan, Blue 2 was awaiting his third onload. At the same time, I then took onboard around 30,000lbs from the recently filled Red 4, who in turn gave a similar amount to Steve Biglands, before turning for home. Red 4, flown by Flt Lt Skelton, was to face a few anxious hours during his recovery as a fuel leak started to eat away at his island fuel reserve. White 4 (Steve Biglands) and White 2 (myself) were once again full to the gunnels, and proceeding in company with Blue 2 (Martin Withers) towards my final refuelling area, Transfer 3. The chances of further problems were statistically reducing with only three aircraft remaining. My own aircraft had behaved impeccably so far, and we had plenty of time to prepare for the last bracket, expected around 5hrs 30mins after take-off and some 2,800nm from Ascension Island. Leading the formation now, my nav radar Flt Lt Wallis and nav plotter Flt Lt Keable assumed the navigational responsibility for the first time. Our recently acquired Carousel inertial navigation system was a great boost to the Victor's otherwise antiquated nav kit. Ernie Wallis's radar system was of no use however because we were not only out of range from the nearest landfall, but also intent on limiting all of our electronic transmissions for fear of alerting any possible enemy surface vessels below. Indeed, virtually all of the refuelling procedures up to this point had been accomplished in radio silence throughout. From a communications point of view, Flt Lt Beer, my air electronics officer, had had little to do apart from maintaining a listening watch on his HF equipment. This would be of vital significance to us later when awaiting the post-attack message with which to gauge the ultimate success of the mission. My co-pilot, Glyn Rees, arranged fuel in the Victor's numerous tanks in preparation for the final refuellings.

Transfer 3 began without incident as we passed fuel for the first time. Blue 2 took on a planned 22,000lbs prior to holding off to my port side. Steve Biglands in the other remaining tanker moved astern in anticipation of his last onload. Straining to recall the met man's weather brief concerning frontal activity in the area around 45 degrees south, I started to lose sight of the stars for the first time that night. Unfortunately for us, and for Steve Biglands in particular as the formating receiver pilot, the ride became very uncomfortable. In next to no time, we encountered severe turbulence associated with convective cloud in frontal activity. Considerable St Elmo's fire was present, as my aircraft started to buck quite violently. Tripping the overworked autopilot, I elected to fly the aircraft manually in an effort to smooth out the larger flight path disturbances. Ernie Wallis continued to pass fuel to the tanker behind. Brilliantly illuminated by the momentary flashes of lightning, he could see that the hose was becoming increasingly unstable. With less than half the transfer completed, Steve Biglands broke radio silence as his probe cracked under the intense gyrations of my hose and basket. The whole mission was now in serious jeopardy, unless a solution could be found to a rapidly deteriorating situation. Firstly, White 4 had not taken enough fuel to complete the planned profile with the Vulcan. Secondly, even if we were to change places, with my taking back the fuel transferred already to Steve Biglands' aircraft, there was no assurance that my own refuelling basket had not been damaged itself in the broken probe incident. This being the case, my capability to refuel the Vulcan subsequently might be affected, or alternatively made impossible where for example the probe tip from the other aircraft might have lodged in my basket. Further delay to refuel however was only going to exacerbate a worsening fuel situation. Any extension outbound by the tankers meant an equal addition to the track miles inbound, incurring a duplicated fuel penalty.

Either way, the initial logical course of action was to change roles with White 4 and attempt to take back the fuel already offloaded, together with the planned transfer to enable me to continue with the Vulcan. Racing through the post-tanking checks, and leaving my nav radar to sort out the HDU, Glyn Rees set up the refuelling tray for the unscheduled onload. Normally, this would be a carefully planned sequence of events that must take account of the critical fuel distribution, otherwise the handling qualities of the Victor, particularly longitudinally, could quickly deteriorate. Hoping that the Vulcan would be able to maintain visual contact with the two of us, I grappled with the controls to place the aircraft astern Steve Biglands' rapidly trailed hose. With the red signal light out and thus ready for contact, I fought for some time to achieve a latched contact between probe and basket. Whilst tossing about like ships on a stormy sea, the fuel began to flow. My skills were being tested to the limit as were the powered flying control units of XH189 during what was turning out to be the most demanding refuelling I had encountered during my time in the tanker force. A few minutes into the transfer, the hose became unstable with the characteristic whipping up and down its length, causing me to break contact. With insufficient fuel received, it took me three to four more valuable minutes in the turbulent conditions to make a further contact, and re-establish fuel transfer. My workload was so intense that I was barely able to monitor Glyn Rees on the fuel tray as those valuable gallons of fuel were being skillfully directed into the appropriate cells. Equally hectic was the activity amongst my rear crew who were frantically trying to keep tabs on the much-extended refuelling bracket – which should have been completed some distance back. My first break came just at that moment as the glorious sight of twinkling stars filled the background around the Victor's silhouette above me, and mercifully, the turbulence subsided. As all three aircraft stabilised once more, the transfer was able to proceed amongst the comparative calm. Paramount in my thoughts was the fact that Steve Biglands' aircraft would not be able to receive any more fuel because of the damaged probe. I therefore warned him not to go beyond that chicken fuel which would permit his assured recovery to Ascension Island. This would mean that I could expect to take on less of the planned transfer than that originally intended. Furthermore, as both tankers had now proceeded down route well past the end of the geographical bracket, more en route fuel would be needed by both aircraft to ensure a safe return. As the implications of the multi-facetted problem began to compound, Steve's refuelling signal lights informed me that I had taken as much fuel as he was able to offer. Accordingly, I eased back and out to the starboard side without delay, to permit his immediate turn to commence his recovery. Brief farewells were made as I re-engaged the autopilot for a brief respite.

We were left with two very significant legacies. Firstly, we still had the integrity of the refuelling basket to prove if we were to pass more fuel. Secondly, as anticipated, the reduced uplift left us woefully short of that needed on the master fuel plan to achieve the mission from that geographical position. There was no point in concerning ourselves unduly with the latter situation, as the problem might not arise if the former could not be addressed. Ernie Wallis promptly re-trailed the hose, as Blue 2 was called astern with a view to inspecting visually my refuelling equipment. The Vulcan's two pilots indicated no apparent damage. To be certain however, there was only one way of proving that the HDU was still capable of functioning normally, and so the Vulcan was cleared for a 'wet' contact. In the restored tranquility, the bomber had no difficulty in quickly making contact, and a nominal transfer of 5,000lbs was successfully achieved. The two-ship pair could at least continue towards the target for the time being.

With the frequent formation changes and the additional refuelling at Transfer 3, we were well over six hours into the mission and around 3,200nm from our departure point. The overriding consideration facing my crew was the fuel situation. The result of hours of formation flying interspersed with high intensity workload refuellings was now glaringly apparent. This was reflected in the depleted contents gauges of the fuel tray. The choices available as I perceived the situation were two-fold: as formation leader, I could call it a day right there, and abort the raid whilst my aircraft had more than adequate chicken fuel to return to base; alternatively, the mission could continue with my own reserves rapidly dwindling to the point where shortly a safe recovery to Ascension could not be achieved, at least not without the aid of a tanker. My crew worked feverishly to consider the options available, calculating points of no return, and flight times against fuel remaining. The reality of our predicament was that, in order to refuel the Vulcan with the expected final transfer necessary for it to reach the target, my own aircraft would be left with insufficient fuel to make the island. At this stage of Operation Corporate, it must be said that a diversion for a tanker to the South American mainland had not really been considered, and as far as I was concerned was out of the question. The only viable alternative was to put one's trust in years of experience in the 'system', and in particular our air commander at Ascension Island. We felt certain that he would be only too well aware of the developing fuel crisis. I could not let the AEO get on the HF radio to inform our headquarters of the predicament for fear of jeopardising the yet unfulfilled mission. With so much effort expended by so many professional airmen to keep this show on the road, I was strongly predisposed to pressing on. Aware however that my ultimate consideration must be for the safety of my crew, I felt obliged to hear their individual opinions for the continuance or otherwise of the mission. Before giving my own views, I asked my colleagues what their decision would be if they were in command. One by one, they unanimously stated that having got that far, the mission should continue. The single most difficult operational decision as aircraft captain that I have ever had to make was thus made easier with the encouragement and support of my crew that night.

The final transfer to Blue 2 went without a hitch, up to the point of casting him off around 500nm from the Falkland Islands. We calculated that we could offer him a sufficient quantity to enable him to press on with the attack, bearing in mind that the inbound wave of tankers would have already been launched to meet him at the recovery RV. By the same token, I had to ensure that I had enough fuel remaining in my tanks at least to get sufficiently close to Ascension Island, in order to stand a reasonable chance of linking with a TAT. At 58,000lbs fuel remaining, I was well below the 78,000lbs chicken fuel state that would have enabled me to reach Ascension. Much to our chagrin however, the Vulcan captain called briefly on R/T requesting the remainder of his expected transfer. Having stretched ourselves to what we considered to be the only reasonable limit, we duly turned north, albeit leaving the hose on offer. Despite turning with us initially, we felt sure that the Vulcan crew with the experienced tanker AAR instructor on board must have been aware of our ever-worsening fuel predicament. Fortuitously, at the next instant he turned away, leaving my aircraft on its own for the first time in seven hours.

A strange silence filled the cabin as I put the aircraft into a cruise climb to the altitude that would give us best range capability. As nothing was going to happen for at least an hour, there was time for us all to reflect and regain our composure. Although the gross weight was quite light at a little less than 160,000lbs, and the engines close to their peak economy at that altitude, whichever way we looked at it, we could only get to within four or five hundred miles of our safe haven. There would still be a lot of South Atlantic left between that area and Mars Bay, the southerly most point on Ascension. My hopes were elevated by the expectation of engineering wing generating that last airframe, and another tanker crew bringing it south to offer me that precious fuel line.

Suddenly, Mike Beer's excited voice cut through the subdued atmosphere with the announcement of "Superfuse"; the Vulcan's HF transmission signalling a successful bombing run. The elation within my crew that we had really helped achieve the attack on Port Stanley's runway must also have been sensed as far away as Northwood. I recall however soon afterwards the strange sensation of learning of the accomplishment of the bombing mission on none other than the BBC's World Service, to which Mike had been tuned. At the time, we were still some five hours flight time from base, with a little under four hours of fuel remaining! From our viewpoint, the announcement to the world whilst so much was still at stake seemed rather premature. Much discussion ensued about the prospect of our not being able to meet up with another tanker. Because of the design of the underside of the nose bay of the Victor, the aircraft had always been considered unsuitable for ditching. The likelihood was that because of a bulkhead to the rear of the H2S radar scanner, the whole aircraft would dive under on impact. A sequence involving the bailing-out of the rear crew, followed by controlled ejection of the pilots was evolved, in an effort to try to anticipate the worst scenario. All appropriate drills having been talked through, the plan was placed on the back burner in favour of concentrating on the more positive prospect of a successful RV.

Mike Beer worked incessantly with the HF radio, attempting to relay our precarious predicament to Ascension. Our situation dictated the need for a tanker to meet us at least one thousand miles south of the island. We also instructed them of the reduced fuel state in the Vulcan so that revised RV arrangements might be made if considered necessary. My expectations were all realised with the ultimate confirmation that a TAT was indeed on the way. Some two hours later, after eleven hours of savouring the comforts of the Mk 3 Martin-Baker ejection seat, we were all ecstatic with excitement as five pairs of anxious eyes searched the clear blue Atlantic sky for that famous crescent wing. My boss Wg Cdr Seymour, on his second sortie that day, manoeuvred his aircraft directly in front of mine after a flawless rendezvous, and offered me his trailed centre line hose. Tiredness was no longer a factor, as the next few minutes would provide the ultimate test of nerve. With hundreds of AAR contacts in the bag, this was to be the most important of my life, literally. There was silence, as I took longer than normal to stabilise in the pre-contact position astern Colin Seymour's hose. There was no point in trying to be too rushed or aggressive. Nor did I feel the usual macho need to make contact in one – a necessity when in company with one's squadron colleagues looking on. The fuel remaining in the tanks as I moved up towards the basket would have kept the engines going for perhaps a little over one more hour. Flying the aircraft as smoothly as possible, I narrowly missed the basket after what I like to think of as the smoothest missed contact that I have ever made. The second approach resulted in my probe clunking home centrally inside the reception coupling. After a brief uneasy moment, the tanker's nav radar transmitted the sweet words "fuel flows": that all-important corollary to the latched contact signifying a positive transfer of fuel. As our tanks filled to that point where recovery to Wideawake Airfield would be possible, the sighs of relief amongst my crew were clearly audible. The final hurdle had been cautiously cleared, and the remainder of the flight was to be entirely uneventful.

Not for us the two hundred or so officers and airmen who met Flt Lt Withers' aircraft to inspect its empty bomb bay, some 1hr 20mins or so after our own arrival. Our experience that night was one to be savoured amongst ourselves and the other tanker crews, some of whom had had hair-raising episodes of their own. A total of 18 tanker sorties were launched during the night of 30 April/1st May 1982 in support of the two Vulcan bombers. A number of crews were called upon to fly second sorties either in support of the inbound recovery wave, or as terminal airborne tankers to assist aircraft returning short of fuel. The participating Victor crews flew in excess of 105 hours, five individual crews amassing flight durations of over 10 hours. Some twenty-three individual air-to-air refuellings took place, with a total of around 635,000lbs of fuel transferred. The refuelling of the Vulcan in support of Operation Black Buck 1 had needed every bit of expertise of 1 Group's tanker force in order to achieve the longest bombing mission in the history of aerial warfare.

Bob's closing remarks emphasize the fact that it was Martin Withers and his crew who quite rightly got the plaudits but the trojan work done by the Victor force was barely mentioned. Rowland White's *Vulcan 607* goes some way to redress the situation and hopefully this book will make a further contribution.

Chapter Nine

Tansor and Desert Storm

When the Falklands war ended the K2s went back to their main task of supporting fighters defending the UK, Tansor operations, and 'trailing' fighters to wherever they were being sent, to the Falklands, to the Middle East or to the USA, to name but a few of their destinations.

With regard to colour schemes on the aircraft, the decision was taken shortly after the conclusion of the Falklands campaign in 1982 to change to 'hemp' from camouflage but the actual changeover took several years to complete which explains the colour variations in formation photographs about this time.

Steve Carty joined Victor operations around April 1986 as a corporal operations controller and has written about the situation before the Gulf War as well as covering the Middle East. When he arrived in Marham, 57 Squadron was preparing to disband as various airframes were being decommissioned and then finally in June, 57 Victor operations effectively became 55 Squadron operations. Here, he tells his story.

Tornado in transit.

Every day there would be a programme drawn up in consultation with Tanker HQ at 1 Group and the Victors would be tasked to refuel various aircraft from around the country as part of routine training to keep all crews current in refuelling procedures and also to extend sortie times for fast jets on training missions and exercises. In addition, Victors would be used to refuel detachments of other RAF aircraft participating in exercises and air shows around the globe.

Our job was to ensure that the crews had the correct information needed for the planned sorties and we provided any navigation and meteorological gen that they required. We would then monitor each sortie and should a Victor have spare fuel we would call around all the fighter units to see if they wanted a practice prod.

In the early days whenever a Victor had spare fuel after a sortie we would always call 5 Squadron or 11 Squadron, operating Lightnings at Binbrook, and 99% of the time they would jump at the chance to get in a quick sortie and would launch an aircraft just to take our fuel. The Victor crews used to tell me that the Lightnings used so much fuel in the climb that they were unable to continue a sortie unless they refuelled at the top of climb. When the Lightnings disbanded in 1988 we sent a Victor to Binbrook to take away all the spare Avtur from the station, which was quite appropriate considering the historical relationship between the two aircraft.

After the Lightnings disbanded the only people we could call to take spare fuel were initially the Phantoms based at Leuchars and Coningsby and the Tornados at Marham and Honington; this proved to be a much harder 'sell' than the Lightnings because the Phantoms and Tornados had much better fuel consumption and the sorties were much more pre-planned, so unless they had an aircraft airborne at the time it was almost impossible to give the fuel away.

I remember one occasion when a Victor had to return to Marham after a refuelling pod fell off on take-off and was still carrying a lot of fuel which he needed to get rid of in order to reach landing weight. As I recall he was carrying around 75,000lbs of fuel which he began dumping while in a holding pattern at 5,000ft west of the airfield. The aircraft landed safely but 10 minutes after landing we received a call from a very upset and irate local car dealer claiming the Victor had dumped fuel all over his display of used cars and the paint on the cars was starting to melt! The good thing about being a lower rank was that there was always someone higher to pass complaints like this on to and so we immediately passed the call on to the squadron leader in charge of operations.

Until 101 and 10 Squadrons were actively operating VC10Ks, the Victors were permanently on standby for Tansor. We constantly had two aircraft with crews on standby to support the jets that intercepted Russian aircraft attempting to penetrate the UK's air defences. The crews and engineers would be on home standby with pagers and would be called in when required. Operations would always be called in first in order to liaise with the air defence at Neatishead and make sure everything was ready by the time the crews arrived. Most of the time Tansor was required at night so it was a common occurrence to be called in the middle of the night. However, at Easter 1988 all the ops guys left Marham on the Thursday afternoon for an Easter away in Wales leaving only one guy to cover Tansor. We returned on the following Tuesday to find out that an hour after we had left Tansor had been called and had

Buccaneers in the Middle East.

been active all through Easter, meaning the poor man had spent over 100 hours straight in the ops room!

In addition to Tansor the Victors would occasionally be called on to participate in secret missions supporting Nimrods which would fly into Russian airspace to monitor Russian military exercises.

I remember one incident around that time when a Victor ran off either the runway or taxiway at Offutt AFB and later had the slogan 'I ran Offutt' painted on the side.

Another time during the mid eighties a detachment of Victors were refuelling (I think Phantoms) across the Atlantic from the US and the Victors stopped off at Lajes in the Azores. At night the groundcrew put the Victors to bed only to be called by the airfield authorities a couple of hours later because someone had left the HP cocks open on one of the aircraft which had slowly dumped thousands of pounds of Avtur on the ramp.

Dick Russell describes some flying before the Gulf War when he was still based at Marham as a QFI and air-to-air instructor.

The Victor OCU continued operating until about 1985 when we amalgamated with 55 Squadron, becoming the Training Flight. Shortly after, 57 Squadron joined us so we were a big happy family as 55 Squadron again.

Just prior to the amalgamation, a Victor with two crews and a supporting VC10 went out to Australia, the excuse being to show the Aussies our refuelling gear. I took the first leg to Wright Patterson Ohio but was short of fuel and had to divert to Griffiss, NY. We didn't have any problems on the third leg to Honolulu but on the last leg to Newcastle, NSW I diverted into Nandi (Fiji) because we were in thick stratus at 34,000ft when suddenly both pitot statics froze almost at the same time and one elevator PFCU warning came on. Before I could talk it over with Keith Handscombe my co-pilot at Marham (he had been the only survivor of the mid-air collision with a Buccaneer), my AEO put out a Mayday call (in the middle of the Pacific!) but luckily no one heard it. Anyway I cancelled it and started a descent to get out of the cloud with a left turn to Fiji. At about 10,000ft the instruments came back but another PFCU started to flicker. We dumped fuel and after landing the AEO redeemed himself by helping the crew chief to get rid of all the water out of both pitots. The PFCUs were diagnosed as faulty pressure switches. The first came on again on the climb out to Newcastle and the second flickered once again, or was it our imagination?

Dick clearly didn't have any problem with his airspeed indicator readings failing when they got iced up and displayed false readings. It is interesting to compare how he handled the situation with the story of the aircraft in the 4 JSTU chapter where the Victor spun after the ASI failed and with the Air France A330 that had pitot icing and was lost in the Atlantic off the coast of Brazil. The other point of interest in this diversion was the PFCU warnings; on the Vulcan there was a control position indicator so if there were any warnings it was possible to check if they were spurious. Dick continues:

On the descent to Newcastle accompanied by two Aussie Hornets I was reading the small print of the en route briefing only to discover that Newcastle runway could only take aircraft with tyre pressures below 195 psi. We were at 250 psi but luckily I wasn't doing the next leg and Paul Millikin, the other captain, left two great dents where we had parked.

We were supposed to show the Aussies our refuelling gear but I suspect the trip was only to get our two crews on a jolly round the world because of the OCU closing and amalgamating with 55 Squadron. I think the CO of 10 Squadron and one of the captains on the VC10 went to one meeting but generally the Aussies kept well away from us. I think things would have been a little different from the way they would have been treated had they come to Marham.

On the way back Paul did the first leg to Darwin and was scheduled to fly the next to Colombo via Butterworth. 1 Group screwed the diplomatic clearance and it was either wait a couple more days or go via the Cocos islands. So Paul and his crew went via the Cocos. Omega had been put in the Victor as the long-term navigation aid but it had not performed well. The VC10 took off first and the Victor used air-to-air Tacan locked on to the VC10 to keep track of their position until within radar range when they peeled off and landed at Cocos and we then went direct to Colombo.

However, on the third leg from Colombo to Bahrain the nose oleo collapsed (not me your honour!). We went home in the VC10 and left the other crew with the problem.

It isn't generally realised that the Victors had operated at and beyond their normal maximum all-up weight in the Falklands so that by about 1985 several were reaching the end of their fatigue lives.

The mid 1980s were fairly uneventful, although we occasionally launched Tansor sorties mainly with the F4 against the Russian Bears coming around the North Cape, probably en route to Cuba although occasionally one would come in to the UK air defence area.

The crews of the Bears seemed to have a sense of humour; on one occasion when the F4 was late arriving and we were shadowing the Bear about half a mile in his eight o'clock position, the pilot of the Bear suddenly throttled back and with his contra-rotating props slowed down much more quickly than we could so that he was suddenly in our four o'clock position.

Some time in the mid 1980s we snuck back into launching sorties in RT silence. Working with the Nimrods, two Victors would take off generally in the early morning; one would refuel the other around Newcastle and return to base. The other would go north and meet up with a Nimrod either going or coming from somewhere around the North Cape of Norway.[18]

At the same time we were using Palermo in Italy as an intermediate for taking and bringing F4s to and from Akrotiri. Looking back it probably saved flying time and therefore fatigue life. We would take the F4s part way and after topping them up would go into Palermo. Then when they were coming home we would launch, rendezvous with them and bring them back. The real problem with that was on departure when we had to fit in with the local airway traffic and very occasionally it all went wrong, and we were delayed on take-off, which threw the rendezvous timing out.

Syd Buxton was a co-pilot on 55 Squadron after the Falklands war and remembers visiting the United States and also the start of the Gulf War.

Plattsburgh Air Force Base, on the shores of Lake Champlain, up in the north-east corner of New York state, was an occasional stop for Victors when operating into and out of North America, possibly because the airfield was, amongst other things, a base for USAF KC135 tankers. On one stopover there, whilst the rest of the crew were replacing the brake chute, there had been a minor embarrassment when a customs team had come around for a random search of the aircraft, assisted by a German Shepherd 'sniffer' dog. Getting the dog up the hatchway ladder was entertaining in its own right – I recall the poor pooch being half-launched off the back of an open pick-up truck. Once inside the cockpit the dog with its handler performed its search in a calm and methodical manner. Of course, there was no contraband or drugs to be found, but the dog did locate an old apple core hidden behind one of the ejection seats!

An apple core was probably not a completely strange thing to find in a Victor cockpit, as the only sustenance supplied for Victor crews usually came out of a sandwich box. I don't know what Valiant crews had in the way of 'food facilities', and I believe the Vulcan had a rather slow soup-can heater, but the Victor K2 had absolutely nothing. Sandwich boxes or bags could vary somewhat around the world, but there was often a piece of fruit included. The USA, like many other countries don't take too kindly to unconsumed food entering the country, so the apple core was examined briefly, eyebrows were raised slightly, and then it was sealed in a rubbish bag. Since the apple core hadn't yet actually left the aircraft cockpit there was no harm done.

On another occasion at Plattsburgh when refuelling had just been completed, the chap operating the refuelling bowser asked if he could come up and have a look inside the cockpit. Once inside I briefly explained the layout to him – the

---

[18]   See *Nimrod Rise and Fall* by same author.

crew positions and the general arrangement of the various equipment panels. After looking around quizzically he pointed towards the rear of the cockpit and asked "Is that all there is?" I suspected he was comparing the Victor K2 to the KC135 tankers that he was undoubtedly more familiar with, where you can wander down the cabin in a way akin to an RAF VC10 tanker, or standard airliner. "Yes," I said, "behind that bulkhead is what used to be the bomb bay but it now only holds extra fuel tanks." He nodded, gazed around for a few more seconds and then asked "Do you guys have to stick a dime in this thing to get it working?" That made me laugh. The rather dated, heavy, clunky switches and dials of the Victor cockpit evidently reminded him of something like an old nickelodeon machine!

In August 1990, 55 Squadron was tasked with providing AAR support for RAF Jaguars participating in 'Reconnaissance Air Meet 90' (RAM 90). RAM was a biennial international recce competition hosted at Bergstrom Air Force Base (AFB) near Austin, Texas, and this was where the Jaguars themselves would be based. For this particular event our Victors would be at Kelly AFB near San Antonio, Texas, about 70 nm to the south west of Bergstrom. I was in a crew that was part of the advance party which flew out to the USA, on an RAF VC10, to begin setting up the detachment, a couple of days prior to the arrival of our Victor aircraft. Once RAM 90 was over, the intention was for our crew to fly one of the Victors up to Ontario in Canada for static display at the Hamilton Air Show. The scene was set for what appeared to be a great couple of summer weeks in North America.

However, a certain Persian Gulf dictator decided that he would escalate his previous sabre-rattling into a full-blown invasion of Kuwait. This occurred as we were beginning the deployment and it was all over the US TV news. We hoped it wouldn't affect RAM 90 but a recall to the UK for the Victor tankers soon came. We learned of the recall whilst the other Victor RAM 90 participants were still airborne, en route to Texas. We had the job of telling them, after they had just landed on a hot Texas afternoon, that they would be going to the hotel for a shower, meal and sleep and then straight back to the UK. That created some very grim faces! Even if the UK MoD had not recalled us so promptly, the USAF staff at Kelly AFB would have forced our hand. Being a large airlift base, Kelly was quickly gearing up to move equipment and personnel to the Gulf and they wanted all the ramp space available for that. Essentially, we were no longer welcome.

As we had positioned out to Texas by VC10, it was decided that the crew I was with would sweep up the detachment party and fly one of the Victors home. We did this on 9th August, flying XL161 back to the UK via a quick refuel stop in Gander, Newfoundland. A total of 9 hrs 30 mins airborne time had us back at RAF Marham late at night – a long and tiring day.

Nevertheless, the very next morning, 10th August, I suddenly found myself being launched in XL164 on a Tansor scramble. Along with Stu Mitchell (capt), Fred Davis (nav), and the AEO, we were called out for AAR support of a Phantom from RAF Wattisham tasked with intercepting an intruder in northern UK airspace. Unusually, it was us in the Victor who actually carried out the final visual intercept, with the Phantom just behind us, not using his afterburner due to his low-ish fuel state. We finally caught up with the intruder well north of the Shetland Islands and it was identified as a Soviet Bear F (the Tu-142, a maritime recce and anti-sub warfare variant of the Tu-95 strategic bomber). Once we were in loose formation with the Bear it was amazing to be able to hear and feel the thrumming of its massive contra-rotating Kuznetsov turboprops. Having been handed a Marham-supplied camera and lens kit, I snapped away at this amazingly fast Soviet turboprop. The photos were processed back at Marham and added, as usual, to the RAF's library of intelligence material.

Being a tanker unit, some 55 Squadron flight crew wore a coveted patch on their flying suit which indicated that individual's successful participation in Tansor intercepts and sightings of ten Soviet Bear aircraft. The design of this 'Ten Bear Badge' incorporated a plan view of a Bear, a Soviet star, and Cyrillic text, all in black, red and yellow. By the time I flew the Victor these Soviet intrusions into UK airspace were becoming much less frequent and I only managed three Bear sightings.

55 Squadron quickly became involved in the air-to-air refuelling trails that were required to move RAF aircraft out to their various bases in the Gulf. For the Victor crews it meant becoming regular visitors to places such as Punta Raisi airport near Palermo, Sicily and RAF Akrotiri in Cyprus. Towards December 1990 we considered ourselves very fortunate to be allocated the international airport at Muharraq, Bahrain as a base for the forthcoming hostilities. Bahrain is a very small Gulf island country but it has no problem with allowing the sale of alcohol, so we were not going to be restricted like many of our RAF and military coalition colleagues based elsewhere in the region! We were also delighted to learn that our own station commander, Group Captain David Henderson, was going to be the RAF detachment commander at Muharraq. Gp Capt Henderson was a popular boss at RAF Marham and we were confident that the needs of our detachment in Bahrain would be well looked after.

55 Squadron began its own deployment of aircraft and personnel in mid-December 1990, to set up base at Muharraq. The crew I was to operate with during the war – Flt Lt Stu Mitchell (capt), Flt Lt Jeff Hesketh (nav) and Flt Lt Ed Billings (AEO) – all left RAF Marham on a dark winter evening for an overnight flight to Muharraq in a RAF C130. Also aboard the aircraft were several groundcrew and a mountain of support equipment and spares for the Victors; we finally arrived in the much warmer Gulf well in to the following day. The build-up of forces and operations, both before and during the Gulf War, have been recounted many times but a couple of memories do stand out for me.

Once the squadron crews, aircraft and equipment had arrived in Bahrain, we quickly geared up to flying regular AAR sorties missions in support of RAF Jaguars, Tornado bombers and Tornado fighters, all working up for their expected mission roles in the likely forthcoming war. One such sortie for my crew occurred on Christmas Eve 1990, but we had to avoid interfering with a televised event.

With so many of the UK's military forces in the region, Bahrain was chosen by the BBC to be the centre of an effort to televise a BBC1 Christmas Eve carol service. This was held in a large hangar right next to where our aircraft were parked. A Victor, with its four Rolls-Royce Conway turbo jets turning and burning, was not a quiet aircraft, so plans were made to get participating aircraft airborne before the event began and return after it was complete. This wasn't considered too difficult as the televised part of the event would only last an hour.

We launched into the dark evening with a full load of fuel but were barely airborne over the waters of the Gulf when we discovered that we had lost all radio communication. Plenty of our missions were conducted in almost total radio silence anyway, a good practice for military operations of this sort, but we still needed working radios for air traffic control and safety purposes, so this complete failure was not a good thing. We set 7600 on the transponder and began flying left-hand triangles with two-minute legs, to signal our plight. We attempted various ways of recovering the radios, somehow eventually managing to recover radio reception, but we could still not transmit in any manner.

Our situation had been recognized by a North American air traffic controller in Bahrain ATC and once we could hear him we were able to signal this by pressing the 'Ident' button when he asked us simple questions. Throughout this process we were reducing aircraft weight by dumping a lot of aviation jet fuel overboard, probably returning it to the very desert sands from which it came. We were pleased to be quickly identified as having a problem because we certainly didn't want to be confused as a possible enemy target dispensing a chemical agent on coalition forces!

Once down to landing weight, we were able to indicate our readiness to return to Muharraq, and this proceeded with no further drama. Having landed, we taxied off the runway, aware that the carol service was still in progress so we stopped some distance away, where there were plenty of airport buildings between us and the hangar. To our chagrin it seemed that the landing had 'revived' our ability to transmit on the radios – who was going to believe we had even had a problem now? We were able to thank ATC for their help and told them we would remain stationary at our present position until such time as we could get some advice from sqn ops.

We couldn't raise ops on the radio so Jeff Hesketh, our nav, offered to exit the aircraft and run over to the portacabin that served as home for 55 Squadron. We hoped to get the aircraft towed to its parking position, thus avoiding interfering with the all-important carol service. Jeff opened the cockpit hatch, dropped over the side and disappeared into the night, toward the bright lights in our crowded corner of the hardstand. Eventually Jeff did turn up at the aircraft with an engineering team. In the darkness, with lights ahead of him, poor old Jeff had fallen into an unseen and quite deep concrete airfield storm drain. He had crawled out with a grazed knee and torn flight suit and must have looked a sight when he arrived at the squadron portacabin.

What of the radio problem? Eventually the engineers found that a large connecting plug in the radio wiring looms was disintegrating and was barely being held together by the pins and wires within. We had been fortunate to get the receiving side of our radios back whilst airborne; the vibration of landing had apparently regained the transmission facility.

David Williams, a navigator by training, was then a wing commander and officer commanding 55 Squadron; he relates the situation in the Middle East covering the period June 1989 to November 1991 from the command point of view.

We had brought a detachment of Jaguars across the Atlantic on the Monday, double staging through Plattsburgh Air Force Base, and landing at Kelly after more than 10 hours flying. We were enjoying our day of rest ready to start refuelling the fast jets

Top: Armed Tornado with drop tanks refuelling from K2 in the Middle East.

Above: Tornado probe safely in the drogue.

Top left: Six lovely ladies, all painted by Andy Price at Muharraq, Bahrain during the Gulf War.

Top right: Gary Weightman relaxing at Punta Raisi.

Above: Victor tankers being prepared at Muharraq by night after unusually heavy rain. (*Stuart Osborne*)

Left: Taxying at Punta Raisi

55 SQUADRON 'DESERT STORM' 1990: MUHARRAQ SWANSONG

MISSIONS TASKED: 299

MISSIONS COMPLETED: 299

R 8,000,000lb OF FUEL TRANSFERRED · AVERAGE 40 MISSIONS PER CREW

Top: Taken at Marham, Al Beedie, OC 55 Squadron, on his last flight. Left to right: Steve Jenkins (captain), Barry Masefield (AEO), Editor of the *Lynn News*, Al Beedie (navigator), Hamish Imber (co-pilot).

Above: Victor K2 formation prior to disbandment 1993.

Left: 55 Squadron at Muharraq overprinted with success statistics.

Left to right from top: 55 Sqn final op detachment in Bahrain; Op Granby/Desert Storm Victors; 55 Sqn Op Granby/Desert Storm aircrew combat ops 'red' scimitar (identical but 'black' scimitar also existed for post-war ops); Standard 55 Sqn badge; unknown provenance (possibly groundcrew); Ten Bear Badge for ten individual sightings of Soviet 'Bear' aircraft whilst supporting UK QRA. (*Syd Buxton & Jim McDines*)

over Texas the next day.

It was early afternoon on Wednesday 8th August 1990, I was walking up the slope of the fairway on the 18th when I saw Flight Lieutenant Peter Jackson standing just behind the green. I was more than a little surprised to see him as he was our ops officer at Kelly Air Force Base and should have been manning the shop. I was playing golf but before I could mark my ball, Peter came up to me and said, "White Cliffs". To many on the Victor force these words would have meant nothing, but having begun my flying career on the Vulcan at the height of the Cold War, I knew exactly what they meant – return to base immediately. Iraqi forces had invaded Kuwait a week earlier and the UK effort was obviously moving on apace. Our home base at RAF Marham was 5,000 miles away and various plans went in and out of my head. We couldn't do much straightaway as the detachment had scattered to the four winds. Moreover, most of the aircrew had been up for quite a few hours and double staging back to Norfolk, against the clock, would be folly. We took off from Kelly early on Thursday morning and double staged through Gander in Newfoundland. Flying east, it got dark over the Atlantic and it was after midnight before the last Victor landed at Marham. I remember being met by the duty ops officer who informed me that we would be busy over the weekend.

Friday was a day to gather our thoughts, because Kuwait was being overrun and Marham was a hive of activity; we were indeed going to fly over the weekend. On Saturday 11th August the Victors of 55 Squadron were involved in the build-up in the Gulf conflict for the first time. We were part of a trail that took Tornado F3s to Akrotiri in Cyprus. We landed in the South of France to refuel and were back at Marham soon after lunch.

Then, on Thursday 16th August, just a week after we were in Texas, RAF Marham was tragically brought into the world of reality. That night, a Tornado was lost over the North Sea whilst preparing for operations in the Gulf. I knew the crew well; the pilot was Bill Green, OC 27 Squadron and a close neighbour of mine. I was to lose more good friends from Marham during the Gulf War but for 55 Squadron, life returned to normal over the following few months. We continued to provide support for air defenders intercepting Soviet bombers operating way up north, to provide receiver training for fighters and to carry on with our own AAR training. We were also involved with trails in support of fast jets – Jaguars, Tornado F3s and Tornado GR1s – making their way to the Gulf. In September, the Squadron took Tornado F3s to Akrotiri and, having refuelled, supported the fighters' onward journey to Dhahran in Saudi Arabia. Some Victors found themselves extremely tight on fuel for the return to Cyprus and diverted into Cairo. Never have I waited so long for a fuel bowser to appear.

By this time, there were Royal Air Force tankers operating in theatre but they were not Victors. The decision had been taken on high that the VC10s of 101 Squadron from RAF Brize Norton would have that honour and would be based at Muharraq in Bahrain. To say that I was envious of their squadron commander, Wing Commander Geoff Simpson, is an understatement

On 1st October, the Commander-in-Chief Strike Command, Sir 'Paddy' Hine, visited Marham – to see the Tornado squadrons in their work-up and to fly with 55 Squadron. The Victor was captained by one of my flight commanders, Squadron

Leader Fred Harbottle, and I was the navigator on this short trip to refuel a pair of Tornados. After the sortie, the C-in-C took me aside to explain why he had chosen to send 101 Squadron to the Gulf rather than 55 Squadron. I don't know whether he saw my disappointment or not, but I recall his parting words: "Your Squadron is highly regarded at High Wycombe and I know we can count on you if you are needed." Nice words that didn't promise anything. I wondered whether we ever would be needed in the Gulf – I doubted it.

We continued to provide receiver training with the emphasis more and more on night refuelling. Then, out of the blue, amid the build-up to Christmas, I was called to see the station commander, Group Captain Jock Stirrup. He told me that four Victors were to deploy to Bahrain to replace the VC10s, which were to move to Saudi Arabia. So, on 15th December we left the Norfolk winter behind. We landed at Muharraq after an eight-hour flight. The warmth of the air struck me as soon as the door opened and I was taken aback by the number of aircraft parked on the tarmac. Muharraq was the base for Gulf Air and was used to being a busy airport, but there seemed to be civilian carriers, fast jets and transport aircraft everywhere. That night we stayed in the Holiday Inn, had a few beers and talked about what would happen in the forthcoming weeks. I don't think anybody in the hotel thought that offensive action was likely – we were simply on a detachment without a date to return. In fact, the Holiday Inn was to become home for the Victor force until the last tanker left Bahrain, some six months later.

Together with my two flight commanders, Squadron Leaders Dickie Druitt and Fred Harbottle, we had decided that, from the outset, we would operate as constituted crews. That is to say, we would always fly with the same crew, unlike back in the UK when we were mixed and matched in an attempt to share the hours as well as spread the experience. So, in constituting the crews, we tried to ensure that less able navigators flew with the more experienced pilots and the inexperienced air electronics operators flew with the more experienced navigators. Surprisingly, nobody specifically asked to fly with anybody and I think we struck a very successful balance in deciding who would fly with whom. No crews stood out from the rest. Dickie Druitt came out to Bahrain with me and Fred Harbottle drew the short straw, remaining at Marham.

My captain was Flight Lieutenant Tim Hatcher and the co-pilot was Flight Lieutenant Tim Walker. My AEO was Flight Lieutenant John Ingham, who before coming to 55 Squadron had been the AEO standardising officer. I like to think that we all got on very well and throughout our four months of flying together, I don't ever remember a cross word.

For the next few days we flew sorties operating on pre-planned tow-lines over Saudi Arabia, primarily at night with the Tornado GR1s. Muharraq was an extremely busy airport and one had to wait one's turn to land. As a tanker, the Victor carried far more fuel that any other aircraft and, inevitably, we were always held off to allow the fast jets to land. Not a problem – under normal circumstances. However, on 20th December there had been an incident on the runway at Muharraq and the fighters were queuing up to land. Not surprisingly, we went to the back of the queue and stayed there. Our fuel gauges dropped so low that Tim Hatcher decided that we would run out of fuel before we could land at Muharraq and so diverted to Dhahran, a mere fifteen minutes away across the water in Saudi Arabia.

The refuelling training sorties carried on day after day, even on Christmas Day. We were coping with the demands on the squadron well and life in the Holiday Inn was very pleasant. Then, at the end of December, I was told to return to the UK to discuss the future of the Victor in any possible conflict. I got back just in time to go to the New Year's Eve party in the officers' mess. After the New Year holiday, I made my way down to High Wycombe, the home of Strike Command. I was surprised to be told that plans were underway to double the strength of the Victor force at Muharraq to eight aircraft. This would mean that the vast majority of my groundcrew would also leave Marham for the Gulf.

On 11th January 1991 I returned to Muharraq and I remember that, on the first Saturday following, a large party was organised by the Tornado force. One of their crews, Flight Lieutenants John Peters and John Nichol, collected the money from those who went. Less than a week later, they were shot down over Iraq.

Around midday on Wednesday 16th January, I received a phone call at the hotel telling me that Group Captain David Henderson wanted to see me late that afternoon. I drove the short distance from the hotel to the airfield and arrived at the same time as John Broadbent from the Tornados and Wing Commander Ray Horwood. I knew Ray well as he had been the OC ops at Marham, and now OC ops at Muharraq. Wing Commander Bill Pixton from the Jaguars was the last to arrive.

You could hear a pin drop as David said: "We are going to war tonight; it starts at midnight." I really never thought it would happen.

By now it was early evening and getting gloomy. I drove back to the hotel and summoned my flight commanders and the captains. I told them that, tonight, we would be refuelling Tornados on their way to bombing targets in Iraq. One captain, I think it was Squadron Leader Paul Millikin my pilot leader, pointed out that some aircrew might have been drinking. "Well they had better stop now," I said, "and get themselves down to the Victor briefing room. I will speak to the whole detachment at eight o'clock."

By the time I addressed the Squadron that evening, I felt sure that everybody who was listening to my words would already know that we were going to war. We were not going to fly over the border with Iraq, but we would be vulnerable from attack by the Iraqi air force; at least one had to assume that would be the case. In fact, it transpired that the vast majority of the enemy air force would never make it off the ground.

As I walked out to XM715 the noise was deafening and the air stank of aviation fuel. It was about 10 o'clock at night and there was a cacophony of sound from running jet engines. Some aircraft would take off very soon; it was about 90 minutes to the border and no offensive aircraft would cross it before midnight – the deadline for an Iraqi climb-down. At 22.50 our wheels left the ground and we climbed via the safe lane to 9,000ft. On a westerly track and flying at 300 knots, it was just like the training flights we had flown over and over again during the past month. With the wing hoses trailed, four Tornados joined us at about 23.30. They would remain with us for as long as they wished before they dropped to low level to dispense their anti-runway area denial weapon system – JP233. The refuelling was carried out in total silence and they took their fuel to suit their plan; we were a flying petrol station. With full tanks, our four fighters dropped out of sight and headed north at high speed. We climbed to 27,000ft and continued north to set up a racetrack just inside the border – and wait; wait for our Tornados to rejoin us, take fuel, and return to Muharraq.

Just before 01.00 four aircraft came out of the dark to replenish their fuel tanks. We would be some of the first to know if an aircraft was lost but our Tornados turned up as expected. They took their fuel and were gone. The following day, one of the Victors had only three Tornados to refuel on the way home. That was because the two Johns were shot down whilst on a low-level daylight mission on Al Rumaylah airfield; both pilots ejected and were taken prisoner.

Syd Buxton describes his first mission of the war.

It was essentially the second wave of effort launched from Muharraq on 17th January. The first wave had launched just before midnight that night. Our mission consisted of a six-ship formation (Two Victor K2s and four Tornado GR1s) and the bombers were tasked with a low-level daylight attack, using 1,000lb bombs, on an Iraqi military airfield. We refuelled the Tornados en route, along the 'Olive Trail' and dropped them off at a point on the Saudi/Iraq border before setting up both tankers in a racetrack holding pattern to await their return. Just before the planned rendezvous time we were listening out on the allocated frequency and were very disheartened to hear the bomber formation discussing a missing aircraft.

A quick discussion between the entire formation resulted in one Victor tanker remaining on station, in case the missing aircraft showed up, and we escorted the three other Tornados back to Muharraq. Our hopes were not high as the returning Tornado crews were sure they had heard their colleagues report being on fire. Sure enough, we would later learn that both Flt Lt John Peters and Flt Lt John Nichol had ejected from a burning aircraft and were now prisoners in Baghdad, the first RAF combat loss of the war. Their appearance on TV, looking battered and bruised, at least confirmed they were alive, and they would eventually go on to recount their harrowing story in the book *Tornado Down*.

It was less than twenty-four hours later that the second RAF combat loss occurred, another Tornado based with us at Muharraq. The RAF Marham crew, Wg Cdr Nigel Elsdon and Flt Lt Max Collier, were lost following a night JP233 attack on an Iraqi military airfield. Sad news indeed, but particularly poignant because the very last two beers I had bought on my officers' mess bar book, at a well attended RAF Marham beer-call in December, just prior to deployment, were for these very two gentlemen.

David Williams carries on his story of 55 Squadron in Bahrain.

The Marham element of the Tornado force at Muharraq lacked a wing commander because Wing Commander Bob Iverson (OC 617 Squadron) was at Tabuk in Saudi Arabia and Wing Commander Nigel Elsdon, who replaced Bill Green as OC 27 Squadron, was undergoing his conversion from the Jaguar to the Tornado when crews deployed to the Gulf. His first sortie at Muharraq was on 18th January and his task was to drop his JP 233 on Shaibah airfield. His aircraft was shot down and both he and his navigator, Flight Lieutenant Max Collier were killed. Tragically, I had lost four friends from the Tornado force, some I had known for many years.

Victors gave refuelling support for both day and night raids by the Tornados as well as providing day refuelling for the Jaguars who were attacking targets in the Basrah region.

With the Tornados we would fly from Bahrain over northern Saudi Arabia towards the border with Iraq, controlled all the time by one of the AWACS aircraft. We would refuel the fighters on one of the many tow-lines that were designated for our use. The vast majority were given the names of fruits – from orange and lemon to loganberry and prune; although the one most used by the Victors was olive. We only used two tow-lines for the Jaguars; they were named Puller and Pusher and were about 100 miles from the coast of Kuwait.

On 26th January a detachment of Buccaneers arrived at Muharraq under the command of Wing Commander Bill Cope to support the Tornado missions. By now 55 Squadron had flown over 70 sorties and Victor operations were running as planned. For every Victor sortie, we provided a reserve Victor; however, the reserve was very rarely required. The more we flew the aircraft, the more serviceable they remained. The tasking was relentless and every crew was either flying a sortie or acting as a reserve for a sortie every day. There were no rest days.

55 Squadron provided air-to-air support right up to the end of the war on 28th February. In total, the Squadron was tasked with 299 missions and, almost unbelievably for an aircraft that came off the drawing boards in the 1950s, the Victor met every single one of those 299 tasks – not one sortie was lost.

Up until now, our work-life balance had heavily favoured work. We now found ourselves with time on our hands as flying ground to a halt. By early March the temperatures were starting to creep up in Bahrain and people turned their thoughts to relaxation – golf and sightseeing, tennis and sunbathing by the pool.

Syd Buxton remembers something that clearly affected the war effort:

Virtually all RAF aircraft in theatre had some sort of nose art applied for the Gulf War. 55 Squadron was lucky to have the artistic talents of Cpl Andy Price, a member of our engineering groundcrew, and he did us proud with his efforts on six of the aircraft. I clearly remember seeing him out on the hardstand, usually late in the evening, under the glare of portable lighting, creating his carefully clad ladies on the left-hand side of the aircraft cockpits, just in front of the cockpit hatch, each one named after the crew chief's lady.

They were – XH671 Slinky Sue (which shortly thereafter became Sweet Sue as it was felt that at a distance, Slinky could be mistaken for Stinky); XH672 Maid Marian (sometimes incorrectly written as Maid Marion – it should be an 'a', not an 'o'); XL164 Saucy Sal; XL231 Lusty Lindy (often incorrectly written as Lusty Linda); XM 715 Teasin Tina; XM717 Lucky Lou. We did have a couple of other Victor K2s participate in the Gulf War but because they were relatively late arrivals at Muharraq there wasn't time to apply such nose art. However, all the participating Victors did have mission symbols applied – rows of small black petrol pumps, applied on the fuselage below and aft of the cockpit hatch.

XM717 had one further unique symbol amongst her petrol pump mission symbols – a small profile of a truck. During operations at Muharraq, with all the chaos of equipment, vehicles and aircraft on the hardstand, XM717 had the misfortune of 'losing' a wingtip on a truck whilst being taxied at night. A new wingtip was dispatched from Marham, quickly fitted and operations resumed.

Unlike practically all other RAF aircraft so adorned for the Gulf War, these six Victor K2s proudly retained their nose art right up until the aircraft were withdrawn from service in late 1993.

Steve Carty fills in some interesting sortie details of the war.

I was given two or three days to prepare to go to Palermo with a detachment of Victors to support the deployment of Tornado GR1s and F3s to Saudi Arabia. Initially we refuelled GR1s from the UK to midway between Sicily and Cyprus and then handed them over to VC10Ks out of Akrotiri which then took them into Saudi airspace. On the first deployment, I flew in the jump seat of the lead Victor with Sqn Ldr Dick Druitt, Sqn Ldr Tony Lovett, Flt Lt Pete Jackson and Flt Lt Barry Munday. It was quite rare that ops guys flew with the Victors rather than in the support C130 so I was very excited to be making the trip.

The refuelling through France went well with some minor adjustments to the refuelling plan due to some problems with the GR1's refuelling abilities. As we flew over Palermo we could see there was very bad weather there and called Palermo ATC to ask how bad the weather was and whether it would clear in the next hour or not. Palermo ATC advised that it was a passing storm and everything would be okay for our return to Palermo.

We dropped the Tornados somewhere between Sicily and Cyprus and began our return to land at Palermo. As we approached there was heavy cloud and we were advised to descend to 15,000ft which took us into the centre of a terrible thunderstorm. The aircraft was being thrown around violently and lightning was flashing across the front windshield and down the sides of the cockpit – I had never experienced anything like it but believed that it must be a normal occurrence and that the crews must be experienced with such situations. Dick Druitt asked ATC to allow us to descend out of the storm but ATC told us to maintain our level. I started to worry when Tony told Dick to watch his attitude because the turbulence had rolled the aircraft more than 45 degrees to the left. The noise from the storm appeared to be louder than that of the engine and seemed like thunderous bangs. Approximately five miles behind us was another Victor captained by Stu Mitchell and he was being told to descend also.

Dick called him and told him to remain at his current level to avoid being in the same situation we were now in. The turbulence was getting worse by the second and the aircraft was now being thrown around like a toy. By now I was terrified and had locked the clips on the oxygen mask into 'bail out' position. I looked behind and

Steve Carty (right) in operations.

Pete Jackson the navigator had switched off the nav radar because it was now useless due to heavy weather and he was sitting looking very tense with his arms crossed. Dick Druitt once again called ATC and advised that we must climb or descend to get out of the weather and once again ATC refused and told him to maintain the level. It seemed to go on forever and so many things crossed my mind which in retrospect were stupid at the time. I had visions of us descending through the cloud straight into the large mountains at the side of Palermo airport or having to bail out because the wings might fall off! My mind kept going back to the story I'd heard of the time a Victor had its tail taken off by a jet on a training mission and none of the crew could escape because of the g force caused by the airframe's fall.

After what seemed like an eternity with me literally screaming obscenities into my mask, someone asked ATC again if we could descend or climb and once again ATC refused. Dick then said that he'd had enough and would climb anyway and divert to the US Navy base at Sigonella and he told Stu Mitchell to do the same. To say I was relieved is an understatement and then as we climbed through the cloud without ATC approval my mind went to the Victor behind and above us and I started worrying that we would pop out of the clouds directly into the other Victor. I think the most joyous moment of my life was when we came through a hole in the cloud in a descending right-hand turn and Sigonella runway was directly ahead of us.

We landed perfectly and I could see the relief on everyone's faces as we exited the runway and taxied in the direction advised by ATC. As we entered a large ramp Tony Lovett looked out of the starboard window and said " Dicky, watch the blast fence" and just before he finished the sentence the aircraft lurched violently to the right and then came to an abrupt stop. Pete Jackson jumped out of his seat and out of the door and then returned to tell us what had happened. Because it was an unfamiliar airfield Dick had been using the taxi markings but hadn't realised that there was no clearance between the wing and the taxiway edge. Along the edge of the taxiway was a large blast fence which had collided with the underside of the starboard refuelling pod and ripped a huge gash in the underside of the pod.

We taxied to the stand and thankfully the C130 carrying the groundcrews was still en route to Palermo so we made a call and had it diverted to Sigonella. That night we spent blowing off steam in Sigonella's officers' mess with a bunch of US reservists on their way to Saudi as part of the Desert Shield build-up and my crew then told me that they had never experienced weather like that before. Between the four of them they had around 75 to 100 years of flying experience so at that point I realised just how bad things had been. I was very nervous about flying again and they told me that the only way to overcome my nerves was to get back into an aircraft at the earliest opportunity.

The next morning we were advised that the engineers had patched up the hole on the pod so we proceeded to the ops room to prepare to fly from Sigonella to Palermo. I was still very nervous and unsure about flying in a Victor again and was considering flying with the engineers in the C 130 but Dick Druitt and Tony Lovett insisted I fly with them.

When we got to the ramp the engineers advised that the previous day's flight had put the same amount of stress on the airframe equal to thirty-nine normal flights and that there were cracks along the joining edge where the wings joined the fuselage!

As the crew walked out to the aircraft I was in the ops room advising Marham and 1 Group of the situation and I was still concerned about flying in an aircraft which was already old and now had done 39 flights worth of stress in one day. Barry Munday was with me and told me that if I forced myself it would be the best thing for me and so I agreed to make the short trip to Palermo.

When I arrived at the aircraft the engines were running and they were preparing to close the doors and taxi. I climbed in the hatch, strapped into the seat and took my helmet which I'd left on the seat the previous day and put it on. Imagine my confusion and panic when I couldn't get it on my head. Because of the adrenalin and worry I didn't understand why I couldn't get the helmet on and I was pushing like crazy, determined to get it on. The crew chief standing outside the door saw what I was doing and climbed through the hatch and thrust another helmet at me. It turned out that during the night when the engineers were carrying out checks on the airframe one of the crew chiefs had been inside the cockpit and had swapped my helmet with his own which was three sizes too small.

The procedure was that when the Victors got airborne I would then go to the radar room at ATC and watch their departure on radar just to make sure that there were no problems because sometimes there would be unserviceabilities with either the Victors or the receivers and changes would have to be made to the refuelling plan at short notice.

On one such occasion I was sitting in the radar room behind the approach controller and while the international language of aviation is English, those guys spoke only enough English for routine air traffic control directions; their conversational English was dreadful and all their conversations with the local Alitalia were always in Italian so we didn't really talk too much. The controller was eating lunch while having a very animated conversation with another controller in between glancing at the radar and speaking to the aircraft in Italian. I heard a familiar English voice over the radio and knew that the first Victor was on his way back to Palermo after completing the first transfer of the trail operation. The controller gave him a vector for the airfield and then spoke in Italian to an Alitalia aircraft also requesting approach to the airfield. As the two aircraft approached, the controller seemed to be paying less attention to the screen and more attention to his colleague with whom he was now engaged in what seemed like an all-out argument. I looked at the radar screen and realised that both the Victor and the Alitalia jet were on a converging heading at the same level approximately 12 miles apart. I tried to interrupt the argument between the two controllers but they were so engaged they ignored me. After a few seconds the approach controller looked at me and I explained what was happening but the guy just dismissed me with a wave of his hand. I then slapped him on the back and shouted in his ear "Airmiss!" He looked at the screen and I pointed to the two blips, at which point a look of absolute fear came across his face and he started shouting at the Alitalia jet in Italian. The Alitalia flight then changed its heading, the Victor descended and all was well but I'm sure that if I hadn't intervened that day, the fate of the two aircraft would have been left to the skill of the aircrew because of a couple of Italians having an argument!

Because the trail officer was an ex Hercules guy, we got to be very close to the C130 aircrews; after one detachment to Palermo we were returning to Marham onboard a C130 with the Victor groundcrews. The C130 was a no smoking aircraft except for in the cockpit so myself and the trail officer (I'd love to remember his name) would go and visit the cockpit for a smoke. As we were crossing the French Alps, the captain asked me if I'd ever flown a C130. I told him I hadn't but would like to try so the co-pilot hopped out of his seat and let me take his place. The captain disengaged the autopilot and told me I now had control. At first it was as if the autopilot was still on but then as we flew over the mountains there were huge updraughts which pushed the aircraft nose up which I was trying to correct by pushing the nose down. The result was a constant up climbing and descending similar to a roller coaster. After around 30 minutes I was tired so gave up on my 'flying lesson' and got out of the seat and climbed out of the cockpit in to the back only to be greeted by the Victor warrant officer. He was white as a sheet and as I passed him he said, "Who the hell is flying this plane?" Realising I'd put them all through an unpleasant experience, I quickly replied, "I don't know but whoever it is is not very good, so you'd better go and have a word with them!"

During September (I think) 1990 we took five Victors and a C130 full of groundcrew and spares to Palermo to operate from there so that VC10s or Victors would trail jets from the UK which would then be handed over to the Victors out of Palermo who would then take them past Cyprus and hand them to the VC10s operating out of Akrotiri. After a week or so at Palermo, the VC10s moved to Bahrain and over a few days the Victors were transferred to Akrotiri.

These trips involved crossing France of course and I remember on more than one occasion where a trail of up to twelve Tornados and five Victors would be delayed with engines running on the ground for up to five hours because the French ATC wouldn't give clearance for overflight. Doesn't really say much about British/French diplomatic relations in those days.

In December 1990 four Victors were deployed to Muharraq, Bahrain to replace the

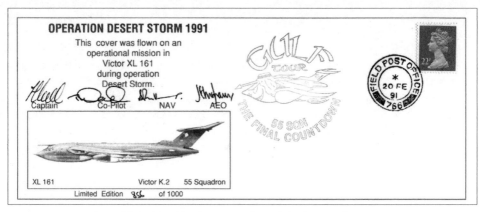

Capt: Flt Lt Tim Hatcher, co-pilot: Flt Lt Tim Walker, nav:
Wg Cdr David Williams, AEO: Flt Lt John Ingham.

VC10Ks which were being moved to Riyadh. I flew in the C130 with the groundcrew which made a refuelling stop at Akrotiri before flying on to Bahrain. I don't remember if the Victors refuelled any jets on the way down but they arrived gradually over the next few days. More aircraft arrived over the next few weeks with a total of eight in theatre by mid January.

After a couple of days handover from the VC10 guys they left for Riyadh and we took over the portacabin they'd been using by the side of the Gulf Air maintenance hangar. The Victors started carrying out familiarisation sorties refuelling Tornado GR1s, F3s and Jaguars and had a regular flying programme much the same as when operating in the UK but obviously with the thought that it was soon going to get real.

The aircrew stayed at the Holiday Inn, Diplomat Hotel and Gulf Hotel with the ops guys and it was a very strange situation to be living in a five-star hotel and driving to the base in what felt like a holiday destination, then changing into combat clothing and practising for war. By early January, Gulf Air had evacuated all their aircraft and personnel to Dubai or Oman and the airfield was totally under military control with the RAF on one side and US Marine C130s on the other side.

When the war actually started on 17th January it wasn't really a surprise although everyone was hoping it wouldn't happen. It was strange to receive the ATOs, air tasking orders, every day and send the Victors off to refuel the Tornados and then sit in the crew room watching Baghdad being bombed on CNN.

The ops crew would receive the ATOs everyday which gave the location of the tow-line, aircraft types and where they were from and it also showed the receivers' target information together with approach procedures for the various airfields.

There were actually very few incidents involving Victors because they were carrying out the same operations as they had done during peacetime albeit under very different conditions though one day a crew told us about the loss of two Tornados.

On the second day of the war one crew reported being shot at by a SAM 7 while returning back to base. Another time a Victor was returning from a tow-line over the Arabian Gulf supporting Jaguars making attacks into Kuwait. We heard lots of panicked chatter on the radio in the ops room as the Victor was being attacked by two Iraqi Mirages. The pilot of the Victor, I think his name was Flt Lt McLaughlin, was flying in a way to try to avoid being locked on by the Mirages but the large slow

Victor would be no match for the fast agile Mirages. After a few minutes of panic we then heard a calm voice saying everything was okay. The Mirages had been shot down by two Canadian Air Force F18s who then requested fuel from the Victor. The relieved pilot was more than happy to give them whatever they wanted.

Another incident was between a VC10 tanker and a Victor. The VC10 was tasked to set up a tow-line a few thousand feet below the Victor's tow-line at night. There was radio silence and the VC10 was flying in cloud and, concerned about the lack of visibility for his receivers, had decided to climb to see if he could get out of the cloud. The Victor was flying level and the VC10 climbed out of the cloud through the Victor's level a few hundred yards ahead of it.

We would often have a Victor on standby to support the US Navy F4G which was used for targeting scud missile launchers. We also would regularly have air raid warnings when scuds were fired by Iraq and we were supposed to evacuate to an air raid shelter by the side of our portacabin, although the air raids were often so frequent that we wouldn't actually bother evacuating or would be so complacent that we would just lie under the ops desk. One time we had an air raid and one crew together with the groundcrew and I were in the shelter lazily putting on our NBC kit when there was a huge explosion outside that shook the ground. I have never before or since seen anyone don NBC kit as quickly as the people there that day. When it happened there had been a couple of avionics guys working on a Victor that was parked on the other side of the airfield in front of the airport terminal. That night when shift change was due, the two guys failed to return to the crew room so a search party went to look for them. They weren't with the Victor and after a long search they turned up looking very happy and slightly inebriated. It turned out that when the explosion happened they ran towards the terminal building in panic looking for shelter. They broke through a door to get inside and found themselves in the airport duty free store so decided to stay and have a few drinks!!

I also remember a crew leaving to go on a sortie and while they were doing their pre flight checks the AEO accidentally inflated the life raft in the cockpit. It took some time to get them out because the inflated raft stopped any of the crew from moving and it took a crew chief with a knife to release them; we had to launch another crew to replace them.

Steve Carty's mention of the attack by two Mirages justified a Victor chaff development that has not been advertised but is described by Syd Buxton.

Some earlier bomber variants of the Victor had been provided with chaff-dispensing equipment, which was fitted in two hoppers in the lower forward fuselage (Mk 1) or later in the 'Küchemann carrot' or 'Whitcomb body' overwing fairings (designed to reduce wave drag at transonic speeds) on the upper trailing surface of the wing (Mk 2). Although these overwing fairings still existed on the Victor K2, the equipment with them had long since been removed to save weight.

It was obvious that AAR was going to be a vital part of the military air effort to force Iraq out of Kuwait, but that could expose the RAF's fairly limited tanker numbers to damage or loss by the largely unknown capabilities of the Iraqi air force. Tankers were thus high value air assets (HVAA) and all the Victor K2 had in the way of defensive equipment was a radar warning receiver which was monitored by the AEO. So, though we might know from which direction the threat was coming, we couldn't stop whatever it was from hitting us! With nothing to really lose, an effort was begun on 55 Squadron to devise a temporary chaff dispenser.

From the flight crew side, Flt Lt Adrian Richardson was the enthusiastic sponsor of work. A basic device was quickly designed and it was reminiscent of a very large, metal, hypodermic syringe but without the needle. I think the tube part was aluminium and its diameter was chosen to fit the sextant mount in the roof of the Victor cockpit. The tube would be packed with chaff and a hand-operated plunger would push a piston up the tube, expelling the chaff into the airflow above the fuselage.

Airborne tests were carried out using Tornado F3s as simulated attackers and there were successes in breaking the lock of their air-to-air radar, so approval was given to carry the device. If I remember correctly, for deployment in the Gulf, about three of these loaded dispensers were clipped to a wooden board which itself was temporarily fixed with bungee cords to the usually unoccupied fifth seat. It was expected that one of the rear crew, nav or AEO, would operate the dispenser, though it was acknowledged this might not be easy if the Victor was manoeuvring to evade an attacker. Thankfully, I don't recall 55 Squadron crews ever having to deploy the chaff in an operational situation.

I should mention that there was one major drawback with the use of the device. There were several air intakes at the rear of the Victor K2, including those on the leading edges of the fin and horizontal stabilisers, for the powered flying control units. I think the troublesome one was the air intake on the top of the fuselage, at the base of the forward edge of the fin (not to be confused with the pair of extending RAT intakes, which were usually retracted in flight). This intake took air to the bomb bay and centreline hose drum unit and a lot of chaff was discovered trapped within and around this area. It was very troublesome to clean out but it was felt that dispensing chaff 'in anger' might just save the aircraft and crew and thus it was worth the inconvenience.

Interestingly, I have since learned that such chaff problems were not new to the Victor K2. Chaff contamination problems were encountered on the Victor B1 with its under-fuselage chaff dispenser. The cooling air intake for the rear equipment bay on the B1 was low down on the rear fuselage and often became clogged with chaff. This problem was apparently countered on the B1A with a modified fairing that improved cooling in the rear equipment bay and minimised clogging of the intake with chaff.

David Williams describes the return from the Middle East.

On 15th March 1991 the vast majority of 55 Squadron left Bahrain on our return to the UK. However, we did not go direct to Marham. We flew to Palermo in Sicily to prepare to support some of the returning fast jets the following day. So, it was not until 18th March that we made the three-hour flight home. Thankfully, all the Victors got airborne; I didn't allow the thought of an unserviceable aircraft to cross my mind.

In the descent to Marham, the Victors moved into formation for the approach to home. Unbeknown to us and unplanned by us, a pair of Tornados joined the

Welcoming party on return from the Gulf. From left: Flt Lt John Ingham,
Gp Capt Jock Stirrup, Wg Cdr David Williams, Air Vice-Marshal Sandy Wilson,
Flt Lt Tim Hatcher, Flt Lt Tim Walker, chief tech Geoff Shilton.

formation to welcome us back to Marham. It was early afternoon on a cold and windswept, but dry Norfolk day that the Victors of 55 Squadron landed one after the other. We were met formally by Air Marshal Sandy Wilson, the Air Officer Commanding 1 Group and our station commander, Group Captain Jock Stirrup. The families were also there; my two young sons had been given special permission to have the afternoon off school.

I can think of many high and many low moments. Many things spring to mind when I think of the forty-four days of the Gulf War but, even now, the most important issue for me as the squadron commander, was that everybody I took to Bahrain returned home safely.

One of David Williams's last flights in August 1991 was to take Johnny Allam flying again in Victor K2 XH672. This was Johnny's first flight in a K2 and Syd Buxton, the co-pilot, kindly gave up his seat to allow Johnny to feel the Victor controls again.

Bill Scragg was a navigator who flew Canberras in Germany, then he did several tours on Vulcans, a ground tour in Germany and was then posted to Marham. He was at Kelly Air Force Base as described by David Williams and Steve Carty and helped move the Jaguars and some Tornados across the Atlantic from Goose Bay. He was in Thumrait, Oman, from 11th August.

In September/November 1990 we got involved moving more fast jets to the Middle

From left; Syd Buxton, David Williams, Johnny Allam, Flt Lt Millikin and Barry Masefield.

East using Palermo and/or Akrotiri for refuelling. We also deployed some Italian Tornados whose pilots had not done a deployment before, 'refuelling in anger'. Because of that, many refuelling 'brackets' were overrun so that some Victors had to divert to Cairo International short of fuel. This caused a minor diplomatic incident which the officer commanding, David Williams, dealt with.

On 14th December 1990, 55 Squadron deployed to Muharraq, Bahrain as part of Desert Shield, guarding against Saddam Hussein going after Saudi oilfields since Iraqi forces were now established in Kuwait. Of course the Victors had long since lost their green camouflage colours and were painted 'desert' brown. Sorties were mostly in support of the F3 Tornados on combat air patrol, Royal Saudi Air Force as well as RAF aircraft taking part.

On Christmas Day we showed the flag and our Victor led twenty-five allied aircraft in a flypast over Bahrain. Then on 16th January 1991 Operation Desert Storm and the liberation of Kuwait began. At first most trips were at night in radio silence taking RAF Tornados across the Saudi desert. They would depart going north towards Iraqi targets. Later Buccaneers flew with the Tornados as laser target designators. Another routine sortie took us to the northern Gulf area so that we were available for the Jaguars operating over Kuwait. We flew in a short racetrack pattern with the hoses already trailed and we often had fuel 'stolen' from us by unannounced Canadian Air Force and US Navy aircraft, CF18s, F4s and 5s. One new departure for us was that we were told to fly with 100% fuel, very unusual because of the penalty of increased speed of usage of fatigue life. Luckily operating from Bahrain was no problem since the airport had a long runway.

Once the air situation was favourable we took some media reporters with us. Bob Fenton did a good article in the *Daily Telegraph*, 20th February 1991.

At 1pm exactly, bang on time, *Saucy Sal* screams down the runway and soars into the blue Gulf sky. The 30-year-old Victor tanker lifts its 50 ton load of fuel to its allotted height and waits for its customers. Behind her a formation of Tornado and Buccaneer fighter-bombers takes off from the same strip on another mission to attack hardened aircraft shelters somewhere deep inside Iraq.

To give them the range they need, the jets will top up their tanks from the plentiful reserves of *Saucy Sal*, high above the Saudi desert. In front of me, Squadron Leader Dick Druitt levels out his craft at the height determined by the 'frag', the fragment of the huge daily allied air battle plan. By his side, Flight Lieutenant Ashford moves fuel from one set of tanks to another. They wait patiently for the fighter-bombers to catch up, then slowly the hoses are reeled out in the slipstream, offering succour to the thirsty Tornados.

"The last thing these guys need at this precise moment is hassle," says Sqn Ldr Druitt. "Our job is to let them set off as quickly and peacefully as possible. We are more than aware of the nerves that must be going on in their cockpits. That's why we try to make it as easy as possible."

Saucy Sal is flying straight and level. There is chatter all around the airwaves as American, British and French aircrews talk to the AWACS radar surveillance aircraft that acts as a flying air traffic controller in skies packed with military jets. The intercom inside the Victor is also alive with talk as flight information and dry humour pass between Druitt, Ashford, Flt Lt Bill Scragg, the navigator and Flt Lt Allan Jones, the air electronics officer.

The desert stretches out to every horizon below us as Sqn Ldr Gordon Buckley edges his Tornado into view of the window on my left. He and his navigator, Flt Lt Paddy Teakle, look over and give us a cheery wave. The far side of them, looking as though they fly wingtip to wingtip, is the plane of Flt Lt Bruce Macdonald and Flying Officer Tony McGlone. After a few minutes flying alongside, they edge across and under the Victor. Buckley goes to the port hose, Macdonald to the starboard.

From the back of the Victor's cockpit, eight feet by six of black dials and switches, Flt Lt Bill Scragg, the navigator, watches them on his periscope. Buckley comes gingerly up to 'prod' the basket trailing at the end of a hose that flutters from the tanker's wing. Twice he 'rims' it, the retractable fuelling probe catching the edge of the basket. But the Tornado makes a good contact the third time and the jet begins to suckle.

Macdonald moves on the other side and takes fuel. Through the periscope they seem close enough to touch, travelling at more than 300 mph, but kept with great skill in exactly the right spot. Once they have finished, it is the turn of the Buccaneer. Within seven minutes, less than three-quarters of an hour after take-off, the formation of pink aircraft are full.

They fly alongside the Victor for another 15 minutes or so before the Tornados come back for a final top-up. Although Druitt has taken the formation 2,000ft higher to avoid cloud the baskets have begun to wave around in turbulence.

"Closing up," says Scragg, his eye fixed again to the periscope, counting down the feet to contact so that Druitt and Ashford know what is going on.

"Closing up ... 10....5 – missed."

"Dropping back…closing up again … 10…5…rim."

Druitt sounds exasperated over the intercom. "Amazing how it can be so smooth until we get to prodding."

Finally the Tornados both make a clean contact and take on fuel. There is as little conversation between the aircraft as possible. We are not far from Iraq. But Druitt and Buckley have a brief exchange to ensure that the Tornados and the Buccaneers know which way the Victor will turn

Final flypast at Marham.

when they part company.

"All right, I'll go right then. Best of luck, lads." With that the Tornados wing north towards the enemy territory and another bombing raid. Their laser-guided smart bombs hang ominously below them as the jets swing away from us. They are quickly out of sight.

Druitt and his crew become noticeably more relaxed now their job is done. Jones breaks out a thermos of coffee for all and Scragg hands out bars of chocolate. Inside the Victor there is little room to move and all four men stay strapped in their seats. There is a strong camaraderie that defies the fact they can only hear each other by speaking into the microphone of their masks. They mix conversation and operational matters with disarming ease.

At the very front of the cockpit sits the fifth member of the crew, acting pilot officer Biggles, the shortest and furriest airman in the RAF. Biggles is a six inches high teddy bear complete with flying jacket, goggles and his own leather helmet; he was sent to the men of 55 Squadron by a Scout Troop from Downham Market, Norfolk next to the air base at Marham. His job is to sit at the top of Druitt's control panel and keep an eye out for other aircraft in the sky. He has flown fifteen missions in a week and is due for promotion.

The Victor turns and climbs to a higher altitude and begins the eastward journey home. 55 Squadron has now flown more than 200 sorties in support of Jaguars, Tornados and Buccaneers as well as a host of other allied jets. Druitt and his men swap jokes as they return from their 25th mission. Although they know they are exposed to far less risk than the fighter-bombers they are constantly alert to the danger of attack or collision with friendly aircraft.

Twenty miles out the jet, designed originally as a nuclear bomber, tips its nose gently down and begins its descent. Because the Tornados took less fuel than Druitt had been led to expect, the Victor has to lighten its load and dump 22,000lb of fuel. Almost all of this will evaporate into the air before it can cause any pollution in the sea..

The final crew of the final flight. From left: Steve Jenkins, Tony Inglebrecht, Peter Lambert, Bill Scragg and Johnny Allam.

Leaving the Gulf, the Victor turns one last time, bringing the distant airfield into view between the stanchions of Druitt's windscreen. Getting clearance from the civilian air traffic controller the Victor comes down on the runway blackened with the rubber from thousands of jets that have landed before. We taxi in to our stand and for the first time for two and a half hours we are free completely. As the crew clamber down the ladder ready for the debrief, a formation of Jaguars taxi to the end of the runway for their sortie.

We have not talked about peace proposals to Moscow or about the war aims of the Allies. The air campaign goes on incessantly and the Victors will continue to play their part as long as other aircraft need their fuel.

During the war, the Victors had flown over hundreds of sorties and never missed a tasked trip, echoing the reliability the aircraft showed in the Falklands campaign. Bill told me that in March the aircraft were used to recover Tornados and Buccaneers using Palermo as the refuelling base. Then that autumn Operation Warden commenced and they were detached to Akrotiri to support Jaguars operating to protect the Kurds in Northern Iraq. Then in 1992 they were again back in Bahrain supporting Tornados over Iraq.

The Squadron was disbanded in 1993 and Adrian Balch has captured opposite the final formation flight from an open para door of an RAF Lockheed Hercules C130.

Postscript

Bill Scragg was on the very final flight, Victor XH672, and someone had the splendid idea of inviting Johnny Allam along. Fittingly, it was on 30th November 1993 to RAF Shawbury for the RAF Museum at Cosford. Still painted on the nose of the aircraft was its name Maid Marian as a remembrance of the Iraqi war.

Epilogue

The life of any aircraft is a finite one, be it civil or military. The drive of technology is remorseless and however advanced an aircraft may be at the start of its life, it will soon become out-of-date and not competitive with newer designs. The Handley Page Victor was no exception but, in the event, its lifespan proved longer than its UK competitors and was an enormous asset in helping the defence of the United Kingdom.

After the Second World War the pace of aircraft development was being driven by the rapid advance of the jet engine. Under the leadership of Sir Frederick Handley Page his firm produced a design which was very futuristic, minimising and delaying the effects of flying close to the speed of sound. Using the latest aerodynamic knowledge obtained not only from the UK but also from the UK's recent German antagonist, the Victor design had the famous crescent wing which minimised the onset of compressibility due to the 'sound barrier' by ensuring that the effect occurred at the same time across all the wing.

The aircraft served throughout the Cold War, initially as a Mk1 carrying a free-fall nuclear weapon and then, as a Mk2 fitted with the larger Conway engines, it hosted the Blue Steel air-launched stand-off weapon. It was then converted into a tanker where not only did it do outstanding service supporting our fighters all over the world but, unexpectedly, made the whole Ascension Island operation possible during the Falklands war. Not content with that, towards the end of its service life it was able to provide vital support to the UK's operations in the Middle East.

Unlike many defence projects, the Victor was an outstanding success particularly as a tanker, able to carry more fuel than the empty weight of the aircraft and being extremely reliable, seldom missing a sortie. This book, with personal accounts from many people who operated the aircraft, makes very clear what an unsurpassed service the aircraft was able to provide, supported by first class and dedicated crews.

Appendix I

Accidents

All aircraft, be they military or civil, suffer from accidents and it is important to examine the causes of these accidents since it is then usually possible to judge whether the aircraft has met the required certification standard both from the engineering and pilot handling viewpoints. However, in the case of the Victor there were certain accidents where the cause of the accident could not be clearly established.

Victor first prototype WB771 14th July 1953
The aircraft was doing low level position-error measurements at Cranfield. As was usual during the tests, the speed was gradually being increased, point by point, and it is alleged that the test pilot, Taffy Ecclestone, did one more run than was on the test plan. Be that as it may, on the final run the tailplane broke off from the fin due to the occurrence of flutter; that is the tailplane started to vibrate and resonate uncontrollably. Accident investigation showed that one of the three bolts holding the tailplane to the fin was already cracked so that in effect only two bolts were holding the tailplane in place during the flight. It was decided to increase the number of bolts holding the tailplane to the fin from three to four and there were no further structural failures of the tailplane during the life of the aircraft.

Victor B2 XH668 20th August 1959
The aircraft was on a test flight from A&AEE doing high speed manoeuvres at 54,000ft when it dived into the sea off Milford Haven, Pembrokeshire. A massive search was conducted to recover the wreckage but it took over a year before the critical components were brought up from the sea; it was then established that the starboard pitot head had broken off due to a fatigue fracture and it was considered that this was the primary cause of the accident. The explanation formulated was that the indicated low airspeed from the failure caused the mach trimmer to retract, the nose flaps to extend and the flaps to come down. The aircraft then went into a high speed dive and there was partial structural break up before the aircraft hit the sea.

There was a view at Handley Page at the time that this explanation may not have been the correct one. I have discussed the accident with Johnny Allam and he felt that it was unlikely that the retraction of the mach trimmer would have caused the pilots any serious problem. Furthermore, he remembers that when the engines hit the water the air brakes were retracted and that Rolls-Royce said that they were running at max continuous power, which seems most unlikely if the pilots were in full control.

The crew were briefed to do buffet boundaries and in the Victor very severe buffet would occur under these circumstances and it was known that the pitot head was liable to damage. There was a view that during one of these very demanding tests the aircraft got into a spiral dive with the speed increasing to .98 mach number at which speed it was known that the aileron jacks were stalled. The pilots at this stage may have tried using rudder to arrest any roll but unfortunately at this speed the normal rolling effect from sideslip effect, lv, was reversed so that instead of returning to wings level the aircraft would have rolled further and without any aileron control it would have dived uncontrollably. The wingtip extensions which had been added to the B2 and the nose flaps would have come off in the ensuing dive.

Peter Baker was a test pilot at Handley Page at the time; later he joined Vickers doing an enormous amount of flight testing of the Concorde and then, towards the end of his flying career, became chief test pilot of the UK Civil Aviation Authority. He was one of the most experienced test pilots of my generation and he has added a comment to this accident.

I think we do know they lost control, the aircraft was overstressed and one pilot did try to get out. I am convinced in my mind that they lost roll power (it was very easy to do at around 0.97M and a steep spiral was easily generated where 1.0M was readily achieved).One had to slow down to recover from such situations and I fear they were not fully aware of that fact. Power off and speed brakes were clearly required and they didn't do any of that for some reason.

As a result of the accident it was thought that extensive further buffet boundary testing was required. It was decreed that this was to be directed under the supervision of RAE at Bedford. An aircraft, XH670, was modified so it could fly with just two pilots and a Javelin squadron was set aside to provide 'chase' – they had problems keeping up!

I did most, if not quite all, of the testing with Harry Rayner. The vulnerability of the pitots was evident in that on one occasion, after particularly severe buffet, one was bent back more than 90 degrees. The trap of lv reversal was avoided by reducing speed before recovery and not using the rudder when at 0.98M or higher (difficult to prevent higher speeds on occasion which inspired me at the end to go supersonic and achieve M1.02 – PE assessed as zero here. Not a popular move).

RAE never spoke to the crew but simply contacted our flight test and told them what they wanted us to do. At the end they declared themselves satisfied. Other than the pitot, nothing broke. After the Victor, Concorde testing was like a walk in the park, where one could pull 2.5g at 60,000ft at M2.0 without buffet.

Clearly we will never know what really happened but on the face of it the official explanation seems unlikely. Because the air brakes were in and the engines were not throttled back, one explanation could be that the crew were anoxic.

Victor B1A XH617 19th June 1960

The aircraft from 57 Squadron caught fire in the air near Diss, Norfolk, when a generator drive failed and penetrated a fuel tank causing a fire to break out. The fire spread steadily through the aircraft which was abandoned but, despite the captain handling the emergency perfectly, only he and the AEO survived. The navigator successfully left the aircraft but was very sadly killed by some object from the aircraft, maybe part of the captain's ejection seat. The co-pilot's ejection sequence did not work for some reason and he was unable to leave the aircraft.

Victor B1 XA917 2nd March 1961
This aircraft was being operated by Handley Page at Radlett doing radar trials and landed in the undershoot damaging the nosewheels. It then ran on to the runway and proceeded more or less normally until the brake parachute was streamed, with a strong crosswind. Without nosewheel steering, the aircraft ran off the side of the runway onto the grass where the nose dug in and the undercarriage collapsed causing damage to the fuselage. Fortunately the crew escaped unharmed.

Victor B2 XL159 23rd March 1962
The aircraft was on a test flight near Stubton in Lincolnshire with a Handley Page test pilot, an A&AEE test pilot, an AEO and two observers. Low speed handling tests were being carried out on the aircraft with the recently fitted production fixed-droop leading edges that replaced the conventional moveable nose flaps. During an approach to the stall at 16,000ft in the landing configuration the aircraft was mishandled and entered a stable stall followed by a flat spin from which the crew were unable to recover, the aircraft sinking at a rate of about 6,000ft/min. Both pilots ejected safely, the co-pilot at 1,000ft and the captain at 400-500ft. One rear crew member abandoned the aircraft successfully, the other two rear crew remained with the aircraft. The aircraft, descending almost vertically, crashed onto a farmhouse at Stubton, near Newark on Trent, killing two residents and injuring two more. Peter Baker comments again.

A Handley Page test pilot was captain of the aircraft, though it was apparently being flown by the Boscombe pilot when it stalled.

The moving nose flaps were replaced on the Victor by a modified leading edge to save weight – the moving flaps needed to be lowered rapidly at given CL which required heavy hydraulic accumulators which could be removed with fixed flaps. The mod was thought to give adequate protection although not quite as good. We suddenly realised that modified aircraft had gone into service without Boscombe having had a look at the mod. The Boscombe pilot took the aircraft to the stall and it pitched up and locked in, the tailplane being now ineffective as it lay in the wing wake. The only mishandling, if you want to call it that, was to take the aircraft to the stall – it was not cleared for stalling!

Victor B1A XH613 14th June 1962
Whilst approaching RAF Cottesmore, at the end of the sortie on a radar approach at 2,000ft, all four engines ran down. The aircraft was being flown by the squadron commander and on giving the order to abandon the aircraft it is believed that the rear crew all left the aircraft in less than half a minute. All the crew survived.

This accident could easily have resulted in the loss of the three rear crew members but the captain made a brilliant, immediate decision to abandon the aircraft. The crew were very well practised in their escape drills and in spite of the nav radar having difficulty passing the nav plotter's seat the rear crew were all out by 1,500ft and the pilots by 1,000ft. Apparently Bomber Command thought this was the first time a complete crew had escaped from a V bomber but in July 1957 Jimmy Harrison, my boss at Avros at the time and flying my aircraft while I was on holiday, successfully got his complete crew out safely when Vulcan Mk1 XA891 had a complete generator failure immediately after take-off.

On the Victor 1 the fuel panel was between the two pilots and contained among other things all the contact breakers for the fuel pumps. The wiring was all carried by a Brieze plug directly under the panel. Normally this was wirelocked but the plug had been removed for maintenance and it was assumed that this had caused the problem.[19]

Victor B1 XA929 16th June 1962
The aircraft was taking off at RAF Akrotiri in Cyprus but apparently the flaps were in the wrong position. It failed to get airborne and by the time the captain realised the problem it was too late. The take-off was abandoned but the aircraft overshot the end of the runway and all the crew were killed. The co-pilot ejected shortly before the crash but did not survive. Dennis Robinson has added some details

> Two switches mounted on Panel A, one above the other, just above the sliding fuel tray AT controlled the main flaps. One was a three-position switch annotated 'UP – TAKE-OFF – DOWN and was used for normal flap selections. The other was a 'gated' switch, annotated 'NORMAL – EMERGENCY DOWN' and was used for emergency flap selections only. The main flaps were powered by a series of gear boxes, torque tubes, universal joints and bevel gearboxes, ultimately attached to a reduction gear box mounted in the roof of the bomb bay and which was driven by a hydraulic motor. Mounted adjacent to the motor was a switch unit containing twelve micro-switches operated by spring-loaded cam mechanisms and four rocker arms notated A, B, C, and D, actuated by a camshaft. The drive for the camshaft was taken from the gearboxes.
>
> Bearing the above in mind, the Board of Inquiry found that the controls in the cockpit were correctly set for take-off, i.e. the main flaps were selected to 'Take-Off' and the nose flaps were selected to 'Auto'. That was the standard operating procedure prior to take-off. In examining the wreckage the same was found with the flaps. The nose flaps were out and the main flaps were at the take-off position.
>
> During interviews with witnesses, it was apparent that the crew chief had thoroughly briefed the groundcrew, only one of whom had seen a Victor before, prior to start-up. The usual pre-start checks had been carried out, the crew chief had climbed on board and the aircraft had taxied out. There was a difference of opinion between the groundcrew as to whether the aircraft had taxied out with the flaps at take-off or with them fully retracted. The Board considered this significant. Other witnesses who had watched the aircraft on its take-off run, albeit from a distance, also gave conflicting information to the Board. Some thought that the aircraft looked unusually clean, others thought that it looked normal.
>
> The most important piece of information came from the duty runway controller

---

[19] See B1 chapter and David Bywater.

situated in the runway caravan. This junior NCO had only just been posted to Akrotiri and had never seen a Victor before. The evidence that he gave prompted the Board to instruct another Victor in transit through Akrotiri to sit on the runway in the position that XA929 was presumed to have sat, and cycle the flaps from up to take-off and back to up. The junior NCO insisted that he had seen much more flap than was evident on this Victor. The Board informed him that that was as far as the flaps on the Victor could go and that they could go no lower. The junior NCO, however, stuck to his guns and insisted that he had seen much more flap. The captain of the commandeered Victor was then instructed to lower the flaps to fully down and the junior NCO stated quite clearly that that was what he had seen.

The Board then examined various components removed from XA929 and concentrated their attention on the flap switch unit. Results from this examination were inconclusive due to the fragmented nature of the unit but the Board felt that this and the setting-up procedure for this unit was the root cause of the accident.

The Board of Inquiry concluded that, taking into account the retraction and extension times for the flaps and nose flaps, a fault had occurred in the switch unit at sometime during the taxiing phase of the aircraft. The fact that the main flaps were seen to have been fully down at the commencement of the take-off run seemed to confirm this. During the run, the flaps were presumed to have moved from fully down to fully up and then back to take-off just as the aircraft impacted the terrain at the end of the runway, hence the loss of lift. With the co-pilot calling out the airspeed and the captain concentrating on the take-off run combined with the known sluggishness of the Desyn indicators, it was considered improbable that the crew were aware of the problem.

As Modification 2352, to introduce drooped leading edges by replacement of the nose flaps was pending, the Board appears to have made few recommendations. The most significant was that the switch box cams be adjusted in a specific sequence of C, D, B and A.

Dick Russell adds a further insight into the problem and the possible cause of the accident.

I was at Marham but flying out of Honington. We were in a crew coach sat behind a 57 Squadron aircraft doing his pre take-off checks. Finishing them, he started to taxi forward and then his flaps moved to up. One of us, Denys Mobberley ran to one of the emergency phones scattered all over the station and made a call to ATC which stopped the take-off. We could have had another Akrotiri accident if Denys had not moved so quickly. The problem was that in the Victor Mk1 the flap selector was in front of the parking brake and as the parking brake was released the left hand could, and in this case probably did, knock the lever to up. The flap lever was moved in the Mk 1A to the centre of the engine instrument panel so that either pilot could operate it and it was less liable to being knocked.

Unfortunately, as with so many accidents it is difficult to be certain what actually happened.

Victor B1 XA934 2nd October 1962

The standard account of this accident states that the aircraft was from 232 OCU and taking off from RAF Gaydon when there was an engine failure. The aircraft was too heavy for an immediate landing and some time was spent burning fuel. Unfortunately, on the approach to landing two more engines failed and the aircraft crashed into a copse several miles short of the runway. The co-pilot was the only survivor and was still in his ejection seat when it hit the ground.

Investigation by AAIB discovered that when the engine failed a piece of metal cut through a fuel feed pipe from the fuselage tanks. Apparently the crew selected fuel from these tanks when starting the approach and the engines failed at this point being starved of fuel. However, what is puzzling is why switching on the fuselage pumps should have caused engine failures even if the fuel pipes were damaged, since the wing tanks would still have been providing fuel.

Moreover, Dick Russell, a QFI who was there, has told me that at that time the drill after an engine failure was to close the adjoining engine and not to parallel the bus bars, so that the fuel pumps on the side of the dead engines would not be operable. Whether this was a factor in the accident and the aircraft was actually short of fuel is not clear but certainly there would probably have been over 25,000lb fuel unusable on the aircraft.

Victor B2 XM714 2nd March 1963

The aircraft, with a crew of five and a Bomber Command 'umpire' took off from Wittering in the early evening to fly a bomber night exercise. The weather was good and the aircraft had only recently been delivered new from the factory. After a normal take-off and after passing 800ft, the co-pilot noticed the No 2 engine fire warning light was illuminated. He told the captain that No 1 engine was on fire but the captain contradicted him with the correct engine details and instructed the co-pilot to tell air traffic control; he then told the rear crew members to check their parachutes. The co-pilot noticed that the undercarriage warning flag, which is activated if speed drops below 160 knots and the undercarriage has not been lowered, was flashing and he warned the captain to watch his speed. The captain replied that he was climbing for height and despite the severe juddering believed that the aircraft had sufficient speed because, it is thought, he believed he was at 100 knots higher speed than was the case. At around 5,000ft the aircraft flicked over to port and fell away partly inverted. The captain ordered the crew to abandon the aircraft but the rear crew members were unable to do so because of the increasing g forces as the aircraft spun down. Only the co-pilot ejected and was unharmed.

It seems that the only possible explanation for an experienced captain losing control in this way was for him to have assumed he had the right speed and that the juddering was not a stall but structural failure caused by the engine fire. In fact, one account did state that the captain shut down the wrong engine when the fire light came on. He then misread his airspeed indicator thinking he was at 240kt when he was actually at 140kt whilst thinking the buffet was due to structural failure rather than pre-stall buffet. Apparently three engines were working perfectly when the aircraft stalled and went inverted.

Victor B2 XM716 29th June 1966

XM716 from RAF Wyton was to give a demonstration flight for an Anglia Television crew. It took off and performed a sharp turn to the right. The aircraft broke up in the air during the turn and crashed nearby. As it was only intended to be a local flight there was no navigator on board. All the crew members died. The subsequent enquiry decided that the pilot had been attempting to put on an impressive display for the TV crew and had exceeded the g limit of the airframe. Unfortunately there have been many accidents caused by display flying, however carefully the pilots are briefed. In this case the display appears to have been impromptu and, again, there have been many more tragic accidents when displays are arranged at the last moment.

Of course, without flight recorders it is impossible to know the exact sequence of events and whether the pilot in this case was indeed to blame.

Victor K1 XH646 19th August 1968
Whilst undertaking a late evening training mission near Holt, Norfolk, the Victor crew experienced extremely poor weather conditions which rendered the ATC radar cover at RAF Watton ineffective. As the fully loaded Victor tanker with four crew began turning out to sea 14,000ft above Holt it collided nose to nose with Canberra B(1)6 WT325 flying in from R.A. Bruggen in Germany with three crew. The crews of both aircraft were killed and the tragedy was tempered only by the fact that miraculously no one in the town was affected by the explosion and wreckage which rained down, with only a few roof tiles damaged. The Victor cockpit burnt out as it lay in a field near Holt Hall while the Canberra broke into thousands of pieces which were scattered over ten square miles around the Holt area. It was indisputably established that neither of the crews nor their aircraft were at fault.

Victor SR2 XL230 10th May 1973
The aircraft was carrying out a two-engined asymmetric approach for landing at Wyton. There was a gusty crosswind from the left of the runway and the aircraft started to drift over the grass. The captain decided to overshoot but unfortunately opened all four engines together so that the two operating engines went up to full power almost immediately but the two idling engines only accelerated very slowly. The aircraft immediately yawed away from the live engines and there was insufficient rudder power to prevent it rolling on its back out of control. All the crew were killed.

The Vulcan had two similar accidents in 1964 and 1965; by a miracle the crew escaped from the second accident. The operating rules were changed to stop the practice on the Vulcan. It is believed that the rules were also changed on the Victor but perhaps the captain of this aircraft, eight years after the last Vulcan asymmetric accident event, did not appreciate the danger of opening all four throttles at the same time when two engines on one side were at idle power.

Victor K1A XH618 24th March 1975
The aircraft was involved in a mid-air collision with a Hawker Siddeley Buccaneer during a simulated refuelling. The Buccaneer hit the Victor's tailplane causing the aircraft to crash into the sea 95 miles east of Sunderland. It bunted over and the negative g forces made it impossible for the crew to escape. The captain managed to reach and pull the ejection handle with the fingers of one hand and although injured was subsequently rescued by a merchant ship. The Buccaneer was undamaged and returned to base.

Victor K2 XL513 28th September 1976

Coming up to rotation at RAF Marham at maximum take-off weight of 222,000lb, the captain saw some sea gulls, heard thumps on the aircraft and thought he had incurred a bird strike; he therefore elected to abort the take-off even though the co-pilot had called 'Decision Speed' during the Victor's take-off run. The braking parachute deployed fully and the aircraft began to decelerate. Neither pilot looked at the ASI after the decision speed had been called until somewhere between the 1,500ft to go point and the end of the runway. The captain then saw that the ASI was not reading, which showed that the airspeed was below 45 knots. After this the rate of deceleration decreased and both pilots realised that the aircraft was going into the overshoot. The AEO warned ATC of their predicament and the crew door was blown open.

The Victor went off the end of the runway at about 25 knots or possibly a little more. The nosewheel collapsed and the port undercarriage bogie began to bog down causing a gentle slew to port. The starboard undercarriage then broke off and embedded itself in the fuselage. The aircraft then swung rapidly to port causing the port undercarriage also to break off, embedding itself in the port underwing tank.

The aircraft stopped and a fire broke out on the starboard side which was probably started by the very hot starboard undercarriage brakes igniting fuel from the split starboard underwing tank. The crew took about one minute to vacate the aircraft. By the time the pilots were leaving the aircraft the fire on the starboard side had got a good hold. The fire crew appeared on the scene just after the last man was out of the cabin. They extinguished the fire quickly and efficiently, thus preventing the whole aircraft becoming engulfed in flames. None of the Victor's crew was injured other than the nav radar who had slight bruising of his left elbow.

This accident was analysed in the RAF magazine *Air Clues* July 1977 by Wing Commander Spry, the mythical air safety officer; he made the obvious point that a take-off should not be abandoned if the aircraft had passed decision speed.

Victor K2 XL232 15th October 1982

The 55 Squadron aircraft was taking off at RAF Marham when an explosion was felt by the crew members. A quick check by the AEO through the rear periscope confirmed that fire and flame were enveloping the aircraft. Speed was immediately reduced and the take-off aborted by the captain, the aircraft being brought to a stop and quickly evacuated by its crew. Despite prompt attention from the fire crew, the aircraft was engulfed by flames from its heavy fuel load and completely destroyed (see opposite). The cause was a catastrophic failure of one of its Rolls-Royce Conway engines with the No 3 engine fuel tank fractured by shattered turbine blades, leading to the aircraft's demise. XL232 was carrying a full fuel load of approximately 55 tons of Avtur on its doomed mission and only the captain's prompt action had prevented a major disaster.

By chance Dick Russell was airborne.

I was down to do an IRT on Barry Neal and, after completion, landed at Waddington to take part in a celebration corporate lunch organised by Simon Baldwin. We carried a co-pilot on the sixth seat to take my place after landing at Waddington. The first part of the IRT was a practice double-engine failure at 100ft followed by a heavyweight

Victor XL232 burning at Marham after an abandoned take-off.

circuit and overshoot from decision height.

We got airborne and after the engine failures climbed to circuit height and turned downwind when we saw a great plume of black smoke stretching from the threshold of runway 24 half way to Swaffham some six miles away.

ATC came up and said discontinue our exercise, well that part of it. The smoke had come from XL232 which had shed a turbine blade at take-off. No one was hurt but members of the crew of 232 broke all records for the 200 yards and the runway needed some major repairs.

Victor K2 XL191 19th June 1986

The aircraft was making an approach in bad weather to Hamilton in Ontario. It crashed into the undershoot. It is understood that the detailed circumstances of this accident are taught within the RAF flight safety training environment as an example of how not to do things. Apparently there was a breakdown in crew co-operation which, when taken with other factors, led to the loss of the aircraft. One report of the accident was as follows.

I was the 'air boss' of the Hamilton show when the Victor crashed. It created a major problem for the show as its tail impinged on the clearances on the main runway, the only one long enough to take some of the military jets, which then had to be closed. We could not move the aircraft until it had been examined and we had to turf out the air attache from Ottawa who had been invited to attend but was involved in something else; he flew in and convened a Court of Inquiry. The committee of the inquiry group flew in via a VC10 which we hoped would stay for static display at the show, no such luck! The bottom line was the aircraft was moved just enough to allow the runway to re-open and the diverted aircraft were gathered in from the surrounding airfields. Fortunately the Victor had planned to come in early.

The Victor had flown in from Marham direct and we had requested that they bring a barrel of British beer to sell at the show. The fire crew said when they got to the aircraft they were amazed to see the crew was pushing out a barrel of beer! Unfortunately the fire crew took the rescued flight crew to their building and somehow the beer never made it to the show.

What happened? According to the story we got from the crew, before they had time to think a better one up, they had an electrical problem when between Quebec and Montreal and they had to cancel their IFR flight plan, so they descended to below the IFR level (9,500ft?) and flew VFR to Hamilton. This of course significantly increased the fuel consumption.

Unfortunately Hamilton is susceptible to local fogs as the warm moist air from Lake Ontario drifts in and is pushed up over the airport where it condenses to form a local fog. We got the word from Toronto control that the Victor was coming in and was going to attempt an approach without its approach aids. The first approach was missed and we got word from the Hamilton tower that they only had sufficient fuel for one more approach and after that they were going to fly over Lake Ontario and eject. They broke out of the crud to find they were significantly off the runway heading and they tried a quick correction, but they just did not have time to correct and they ran off the runway into a gully, driving the undercarriage oleos up through the wings.

It was our understanding that the aircraft was one of the newer Victors and it had recently had its life extended. The aircraft was scrapped and the nose section was donated to the Canadian Warplane Heritage Museum. I believe they eventually disposed of it as it did not fit into their collection mandate.

It is disappointing that it has not been possible to get a more definitive report of this accident. The primary cause of the accident seems to have been the decision to dump diversion fuel rather than divert just because the captain thought he would have no trouble landing. In the event the weather was not suitable for a visual approach and they were forced to land regardless or dump the aircraft in the lake. Allegedly there were issues around captaincy of the aircraft, unauthorized departure from plan to go sightseeing over Niagara Falls, wrong pressure setting resulting in illegal low flying, issues with nav aid set-up and task sharing on approach.

Victor K2 XM715 3rd May 2009

This luckily was an incident not an accident but I felt it worthy of a mention in this book.

On 3rd May 2009 during a 'fast taxi' run at Bruntingthorpe Aerodrome, XM715 made an unplanned brief flight reaching a height of between 120-130ft before being landed straight ahead. The aircraft did not have a permit to fly. The Civil Aviation Authority (CAA) stated that they would not be conducting an investigation. The causes have been identified as the co-pilot failing to reply to the command 'throttles back', thus resulting in the pilot having to take over the control of the throttles himself, resulting in a brief loss of control of the aircraft, causing it to leave the ground. No legal action was taken by the CAA against either the crew aboard XM715 or the operators of Bruntingthorpe.

Shortly after this event I was watching the Vulcan at Wellesbourne Mountford doing a similar fast taxi run and was very impressed by the technique employed. The engines were opened up to full power and the aircraft accelerated to 100kts. The power was then reduced and the pilot, in this case Martin Withers of Falklands fame, only then pulled the nose up as the aircraft decelerated. In this way there was no chance of the aircraft getting airborne.

Unplanned flight of XM715 at Bruntingthorpe.

Discussion on accidents

Reviewing all the accidents, there did not seem to be a design weakness in the aircraft though clearly it was important not to let it stall since it would then go into an uncontrollable spin. What perhaps is surprising is that the causes of the accidents in certain cases were not clearly established or the official findings did not seem to take all the issues into account.

Aerodynamic issues, XH668, XL159

Dealing first with the aerodynamics of the aircraft, the high-set tailplane meant that the aircraft could not be stalled since it was virtually irrecoverable once the tailplane was in the turbulent wing wake. The Handley Page test pilots and the Avro test pilots, when we were developing the K2, would only go as far as heavy buffet, called 'the hammer'; it was a very heavy high amplitude affair which literally shook the whole aircraft quite violently, particularly when clean. If the aircraft was stalled it would go into a spin and was not recoverable using normal aircraft controls so that intentional stalling was forbidden. However in the life of the aircraft two recoveries were made after unintentional stalling by using the braking parachute. One of these incidents was in Australia and fully described in the 4 JSTU chapter. The other event was in Victor XL233 when Peter Baker was doing mach trimmer runaways to clear the modified leading edge.

At the high speed end of the flight envelope the aircraft could go supersonic but was not of course designed to be flown or operated in this regime. Consequently it did not matter that at .98M and above the aileron jacks were stalled and ineffective. Nor did it matter that at this speed the rolling moment due to sideslip, $1v$, was reversed. No money or time could be justified modifying the aircraft to sort these characteristics out. However, it was clearly important to be very careful at high speeds to keep the wings level with very little g and it was flying in this area that almost certainly caused the loss of XH668.

Aircraft design issues XH617, XH613, XA929

The loss of an alternator drive shot going through the fuel tank, XH617, was basically due to the alternator being mounted on the airframe and the engine driving the shaft. This arrangement caused stress and fatigue on the shafts and in fact there were a number of failures due to this design feature but luckily only one was catastrophic. The engine was modified to permit the alternator to be mounted on the engine compressor case.

The cause of the loss of power on XH613 was found in the wiring in the fuel panel. The K2 panel was subsequently completely redesigned.

The take-off accident of XA929 was attributed by the Board of Inquiry to a fault in the flap switching unit. As far as is known no similar incidents occurred during the life of the aircraft. However apparently on the Mk1 it was possible to knock the lever into the up position and this was changed on the Mk 1A.

Engine malfunction, XL232, XA934

The failure of the engine in XA934 apparently damaged the fuel pipes and caused the engines to fail but it is suggested that there may have been other contributing factors.

The aircraft only had one catastrophic engine failure which resulted in an accident causing the loss of an aircraft but, thankfully, not any crew. This was in contrast with the Olympus engine in the Vulcan which was not nearly as reliable.

Apparent pilot error XA917, XM714, XM716, XL230, XL191

In any accident investigation it is very easy to blame the crew if they are killed in the accident. On new aircraft flight recorders help the accident investigators not only recording the key flight parameters but also recording the crew intercom. Unfortunately, at the time of these Victor accidents no such aids were available and pilot error was assumed, rightly or wrongly.

With regard to the accident in Canada, XL191, unfortunately approaches to airfields all over the world are littered with aircraft which have crashed trying to land in bad weather and this accident was particularly unfortunate in that allegedly diversion fuel had been dumped. Having dumped the diversion fuel the captain had no alternative but to come below his approved minima for the airfield and he was extremely lucky to have been able to force land the aircraft without loss of life. The terrible accident to the Vulcan at London airport is a perfect example of how things can go wrong coming below minima (see *Vulcan Test Pilot*). I must admit to having been lucky in my flying career in that I have come below my minima several times and got away with it, but, in retrospect, each time it was a foolhardy thing to do.

Aircraft collision XH618

The loss of a tanker aircraft through poor flying by a receiver aircraft is an unavoidable hazard. Luckily it is a very rare occurrence, but tragic when it happens. Proper training and supervision is the main safeguard. It can be argued that the United States system using a boom is a safer and easier way of refuelling, certainly for large receiving aircraft.

Bird Strikes XL513

It is not entirely clear why the pilot thought there had been a bird strike but though the aircraft was destroyed it was very fortunate that no-one was killed. The accident certainly looks like a clear-cut case of pilot error trying to abandon take-off after decision speed had been reached.

Mid-air collision XH646

The collision between the Canberra and the Victor should never have happened since both aircraft were under radar surveillance. The weather was very bad at the time and it is suggested that the radar performance was downgraded by heavy rain.

Victor Bases in the UK

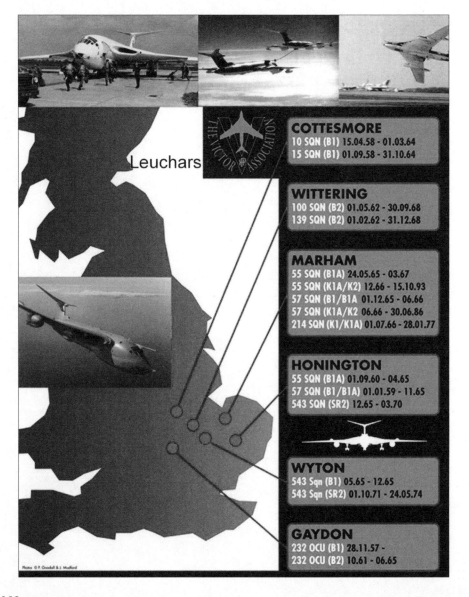

Leuchars

THE VICTOR ASSOCIATION

COTTESMORE
10 SQN (B1) 15.04.58 - 01.03.64
15 SQN (B1) 01.09.58 - 31.10.64

WITTERING
100 SQN (B2) 01.05.62 - 30.09.68
139 SQN (B2) 01.02.62 - 31.12.68

MARHAM
55 SQN (B1A) 24.05.65 - 03.67
55 SQN (K1A/K2) 12.66 - 15.10.93
57 SQN (B1/B1A) 01.12.65 - 06.66
57 SQN (K1A/K2) 06.66 - 30.06.86
214 SQN (K1/K1A) 01.07.66 - 28.01.77

HONINGTON
55 SQN (B1A) 01.09.60 - 04.65
57 SQN (B1/B1A) 01.01.59 - 11.65
543 SQN (SR2) 12.65 - 03.70

WYTON
543 Sqn (B1) 05.65 - 12.65
543 Sqn (SR2) 01.10.71 - 24.05.74

GAYDON
232 OCU (B1) 28.11.57 -
232 OCU (B2) 10.61 - 06.65

Photos © P. Goodall & J. Mulford

Appendix III

Acronyms

A&AEE	Aircraft and Armament Experimental Establishment
AAPU	Auxiliary Airborne Power Unit
AAR	Air to Air refuelling
AEO	Air Electronics Officer
ASR	Air Staff Requirement
CFS	Central Flying School
ECM	Electronic Counter Measures
ETPS	Empire Test Pilot School
F/S	Fire/Security
GPI Mk 6	Ground Position Indicator
H2S	Early radar fitted to Victors and Vulcans
HDU	Hose Drum Unit
HTP	High Test Peroxide
IFF	Identification Friend or Foe
ILS	Instrument Landing System
IMC	Instrument Meteorological Conditions
IMN	Indicated Mach Number
INS	Inertial Navigation System
IRT	Instrument Rating Test
ITP	Instruction to Proceed
JSTU	Joint Services Trials Unit
MOD	Ministry of Defence
MOD(PE)	Ministry of Defence Procurement Executive
MPA	Marine Patrol Aircraft
MRR	Maritime Radar Reconnaissance
NATO	North Atlantic Treaty Organisation
NBC	Nuclear Biological Chemical suit
NBS	Navigation and Bombing System
NOTAMs	Notices to Airmen (OR Not to worry about the next morning NOT AM!)
NTP	Navigation Terminal Point
OCU	Operational Conversion Unit

ORP	Operational Readiness Platform
PAWS	Pan American World Service
PFCU	Powered Flying Control Units
QFI	Qualified Flying Instructor
QRA	Quick Reaction Alert
RAE	Royal Aircraft Establishment
RAM	Reconnaissance Air Meet
RAT	Ram Air Turbine
RBSU	Radar Bomb Scoring Units
RSnn	Readiness State nn minutes
RTB	Return to Base
RV	Rendezvous Point
SAC	Strategic Air Command
SOP	Standard Operating Procedure
TANSOR	Tanker Sortie Defence UK
TFR	Terrain Following Radar
VMC	Visual Meteorological Conditions
WRE	Weapons Research Establishment, Woomera

INDEX